MACHIAVELLI AND MYSTERY OF STATE

Machiavelli and Mystery of State

PETER S. DONALDSON

Professor of Literature
Massachusetts Institute of Technology

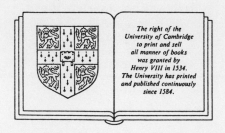

The right of the
University of Cambridge
to print and sell
all manner of books
was granted by
Henry VIII in 1534.
The University has printed
and published continuously
since 1584.

CAMBRIDGE UNIVERSITY PRESS

NEW YORK

NEW ROCHELLE   MELBOURNE   SYDNEY

For Alice

Published by the Press Syndicate of the University of Cambridge
The Pitt Building, Trumpington Street, Cambridge CB2 1RP
32 East 57th Street, New York, NY 10022, USA
10 Stamford Road, Oakleigh, Melbourne 3166, Australia

First published 1988

Printed in the United States of America

Library of Congress Cataloging-in-Publication Data

Donaldson, Peter Samuel, 1942–
Machiavelli and mystery of state.
Includes bibliographical references.
1. Machiavelli, Niccolò, 1469–1527 – Contributions
in political science.   2. Political science – Italy –
History.   I. Title.
JC143.M4D65   1988   320.1′092′4   88–6136

British Library Cataloguing in Publication Data

Donaldson, Peter S.
Machiavelli and mystery of state.
1. Politics. Theories of Machiavelli,
Niccolo, 1469–1527
I. Title
320.5′092′4

ISBN 0 521 34546 4

Contents

Preface

Perhaps the most notorious passage in Machiavelli's *Il Principe* comes in Chapter 18, where the duplicity of the fox and the violence of the lion are set as models for political conduct, and where the author writes that, though a prince should conduct himself in accordance with the moral virtues when he can, "if the necessity arises, he should know how to follow evil." These words have often been taken as a sign of Machiavelli's decisive break with the past, with biblical and classical traditions according to which the office of a prince was an inescapably moral one.[1] Yet, in making these recommendations, Machiavelli was attempting to place his own teachings in an ancient tradition of secret political instruction. The legend of Achilles and Chiron the Centaur is his text:

It must be understood that there are two ways of fighting, one with laws and the other with arms. The first is the way of men, the second is the style of beasts, but since very often the first does not suffice it is necessary to turn to the second. Therefore a prince must know how to play the beast as well as the man. This lesson was taught by the ancient writers who related that Achilles and many other princes were brought up by Chiron the Centaur, who took them under his discipline. The clear significance of this half-man and half-beast preceptorship is that a prince must know how to use either of these two natures and that one without the other has no enduring strength. Now since the prince must make use of the characteristics of beasts, he should choose those of the fox and the lion.[2]

Machiavelli's own principles, where they conflict most directly with conventional political morality, are thus held to have been prefigured in an ancient legend of secret instruction with a veiled or hidden meaning. What Chiron taught Achilles is not revealed, but, by telling

---

[1] See, for example, Reginald Pole's *Apologia*, discussed in Chapter 1, this volume.
[2] *The Prince*, trans. and ed. Thomas G. Bergin (Northbrook, Ill., 1947). Citations of *The Prince* in English will be from this edition and those from *The Discourses* from the Bernard Crick edition (Harmondsworth, England, 1970).

the story of his preceptorship, ancient writers "covertly"[3] taught princes what could not be stated openly.

According to Pindar, what Chiron expounded was the *agraphoi nomoi,* the unwritten or unstated principles by which human society was constituted (*Pythian Odes,* VI, 21–7). However, for Pindar as for other authors, the content of these unwritten laws was respect for parents and fear of the gods.[4] Machiavelli has reversed the moral sign of the story, and locates its meaning not in its conventional and pious content, but in the half-bestial character of the instructor and in the covert mode of his instruction.

This book is a study of six figures – five writers of political texts and one printer of political literature – for whom, in various ways, Machiavelli was associated with ancient and secret knowledge, with mysteries of state or *arcana imperii.*[5] Machiavelli is so often thought of as an ancestor or precursor of contemporary modes of political thought – scientific, positivist, value free or other – that such an association may come as a surprise; yet there were passages in *Il Principe* and *I Discorsi* that could, like the story of the education of Achilles, be read as points of intersection between Machiavellian and sacral conceptions of politics. In *Principe* 18, Machiavelli does not reject ancient traditions so much as claim that his own work expresses their hidden sense.

Reginald Pole, Stephen Gardiner, John Wolfe, Arnold Clapmar, Gabriel Naudé, and Louis Machon attempt, in various ways, to assimilate Machiavelli to traditions of political mystery of ancient origin. Drawing on Greek, Latin, or biblical sources, they tend to see in Machiavelli's works a revelation of the ancient arcana of kingship. Cardinal Pole regards the appearance of *Il Principe* as a manifestation of the

---

[3] "Questa parte è suta insegnata a' principi copertamente dagli antichi scrittori." References to Machiavelli are to *Niccolò Machiavelli: tutte le opere,* ed. Mario Casella (Florence; 1969).

[4] George Thomson provides a very full and valuable note on the *agraphoi nomoi* in his edition of *The Oresteia of Aeschylus,* 2nd ed. (Amsterdam and Prague, 1966), II, pp. 200–2. For a fascinating study of how Machiavelli's treatment of the Chiron story influenced later portrayals of him in France, see Heather Ingman, "Machiavelli and the interpretation of the Chiron myth in France," *Journal of the Warburg and Courtauld Institutes* XLV (1982), 217–27. Ingman emphasizes the change in Chiron's moral significance but does not explore the association of Machiavelli's advice with secret teaching.

[5] This expression is discussed at length by Clapmar and Naudé, and appears in Pole, Gentili, and Machon. See Chapters 1, 3, 4, 5, and 6, this volume. Its source is Tacitus, *Annals* 2:36, and is used in reference to a proposal made by Gallus that magistrates be elected five years in advance. "There was no doubt," Tacitus comments, "that the proposal went deeper than this, and trespassed on the arcana of sovereignty" ["haud dubium erat eam sententiam altius penetrare et arcana imperii temptari"] (trans. John Jackson in *Tacitus II,* Loeb Classical Library [London and New York, 1931]).

mysterium iniquitatis of Thessalonians, a signal of the approach of Antichrist before the Last Days. Bishop Gardiner uses Machiavelli to prepare a secret manual on the governance of England for Philip II, and
tries to show that the apparent amoralism of the techniques he recommends is justified by biblical notions of kingly license. John Wolfe's
publication of surreptitious editions of Machiavelli's works was influenced, as its preface indicates, by the belief that Machiavelli was an
unmasker of the arcana of tyranny. Arnold Clapmar's *De arcanis rerumpublicarum* associates the "reason of state" tradition that derived
from Machiavelli with the Tacitean *arcana imperii* and with Roman
legal principles according to which the sovereign was exempt from
law. Gabriel Naudé's *Coups d'état* draws a portrait of the effective politician or *esprit fort* analogous to that of the ancient magus. Louis Machon composes a sustained and elaborate defense of Machiavelli according to which all of his central doctrines may be found in the Bible.

Efforts to read Machiavelli as the reviver or reviser of an ancient
mystery of statecraft now seem strained; yet the facts concerning the
publication of his major works, as well as their subject matter, offered
a foothold for such a reading. *Il Principe* and *I Discorsi* were both published posthumously. In the dedication of *Il Principe*, Machiavelli could
easily be thought to be addressing his work to the dedicatee alone, as
a private manual of statecraft. In the body of the text, he often adopts
a confidential tone, using the second person singular as if he had an
audience of one, and he counsels his implied reader to discard certain
aspects of Christian morality, when necessary, and to create and sustain
several kinds of illusions and fictions for political effect. In the dedication of the *Discorsi*, he casts himself in the role of rediscoverer of
ancient modes of political thought. He compares his own teaching, at
its morally most problematic point, to the secret indoctrination of
Achilles into the unwritten laws. These and other promptings of the
text, together with the Renaissance belief in ancient secret traditions
of all kinds, gave rise to a rich and varied pattern – which sometimes
takes on the consistency and sequence of a tradition – in which Machiavelli's real subject was thought to be the *arcana imperii* of the ancient
world, and according to which his apparent amoralism might be explained as the special license of the sacred ruler.

The myth of the arcana may also help us to make sense of certain
well-studied patterns in the transmission of Machiavelli's ideas. From
the start, beginning even before the publication of *Il Principe* and the
Discorsi in 1532, Machiavelli's works were plagiarized, borrowed, and
quoted without attribution. Plans were made for expurgated editions
to be published under a false name, and surreptitious editions were

published. Many of these patterns owe something to Renaissance ca-
sualness about literary property and something to the constraints of
censorship. But they may also derive from a habit of regarding Machiavelli as the purveyor of the arcana. For the figures studied here,
secrets of state lead a double and unstable existence: If they are divulged to readers, they are no longer secrets; their mystery is compromised. The publication of the arcana, whether by Machiavelli himself or by his imitators, is necessarily a double act whereby what is
revealed is also somehow concealed – by ambiguity of discourse, by
limitation of circulation of the text, by falsification of the facts of publication, or in other ways. Machiavelli was thus linked to the myth of
the *arcana imperii* not only by identifying his work as part of an ancient
tradition, but by ambiguous acts of publication. The complicated history of the transmission of Machiavellian thought studied by Gerber
and many others may be partly understood as deriving from the paradox inherent in the public dissemination of mysteries of state.

   In certain ways, the work presented here may be thought of as a
modest revision of that of Ernst Kantorowicz, from whom I draw my
title. In his seminal article "Mysteries of state: an absolutist concept
and its late medieval origins,"[6] Kantorowicz attempted to trace the
origins of seventeenth-century notions of the sacredness of royal power
to the jurists of the twelfth and thirteenth centuries, who adapted and
revised claims that had previously been made for the pope so that
they would apply to Frederick II. But these claims, in their turn, derived from the divine pretensions of the ancient Roman emperors,
and the roots of these pretensions were earlier still. In its tracing of
origins, Kantorowicz's influential work displays its own continuity with
the early modern texts he sought to locate in a tradition of "mystery
of state," for the search of origins and ancient sanction is a pervasive
concern of much political writing of the period.

   The present study is less concerned with origins and more concerned
with how the revival of "mystery of state," which Kantorowicz has so
well described, coincided and combined with the Machiavellian strand
of Renaissance political discussion. Kantorowicz does not mention
Machiavelli in his accounts of late Renaissance claims concerning the
sacredness of kings, but Machiavelli was a pervasive presence in Renaissance political discourse, and several of the chapters in the present
volume argue for the central importance of his texts in the Renaissance
recasting of the old idea that kingship was a mystery. In fact, so in-

---

[6] *Harvard Theological Review* XLVII (1955), 65–91.

terconnected were "Machiavellism" and the ideology of sacred kingship in the period that one can regard them as variants of the same discursive system. In a way that might be compared to Freud's position in twentieth-century psychological theory, Machiavelli's innovations established new terms and new modes in political writing and political life. He was so important a figure that nearly all political discussions had to take account of his work and orient themselves in relation to it, whether by absorbing him, condemning him, or defending him, or by some more complex placement in relation to him. The "mystery of state" we find in James I (a favorite source for Kantorowicz) or in the French absolutist authors of the seventeenth century is a concept framed in relation to Machiavellian assumptions and Machiavellian themes, especially in relation to Machiavelli's central insights into the role of illusion and fiction in politics.

Some of the figures studied here attempt to define political mysteries, or *arcana imperii*, as alternatives to what they think of as the dangerous or evil influence of Machiavelli; others defend Machiavelli as if he himself were the purveyor of sacred and ancient doctrines. The divergences in moral valuation are great – from Cardinal Pole, who thought *Il Principe* was directly inspired by Satan, to Louis Machon, for whom Machiavelli "spoke like a saint" – but they ought not to obscure those convergences of theme and terminology that make the authors, statesmen, and publishers studied here users of and contributors to a discernible variety of political discourse, whose terms and questions were set – not unchallengeably or unalterably, but nevertheless decisively – by Machiavelli's major works.

In using the term political discourse for the subject matter of this book – rather than political theory or history of political ideas – I have in mind several but by no means all of the meanings this term has recently acquired. "Discourse," as used here, refers not only to the content of texts and the history of that content, but to patterns in the production and use of texts. Attention is paid to publishing history and to other particulars of the transmission of the text, not as "background" or to supply evidence for the stabilization of meanings, but because the way in which political texts were produced and circulated is an essential piece of the story of "mystery of state": By analogy with other supposed ancient arts, the occultation or secret transmission of the text is itself a significant aspect of the mystery. Attention is also paid to how political texts determine and are determined by the discursive roles they specify or suggest: The role of counselor, especially "secret counselor," becomes something very different from what it

had been in the Middle Ages when the medium of counsel is a secret
or private treatise. What biographical narrative there is in this book
has the description of such discursive roles as its aim.

In keeping with this emphasis, the following chapters not only point
out ways in which Machiavelli's texts were described as if they were
a kind of secret manual or breviarium, but also show how that very
view of Machiavelli was both manifested in the mode of publication
(or circulation) of the texts produced by the authors studied here and
embodied in the writer–reader relation the texts imply. If Machiavelli
had revived or revealed an ancient and secret art of politics, to imitate
his work of innovation or recovery might mean to produce one's own
arcana – that is, to withhold one's work from publication and transmit
it secretly to kings, to publish in a limited edition, or to publish surreptitiously. Such texts deal with arcana; they are themselves in some
sense arcana; and their authors or publishers present themselves as
the purveyors of a secret wisdom.

In studying the transmission of texts believed to be political arcana,
and in studying the shifts in the counselor–ruler relationship implied
by those texts, the question of the relation between printed books and
manuscripts is often of special importance. In the age of the printing
press, the difference between "secret" and "open" knowledge could
be thought of as an opposition between what was spoken and what
was written, as previously, but now it could also be thought of as the
difference between what was handwritten and carried by hand in a
diplomatic pouch and what appeared in a printed book offered for
sale to the public. This doubling of what might be meant by the word
"book" was a necessary component of Renaissance conceptions of the
arcana and figures especially in Gabriel Naudé's exposition of the *coups
d'état;* it was also, I suggest, a determining factor in the way Machiavelli's work was received. If Machiavelli had written at a time when
there was only one kind of book, or if he had written one kind of
book instead of leaving a manuscript addressed to a prince that was
printed after his death, attempts to associate his teachings with the
arcana imperii would have had to take a different form.

This book, then, is intended as a contribution to the history of Renaissance political discourse, an exploration in detail of several instances
of the Machiavellian legacy that have in common some exploitation
of the notion of Machiavellism as *arcana imperii,* or mystery of state.
"Influence" is too limiting a term to characterize Machiavelli's place
in Renaissance political culture. The present attempt to specify that
place takes cognizance not only of the history of the reception of Machiavellian ideas but also of the history of their misconstruction or

rejection. It attends to ways in which older discourses were recast in the attempt to take account of Machiavelli; to changes in the way political texts were produced and circulated; and to transformations of the roles of writers, speakers, hearers, and readers of political discourse in the wake of Machiavelli's innovations.

The specifically *literary* use of Machiavelli is not directly addressed, but the ideological and discursive patterns discerned here have some bearing on current efforts to redescribe the relation of Renaissance literature and politics. In particular, the following pages may corroborate Stephen Orgel's wise suggestions concerning the confluence of Machiavellian and sacral theories of kingship in the Jacobean theater (*The Illusion of Power;* Berkeley, 1975, pp. 42–3). The sections of Jonathan Goldberg's *James I and the Politics of Literature* (Baltimore, 1983) that deal with the *arcana imperii* also reach toward new ways of understanding Renaissance mystery of state as it relates to literature. My work here extends that of many other literary and historical scholars who have regarded the Machiavellian and sacral traditions as closely interwoven, and in future contributions I plan to apply the findings of *Machiavelli and Mystery of State* to canonical literary texts, especially those of Shakespeare.

My long-term scholarly debts include those to William F. Church's *Richelieu and Reason of State* (Princeton, N.J.: Princeton University Press, 1972); to Kantorowicz's article from which I draw my title, as well as to his book *The King's Two Bodies* (Princeton, N.J.: Princeton University Press, 1957); to the work of John Pocock; and to the various specialized studies acknowledged in the notes. My dissertation adviser, William Nelson, is not alive to read the second book that developed out of his suggestion for a dissertation topic, but I would like to record my appreciation for his help and his example. I wish to thank Michael Moore, Claudia von Canon, Paul Kristeller, Joseph Mazzeo, Sir Geoffrey Elton, and John Pocock for assistance while emphatically absolving them of responsibility for the use I have made of it. I have been assisted by grants from MIT, the National Endowment for the Humanities, and the American Council of Learned Societies, and by the courtesy and skill of many librarians, especially at the British Library, the Bibliothèque Publique de Bordeaux, the Escorial, and the Houghton Library at Harvard. I wish to thank Alvin Kibel, Bruce Mazlish, and Richard Douglas for their collegial support at particularly crucial points in my career. As always, I am grateful to my parents and my children. My greatest debt is to my dear wife, Alice, who was a loving and patient companion as I completed a difficult project. My work is dedicated to her and to our partnership in life.

A version of Chapter 1 appeared in *Leaders of the Reformation,* edited by Richard L. DeMolen (Cranbury, N.J.: Associated University Presses, 1984), and Chapter 2 expands material from my introduction to *A Machiavellian Treatise by Stephen Gardiner* (Cambridge: Cambridge University Press, 1975). Early versions of these and other chapters were presented as papers at meetings of the Modern Language Association, the Anglo-American Conference of Historians, the New England Renaissance Conference, the annual meeting of the American Association of University Professors of Italian, and the Columbia University Seminar on the Renaissance.

1

Machiavelli and Antichrist
Prophetic typology in Reginald Pole's *De Unitate* and *Apologia ad Carolum Quintum*

In the *Apologia ad Carolum Quintum* (1539)[1] Reginald Pole claimed to know, on the basis of a conversation with Thomas Cromwell some ten years earlier and subsequent inquiry into Cromwell's views, that Machiavelli's *Il Principe* had been the inspiration behind Henry VIII's decision to break with Rome, declare himself head of the church, and seize the property of the English monasteries. The *Apologia* remained unpublished until A. M. Quirini's edition of Pole's letters appeared (1744–57). After that, Pole's views were influential in fixing the image of the Henrician polity as Machiavellian in character. To A. F. Pollard, for example, Henry VIII was "Machiavelli's *Prince* in action." Since 1905, however, when Paul Van Dyke devoted an appendix to his *Renascence Portraits* to an examination of the *Apologia*, it has been more common for historians to dismiss Pole's claim that Cromwell knew Machiavelli so early and made *Il Principe* the basis of his advice to Henry VIII. Many of Van Dyke's arguments were accepted by G. R. Elton in *Tudor Revolution in Government* (1953) and "The political creed of Thomas Cromwell" (1956).[2]

Pole's views on Machiavelli appear in a work that, like the closely related *De Unitate* (1536, published 1539), is permeated by a typological vision of history. The events and persons of Pole's own time are seen as fulfillments or partial fulfillments of biblical models. Pole's typology is quite complex and, though it derives from time-honored medieval traditions of biblical exegesis, somewhat original in its method and in the particular place it finds for current events in the biblical sequence of the Last Days. Pole's works have a place in the history of sixteenth-

---

[1] The *Apologia* is printed in Angelo M. Quirini, ed., *Epistolarum Reginaldi Poli S. R. E. Cardinalis et aliorum ad ipsum collectio* (Brescia, 1744–57), I, pp. 66–171.
[2] Albert F. Pollard, *Henry VIII* (London, 1905; repr. 1951), p. 353; Paul Van Dyke, *Renascence Portraits* (New York, 1905), pp. 377–418; Geoffrey R. Elton, *Tudor Revolution in Government* (Cambridge, 1953), pp. 71–6; Elton, "The political creed of Thomas Cromwell," *Royal Historical Society Transactions*, ser. 5, VI (1956), 69–92. See also T. M. Parker, "Was Thomas Cromwell a Machiavellian?" *Journal of Ecclesiastical History* I (1950), 63–75.

century apocalyptic thought now being written, and, as Pole's apocalyptic vision shaped his report of the facts, it is helpful to examine
his view of sacred history, and particularly the role he assigned to
himself in the unfolding of scriptural prophecy, to assess how his bias
might affect his telling of a story like that of his meeting with Cromwell.

This chapter is concerned with Pole's use of prophecy and with the
question of Machiavelli's availability in England in the late 1520s. But
our primary interest here is in the relationship between Machiavellian
and biblical discourse: in the ways in which old doctrines of the sacredness of kings and their office were reformulated in order to meet
the challenge posed by Machiavelli, and in how that reformulation
created new roles in the writing of political texts and the speaking of
political counsel. Pole opposed Machiavelli and regarded his doctrines
as an essentially secret teaching whose poison was spreading through
Christendom. Yet, in opposing Machiavelli, Pole himself became in a
sense an author of political arcana and tried to find a biblical precedent
for such a role. The texts discussed in this chapter belong to a tradition
of political prophecy whose explicit origins are biblical; they represent
a special form of prophetic discourse, shaped by opposition to Machiavelli and by the belief that Machiavelli had written a secret text.
Pole's themes, his conception of the chronology of sacred history, and
indeed his own view of his prophetic or quasiprophetic mission were
all deeply influenced by the complex interplay of occultation and revelation he thought he had discovered in Machiavelli's *Il Principe* and
in the contemporary events it inspired.

Before proceeding to the texts, a brief account of the spiritual and
political crisis Pole experienced at the time of their composition is in
order.[3] Pole had from early childhood a complex and potentially ex-
plosive relationship to the king. Pole's mother was the daughter of
George, Duke of Clarence, and the niece of Edward IV. Her brother
Edward was executed in 1499 because of the potential danger he represented to the Tudor claim to the throne. Pole was born in 1500,
and his father, Sir Richard Pole, died in 1505. Henry VIII came to
the throne when Reginald Pole was nine; he favored the Poles, and
especially young Reginald, whom he generously supported at Oxford,
where he was king's scholar at Magdalen from 1513, and then at Padua,
where he went for an extended period of study in 1521. Pole was

---

[3] In what follows I am partly following Wilhelm Schenck, *Reginald Pole: Cardinal of
England* (London, 1950), pp. 1–86, and Dermot Fenlon, *Heresy and Obedience in Tridentine
Italy: Cardinal Pole and the Counter Reformation* (Cambridge, 1972), pp. 24–44, but I
develop the theme of prophecy somewhat differently than Fenlon, and the attempt to
explore the psychological dimension of Pole's spiritual crisis is my own.

very, perhaps excessively, grateful: In the hope of serving his benefactor with the fruits of his study, he devoted himself to his books to
the point of injuring his health (*De Unitate*, Sig. Bir).[4] In this zeal we
may perhaps see an attempt to resolve ambivalent feelings: Pole was
a boy without a father, and the man who, as kinsman and benefactor,
in some measure supplied his place sat on a throne that might have
passed to his grandfather, to his uncle (whom Henry VII had killed),
or to his brother. Beneath his childhood loyalty lay great bitterness
that comes to the surface in later references to his uncle, as in this
passage from the *De unitate*, in which he points up the irony of his
own defense of Mary Tudor's right to the succession:

If your father came back to earth now and saw me, the nephew of that man
whom, though utterly innocent as everyone knows, he took pains to have
killed because he was too close to the throne and capable of later becoming
an impediment to his descendants; if he saw me, offspring of that house he
considered dangerous, defend the right of inheritance [i.e., Mary's] against
which you, his son, are taking action! What an extraordinary thing it would
seem to him. He would then clearly see how weak human reason is when it
tries to remove all obstacles to the perpetuity of a dynasty. For what moved
him to the murder of my uncle, who was unanimously judged to have been
completely innocent all his life (like a one year's child, as Scripture says), was
only that he saw in him the nephew of King Edward, the sole living male in
the line that could one day be the source of fresh revolts to establish that
man's right to the throne against that of his own family. . . . And it is I, who
come of the same family, son of the sister of the man whom he had killed
because he feared he could become an obstacle to his children, it is I who
take up the defense of his granddaughter against his son's opposition when
he himself had thought that that murder would assure the protection of his
line. (Sig. Oiiv-Oiiir)[5]

Here an ironic loyalty to the Tudor succession mixes with bitter anger
at the loss of his uncle.

The turning point in Pole's attitude to the king came in 1535, when
Thomas More and John Fisher were executed (Sig. Svv). This was
only one of a number of acts by which Henry moved away from obedience to Rome (the king's divorce, his assumption of supremacy over
the English church, the desecration of the shrine of Thomas Becket,

---

[4] References to the *De Unitate* are to the Blado edition (Rome, 1539), *Reginaldi Poli
Cardinalis Britanni, ad Henricum octavum Britanniae regem, pro ecclesiasticae unitatis defensione,
libri quatuor*. For the date of this edition, an account of its differences from the P.R.O.
MS sent to Henry, and arguments concerning the need for a critical edition, see Thomas
F. Dunn, "The development of the text of Pole's *De unitate ecclesiae*," *Papers of the Bibliographical Society of America* LXX (1976), 455–68.
[5] Translations, unless otherwise attributed, are my own throughout.

and the dissolution of the monasteries were others). But for Pole it was perhaps the most personally painful, and it precipitated his own crisis of obedience. This was the major crisis of Pole's life, transforming not just his attitude toward Henry but his whole religious life, his conception of history, and his Latin prose style.[6]

Pole's life was first touched by the changes taking place in Henry's England when he returned from Padua in 1527 and had his conversation with Cromwell about Machiavelli's ideas (and their relevance to Henry's intended divorce). In 1529 he left for study in Paris, but while there was asked by the king to act as royal emissary in obtaining an opinion on the divorce from the University of Paris. He later claimed to have resisted this task and to have delegated it to Edward Fox. What Pole's actual role was remains unclear, but it is evident that bribery was involved, whether Pole knew of it or not. It seems likely that whatever role Pole played in the mission, he could not have then held such an uncompromising view of the divorce as he was later to do. In 1530 Henry VIII offered Pole the See of York on condition that he declare his opinion of the divorce. Pole tried to devise an acceptable compromise, but when the time came to explain it to the king, he became tongue-tied and then found himself, despite his plan, condemning the divorce to the king himself in the strongest of terms. He attempted to conciliate the king afterward, but as his position had not really changed, he was unsuccessful. He was allowed to leave England again in 1532 because, according to Eustace Chapuys, the imperial ambassador, he threatened to speak his mind publicly if made to stay. Abroad again, Pole retained his various benefices and royal pension, and Henry made further efforts to persuade him of the rightness of his cause. At this time the breach was not permanent, but it was soon to become so. In Italy, Pole's studies took a theological turn and, influenced by the intense piety of Gasparo Contarini and his associates in the Oratory of Divine Love, and by other currents of religious feeling in Padua and Venice, Pole experienced something of a religious conversion. In the words of one member of his circle, "Pole is studying divinity and *meteorologizei*, despising things merely human and terrestrial. He is undergoing a great change, exchanging man for God."[7]

---

[6] His style loses polish and urbanity and gains in vehemence at this point. See Noëlle-Marie Egretier, ed., *Défense de l'unité de l'Église* (Paris, 1967), pp. 36–41 and refs., but see also Dunn, "The development of the text," pp. 464–7.

[7] Fenlon, *Heresy*, p. 36, citing a letter of John Friar to Thomas Starkey; J. S. Brewer, James Gairdner, and R. H. Brodie, eds., *Letters and Papers, Foreign and Domestic, of the Reign of Henry VIII* (London, 1862–1910), IX [no. 917]. This collection will be cited hereafter as *L.P. Meteorologizei* [Gk.] means "he speaks of high things, spiritual matters."

Thus, when Henry VIII set Thomas Starkey the task of getting Pole to declare his views on the supremacy in 1535, it was a far more religiously committed man with whom they had to deal. Pole's answer took the form of a treatise, the *De Unitate*, which was sent to Henry in 1536. It is a scathing attack on Henry VIII and on his policies, and it led to a complete break.

Pole's family had remained in England, and in 1538 Reginald Pole's elder brother Henry was executed. His aged mother was imprisoned, and later (1541) she too lost her life as a result of her son's rebellion. Pole knew of the danger, and in fact this aspect of his allegiance to Rome – that he had to abandon his family to likely death to proclaim it – helps explain why his conversion was so thorough, his position in regard to Henry so uncompromising. The personal stakes were too high to permit halfhearted solutions: In the *De Unitate* he adopts the role of the zealot and the prophet, casting earthly attachments aside in favor of identification with biblical exemplars of selfless devotion, cutting ties not only to his king but also to his family. Having put them at risk, he rejects the claims of his human family, and the church becomes his mother:

I have seen you kill those who were dearer to me for Christ's sake than my own parents [More and Fisher]: I see your hand now make every effort to destroy the unity of the Church of Christ and to break off, so much as lies in your power, a large part of it, that unity that ought to be dearer to me than my parents and my country, dearer than the entire creation. Now I am not completely silent, but my mother the Church has taught me to speak, and in this decisive and perilous moment at which she finds herself should I not raise my voice? Should I not speak? Should I not cry out? (Sig. Svv)

Pole may have had Saint Cyprian's well-known saying in mind: One cannot have God for a father who has not the church for a mother. Henry, by rejecting one, had lost the other, whereas Pole, in his own understanding of these events, was drawing nearer to his heavenly parents by rejecting the king who had been a symbolic father to him, but at the terrible cost of abandoning his mother to Henry's revenge. Only by recourse to the transcendent, among biblical examples of martyrdom and sacrifice, could he find solace (and sanction) for the course of action his conscience thrust upon him.

Dermot Fenlon has written brilliantly of Pole's spiritual life at this time, relating Pole's experiences to those of the *spirituali* influenced by Juan de Valdes and to other traditions of piety and meditation. Pole's was an intensely personal conversion, but it also entailed the adoption of a scriptural attitude toward history and politics:

At Venice, in the Benedictine setting of S. Giorgio Maggiore, and at Padua, in that of S. Justina, Pole now came into contact with the new Biblical scholarship, and with a style of exegesis which began profoundly to influence his whole cast of mind. He attended lectures on Isaiah given by the Hebrew scholar Jan van Kempen (Iohannes Campensis) whom Contarini had summoned to S. Justina; there, too, he became familiar with the Scriptures as expounded by the Benedictine scholar Isodorus Clarius. From this time forward, we find in his writings a pervasive consciousness of God's continuous dealings with mankind in history. Pole's thought becomes from this date permeated by the Bible. The effect may be described as follows. He learnt to apply the Bible as an interpretative key to history, including the events of his own time. Time became for him the movement of providential history; he began to read events in the light of what the Scriptures yielded.[8]

In consequence of this new scriptural orientation, Pole's works in which English history is at issue, especially the *De Unitate* and the *Apologia*, place current events in the larger sequences of sacred history and relate contemporary persons to their biblical (and especially apocalyptic) counterparts. Pole's personal crisis thus came to seem part of the larger historical crisis as the tragedy of More and Fisher, the suffering of his family, and his own agonies of conscience became part of the universal anguish that marked the coming of the Last Days. Pole's resistance to Henry was like that of the prophets opposing the wicked kings of Israel, his testimony like the witness the church would be called upon to make against Antichrist.

The *De Unitate* was finished in early 1536 and sent to Henry VIII in May. In the same year, Pole was made a cardinal and shortly thereafter was appointed papal legate to England at a time when Henry faced serious domestic resistance. Pole's two legatine missions ended in failure. It was during the second of these (1538–9) that he visited Emperor Charles V and attempted to convince him to invade England. The *Apologia* was probably written as an elaboration of the verbal arguments Pole had made to Charles in person. Van Dyke dates its composition between August 1538, when Henry VIII was excommunicated, and early 1539, after Pole read Richard Morison's treatise defending the execution of Pole's brother, Henry Lord Montague, and that of Henry Courtenay, Marquis of Exeter (late January 1539).[9] Charles did not invade England, nor did he share Pole's view of the threat Machiavelli posed to Christendom, for in 1550 he licensed the Spanish translation of the *Discorsi* and stated, in the text of the *privileg*, that he considered the book "very useful and profitable" and had

[8] Fenlon, *Heresy*, pp. 30–1.
[9] Van Dyke, *Renascence Portraits*, pp. 387–8.

commended it to his son Philip.[10] Pole apparently made subsequent efforts to oppose Machiavellian influence: An English traveler to Italy who met Pole reported to the Privy Council a plan of Pole's to do all he could to see that the book was banned; he set his nephew, Henry Huntington, the task of translating portions of Osorio's *De Nobilitate* (1542), which contains the first published attack on Machiavelli; another early critic of Machiavelli, Lancelotto Politi (*De libris christiano detestandis*, 1551), may have known Pole's views, for his own argument is quite similar; so it seems quite likely that Pole's anti-Machiavellian opinions had some subsequent influence, despite the *Apologia*'s remaining unpublished in the sixteenth century. All of Machiavelli's works were placed on the first papal Index in 1559.[11]

Pole's apocalyptic typology: Machiavellism as secret doctrine

In the *Apologia*, Pole's central argument is that the actions of Henry VIII – his claim to be head of the church, the desecration of shrines and monasteries, his manipulation of statute to achieve the death of his opponents – all flow from adherence to a secret doctrine, namely, that of Machiavelli's *Il Principe*, which is satanic in inspiration and whose influence in England is a sign of the coming of Antichrist. Pole's story of his meeting with Thomas Cromwell (pp. 133–6) is designed to reveal how Pole came to know about this doctrine, while at the same time demonstrating that Cromwell wanted to keep it secret.

The *Apologia* is structured so that the recital of Henry VIII's enormities builds suspense for the revelation of Machiavelli as the key to his policies:

But this will be seen much more clearly when I reveal the sources of his counsels, from which those actions derive. (p. 111)

I say only what all would have said had they the same opportunity to know that I have had. For the inmost core of their counsel or should I say their doctrine, which the king, now inclining wholly to tyranny, set up as the new pattern for his actions and upon which the rest of his plans depended, was

---

[10]Adolph Gerber, *Niccolò Machiavelli: Die Handschriften, Ausgaben und Ubersetzungen seiner Werke im 16. und 17. Jahrhundert* (Gotha, 1912–13; repr. Turin, 1962), II, p. 4.
[11]Letter of John Legh to Privy Council, *L.P.* XV, 337 [no. 721]; Hieronymus Osorius, *De nobilitate civili, libri duo* (Lisbon, 1542), fols. 98ff.; letter of Pole to Catherine Pole, Bodleian MSS Carte 78, fol. 251r; Ambrosius Catharinus [Lancelotto Politi], *De libris christiano detestandis, et a christianismo penitus eliminandis* [printed as coll. 339–44 of the *Disputationes* appended to the author's *Enarationes in quinque priora capita libri Geneseos*] (Rome, 1551–2). Friedrich Heinrich Reusch, *Die Indices librorum prohibitorum des sechzehnten Jahrhunderts* (Tubingen, 1886; repr. Nieuwkoop, 1970), p. 198.

easy to judge from the slaughter of those nobles that eventuated. And because I happened to discover this doctrine, I was able to predict what has actually happened. This is not because I was led by any special prescience, but because I knew the counsels of these men. (p. 114)

And now I shall reveal, as I promised, the inmost counsel of the man who (along with his subordinates) alone was grieved that the king was returning to better thoughts. (p. 117)

When Henry wavered about seeking a divorce, Satan sent "one of his own privy councillors" with "more ample orders" in order to strengthen the king's intention to gratify his lust. Pole knows "what those orders were, who brought them, and by whom he was sent" (p. 118), but he delays many pages before revealing that the *nuntius Satanae* was Cromwell (p. 126) and that it was Machiavelli who wrote the text that he used to corrupt the king (p. 137). Even in the actual story of the meeting between Pole and Cromwell, the title of *Il Principe* and the identity of its author remain concealed, as we shall see.

The meeting took place at a time when Henry was seeking advice about his divorce. Pole had just returned from Italy, and Cromwell, welcoming him home, drew him into a conversation about the duties of royal counselors, hoping to find out which way Pole inclined on the divorce question. Pole thought one should tell kings what was honorable, honest, and useful. Cromwell thought this naive: Such ideas were very well in school debates but useless and even dangerous at court, for what princes wanted was not always honorable or honest. This fact could not be taught in schools, and so scholars newly come to court were in some danger of bringing trouble upon themselves and those closest to them through their lack of experience. Cromwell's own opinion was that the counselor should try to find out what the prince really wanted ("quo tendat voluntas principis") and help ensure that the prince got his way without appearing to be irreligious or immoral. Cromwell recommended that Pole read a book (if he read at all; experience was a better teacher) by a perceptive modern writer who based his views on experience rather than on dreams like those to be found in Plato's *Republic*. Pole did promise to read it, but it was never sent because, Pole thought, Cromwell could judge his real reaction from his face. However, when Pole discovered from those familiar with Cromwell's "secret studies" what book was meant, he took no less pains to get a copy than one might to intercept the secret orders of an enemy in the hope of discovering his plans.

For Pole *Il Principe* was written by Satan in the same sense in which Scripture was written by God (p. 137). It was a new doctrine, a *nova ars regnandi* (p. 151), rejecting entirely the traditional basis of statecraft in the kingly virtues and the common good. Machiavelli's doctrine transferred the *arcana imperii* to the custody of the lion and the fox (p. 140), that is to say, based the security of the state on the use of force and fraud.[12] Pole considered the doctrines of *Il Principe* literally satanic in origin: The book bore the name of the man on its title page but was "written by the finger of Satan" (p. 137).

Pole also saw Satan's hand in the transmission of the text, for Cromwell, who was to corrupt Henry with Machiavelli's ideas, had first to be corrupted by demons. Indeed, Pole speaks of him as having become wholly inhabited by them, with little of his human identity left, before he could become the conveyer of Machiavellian influence to England (p. 126). This influence was the turning point in Henry's reign. Basing his advice on Machiavelli's supposed rejection of absolute standards of morality and advocacy of the use of religion as an instrument of policy, Cromwell convinced Henry (pp. 118–23) to declare himself head of the church and seize the property of the monasteries. In taking these steps, therefore, Henry was in fact yielding to Machiavellian (and thus demonic) influence. But in Pole's account, Henry did not know the source of these ideas, for Cromwell mentioned no source. Without naming Machiavelli, Cromwell nevertheless transmitted the essential core of Machiavellian doctrine to Henry, who thenceforth embodied that doctrine "to the letter" (p. 146) in his policies. The king became a "disciple" (pp. 144, 151) who manifested the teachings of his master more exactly than the Disciples embodied those of Christ. Thus Machiavelli's ideas are the doctrines or dogmas of Satan (pp. 114–15 and passim), and *Il Principe* is treated as the apocryphon, or secret book, that embodies them and is kept concealed not only from Pole but even from the king, who became an adherent of Machiavellism without knowing it.

Machiavelli could be thought of as the purveyor of a secret doctrine partly because, at the time of his purported influence on Henry VIII, *Il Principe* existed only in manuscript. It was published in 1532, but even after it was widely known it was often thought of as a book that dealt with the *arcana imperii* or secrets of rule.[13] This view was partly

---

[12] "Et ideo arcanum illud imperii tuendi cum omni securitate, atque felicitate, ad leonis violentiam, et vulpis dolos transfert" (p. 140). Pole's use of the term *arcanum* in this context reflects Machiavelli's own comparison of his teaching concerning the lion and the fox to the secrets of state taught to Achilles by Chiron and allegorically hinted at by ancient writers (*Prin.* 18).

[13] This association between Machiavelli and the *arcana imperii* will be touched on frequently in the following pages, especially in Chapter 4. See also Anna Maria Battista, "Direzioni di ricerca per una storia di Machiavelli in Francia," *Atti del convegno inter-*

a consequence of Machiavelli's self-presentation in his works. He characterizes himself as an innovator, a discoverer or rediscoverer of "new modes and orders" (see *Disc.*, preface; *Prin.* 15); he addresses his reader with an almost conspiratorial intimacy; he compares his own doctrine to the secret instruction of Achilles by the Centaur (*Prin.* 18). That doctrine itself, with its emphasis on secrecy, deception, and dissimulation, also lent credence to the notion that he was revealing the "secrets of rule" hinted at by Aristotle, Tacitus,[14] and other ancient writers: Surely if the Tacitean phrase *arcana imperii* meant anything, it must refer to these teachings of Machiavelli, which seemed, by making ordinary readers privy to the moral license by which princes achieved their ends, to disclose the trade secrets of statecraft. In addition, there was a built-in paradox in the publication of such secrets, for if these really were the techniques by which clever men gained power over others, then publishing them for all to read could only weaken their effectiveness. From this paradox grew a tradition of interpretation that saw Machiavelli as the revealer of princely secrets to the masses. For those who followed this line of interpretation, Machiavelli was secretly democratic in his sympathies and published the arcana in order to alert the populace to the deceptions of their rulers.

Cardinal Pole held no such views of Machiavelli's intentions, but his *Apologia* nevertheless provides the first evidence of such an interpretive tradition, for Pole says that on a trip to Florence he was told by Machiavelli's fellow citizens that the author himself claimed that he had written *Il Principe* only in order to hasten the downfall of the Medici (p. 151).[15] Pole rejects this story as excuse making. But if he rejects the idea of an antityrannical Machiavelli, he nevertheless seizes upon the paradox that lies at the heart of this story and makes it an essential part of his own analysis of Machiavellism. There is an inherent contradiction in the publication of political techniques that would work better if they remained secret. For Pole, this contradiction reflected the opposition between satanic concealment and divine revelation in the workings of the historical process. Machiavellism was a doctrine of secrecy and deception that contained the seeds of its own destruction, for the more widely it was known, the more its secrets would

---

nazionale su il pensiero politico di Machiavelli e la sua fortuna nel mondo (Florence: Istituto nazionale di studi sul Rinascimento, 1972), p. 63n; Hermann Hegels, *Arnold Clapmarius und die Publizistik über die arcana imperii im 17. Jahrhundert* (Bonn, 1918), p. 49.

[14] See, for example, Tacitus, *Annals* 2:36; Aristotle, *Politics*, 4:13, 5:8.

[15] The notion of Machiavelli as a hater of tyranny who wrote with the secret intention of ruining the Medici is also found in Giovanni Matteo Toscano, *Peplus Italiae* (Paris, 1578), p. 52, and in Alberico Gentili, *De legationibus libri tres* (London, 1585). See Chapter 3, this volume.

stand revealed. This paradox illustrated, in extreme form, the self-defeating character of all human attempts to hide the truth; what Pole took to be the unprecedented espousal of dishonesty in *Il Principe* was a sign of the approach of the biblically predicted time when evil would stand fully revealed. We must follow Pole's attempt to link Machiavelli's text to biblical archetypes of secrecy and concealment in some detail.

Pole's apocalyptic typology: occultation and revelation in history

Pole saw Machiavellism as preeminently a doctrine of concealment. The "entire doctrine of Cromwell and Machiavelli" was contained in the idea that the prince should serve his own desires "under pretext of religion" (p. 145). Pole's reading of Machiavelli was an intense but somewhat narrow one. Only the phrase *via media* (p. 138) suggests any acquaintance with the *Discorsi*. Of *Il Principe* he knows chapters 15–19 (Cromwell's reference to Plato, p. 135, paraphrases *Prin.* 15; the discussion of how to avoid being hated, p. 147, refers to *Prin.* 19). What Pole knows best about *Il Principe* are those passages in which the appearance of religion and virtue is said to be more useful than the actualities:

He who wishes always to follow truth and faith and religion will never live safe from snares. But neither will he who openly neglects religion find a better state. When then is to be done? Holding a middle course, as prudence dictates, you will observe religion when your advantage instructs you; when it dictates otherwise you will not be so scrupulous that you will not swerve from it, nor on the other hand so rash that you will openly reject it. (pp. 138–9; cf. *Prin.* 18)

What he says of religion . . . he expresses in clearer words concerning all the virtues which religion requires to be observed: piety, faith, justice, liberality, clemency; to possess and observe these is most harmful for princes, but to display the appearances of them, and to be able to use them appropriately as advantage dictates – that is always profitable. (p. 139; *Prin.* 18)

Truly that prince will excel in proportion as he knows how to simulate and dissimulate, and let him be careful in this business to show that while he rejects those virtues about which, when philosophers write about them they make their books so admirable, he nevertheless holds religion, faith and justice in great esteem, and that he follows them without reluctance. And it will be profitable to demonstrate this even by some deed, as is advantageous. In fact it is not prejudicial to employ these virtues from time to time. But he concludes that to be addicted to them, and to show oneself as, and actually to be a persistent observer of them, has never been profitable to anyone. (p. 140; *Prin.* 18)

Pole was quite familiar with chapter 18, and indeed takes it for the whole of Machiavelli's thought.

In the *Apologia* this Machiavellian motif of dissimulation is set in contrast to the biblical theme of revelation. What men most try to hide is often brought to light by providential discovery or by the very publicity that attends the attempt to conceal. For example, Machiavelli had advised the prince to avoid being hated at all costs (*Prin.* 17, 19), yet had also advised the simulation of virtues:

And this least of all escapes his notice: that if the simulation is recognized, it is not possible to avoid hatred, and therefore he diligently warns the prince to be careful lest he be caught simulating the virtues. But that, most foolish and impious of men, lies not within man's power; the matter rests with God who knows of all things and reveals them when he wishes to do so. The words of His Son are "there is nothing hidden that will not be revealed, nor can a city on a mountaintop be hidden." Indeed, even if the simulation of a private man may be hidden for a time, how much more difficult it is for a prince, whose every word and deed, even his sighs, groans, and every gesture of his body (which so often express the soul) are noted. It cannot be, and nature herself says that nothing simulated can be eternal. (p. 147)

Henry VIII himself is a fine example of the ironic character of the project of concealment: "The more he has labored to hide his lusts and wicked desires, the more divine providence has revealed them, to his shame" (p. 148). "When he sent round to all the universities to obtain support for his divorce, he merely advertised his lust, and made himself a laughing stock for taking such pains to prove himself incestuous!" (pp. 148–9). In this case, the act of concealment itself is the means of revelation; in others, as in Pole's chance encounter with Cromwell, providence assists. In all cases what is hidden eventually comes to light. Behind this contrast of occultation and revelation lies the apocalyptic notion that the work of Satan is a secret work, and that as the Last Days approach, Satan's power will greatly increase and its increase will be accompanied by its revelation to all. When Antichrist's power is complete, his revelation will also be complete, and he will be ripe for destruction. The key biblical text for this notion is 2 Thessalonians 2:

Let no one deceive you in any way; for that day will not come, unless the rebellion comes first, and the man of lawlessness is revealed, the son of perdition, who opposes and exalts himself against every so-called god or object of worship, so that he takes his seat in the temple of God, proclaiming himself to be God. . . . And you know what is restraining him now so that he may be revealed in his time. For the mystery of lawlessness is already at work [Vulgate: *nam mysterium iam operatur iniquitatis*]; only he who now restrains it will do so until he is out of the way. And then the lawless one will be revealed, and the Lord Jesus will slay him with the breath of his mouth and destroy him by his appearing and coming.[16]

The god-challenging motif of this passage is crucial to Pole's attempt to identify Henry VIII as a precursor of Antichrist, and will be discussed later. For now, we are concerned with the relation between concealment and revelation: Antichrist works in mystery, but only until the proper moment when he stands revealed. Pole clearly thought of his own age as the time when the secret works of Antichrist were being revealed, despite themselves, more fully than ever before, and believed that this revelation marked the start of a new·phase of sacred history. In Henry VIII's manipulation of English law to secure the death of his opponents, Pole saw the mystery of evil,

if I should call that a mystery which is so openly manifested by anyone who, in the spirit of Antichrist, assails the servants of Christ and precedes his coming. But if Antichrist is revealed by the open performance of the works of Antichrist, and if the works of Antichrist are those that the prophet Daniel distinctly set forth and Paul enumerated: to proffer speeches against the Most High and persecute his saints, to rise so high in one's pride that one thinks he can change the laws and the times, then who ever displayed the works of Antichrist so openly and less mysteriously? (pp. 155–6)

Antichrist worked in secret in the past, but in Henry VIII he works openly:

Who would ever try this except he who worked openly in the spirit of Antichrist, and no longer in mystery? (p. 157)

These are not so much mysteries, are they, or even the now open evidence of the working of Satan and the reign of Antichrist? For could Satan himself, if he had come and were already revealed, have exalted his throne any higher? I think he could not. (p. 159)

Henry VIII remains a type or a precursor (p. 169) of Antichrist. But his resemblance to the archetype is exact: he

so closely expresses the kingdom of Antichrist *in typo* that if I wanted to examine the exact words that are spoken of the reign of Antichrist, I should not find even one word that he does not embody so closely that a painter could never present a more exact image of anyone. (p. 169)

[16]Biblical texts are cited in the Revised Standard Version.

He so embodies the form of the reign of Antichrist that it has never been seen, these many centuries, in such open form in any other king or tyrant, Christian or infidel. (pp. 167–8)

This closeness of approximation to type, and the transition from the *in mysterio* of earlier tyrants to the *palam* or *aperte* of Henry VIII is of the greatest importance for our attempt to define Pole's use of apocalyptic models. For in insisting that Henry is a more open and more complete approximation of the archetype than has been seen before, Pole adopts a progressive or historicist approach to the biblical texts, seeing the events of his own time as part of an unfolding process rather than as static reflections of unchanging biblical models. According to Firth, such an emphasis was a special mark of the sixteenth-century *Protestant* apocalyptic tradition: "If [an author] asserts that the revelation of such corruption at one time rather than another is particularly significant, or that by its recognition and defeat a new era in history has begun, then we are dealing with the first signs of the apocalyptic tradition in Protestant historiography."[17] Pole has a similar understanding of his own era.

Thus Pole saw the ironies of Henry's career and the ironies of Machiavellian dissimulation as closely related, and placed both in the context of Antichrist's self-concealment and eventual revelation. There had been wicked kings and wicked counselors before: The inescapable power of sin ensured that political life, like the rest of life, would be morally flawed. But to sin *ex fragillitate* (p. 143), out of human weakness, was one thing, and to embrace sin as a willfully adopted, explicit political principle was another. In Pole's view, the explicit commitment to evil of *Il Principe* and the manifestation of this principle in Henry's actions was something wholly new in the world, marking a distinction between Henry VIII and all previous tyrants and connecting him with Antichrist. The argument Pole makes for the novelty of Machiavelli's "new art of ruling" is thus also an argument concerning the chronology of sacred history, which must enter a new phase as biblical archetypes come closer to fulfillment or are approximated in radically new ways.

Pole's periodization of sacred history is relatively free of the numerical calculations that were often made by apocalyptic writers. His use of Revelation itself, from which most such schemes derive, is very sparing, and though Daniel provided a variety of numerical sequences as well, Pole, who uses Daniel frequently, always breaks his citation

---

[17]Katherine R. Firth, *The Apocalyptic Tradition in Reformation Britain 1530–1645* (Oxford, 1979), p. 7.

off just as the numbers become specific (e.g., the "time, two times and half a time" of Daniel 7:25). Nevertheless, his view of the character of the era in which he lived, and of its relative place in the sequence of apocalyptic events, is clear. The Machiavellian age would be that period foretold in Revelation 20 in which Satan was released from his bonds for a time and in which Antichrist would appear. Before his own age was the period after Christ came and during which Satan was bound; after it would come the defeat of Antichrist and the Second Coming. This sequence can be observed in Pole's extended argument that the desecration of saints' shrines could not have taken place unless Satan had been released from bondage (p. 101) because the power of Satan over the bodies of saints had been reined in since the coming of Christ (p. 102); in his claim that Henry represents Antichrist in a new way; and in his prediction of Henry's fall (pp. 167ff.), which will mirror that of Antichrist. The insistence upon the exact similarity between Henry VIII and Antichrist (pp. 157, 159, 167–8) seems to leave no room for tyrants to come who will be just a bit worse than Henry and just a bit short of Antichrist, so it seems that Pole thought that his own period (the unbinding of Satan) would be brief and that Antichrist would shortly appear. Perhaps Henry would become Antichrist himself, or would be revealed to have been Antichrist himself all along; Pole's falling short of asserting complete identity may be scrupulosity. Having begun with the composition of *Il Principe* ("by the finger of Satan"), this era would end with the full revelation of Antichrist.

Pole thus has a place in the history of the revival of "historicist" exegesis of the apocalyptic material in the Bible. Recent studies (those of Firth, Patterson, and Bauckham)[18] have agreed in finding the main medieval tradition a relatively ahistorical one in respect to apocalyptic. Augustine's views dominated, and for him, unlike many of his predecessors who expected an imminent end and saw scriptural prophecy unfolding in their own time, the Last Days are far off, and the archetypes of apocalypse tend to become ideal types rather than historical realities. As such they are still intimately relevant to experience, for every wicked king is in some sense Antichrist and every man is Adam; but the watchful assessment of current events for evidence of the changing of the times falls into disuse. It survives, as the labors of

[18]Firth, *The Apocalyptic Tradition;* Lloyd Patterson, *God and History in Early Christian Thought* (London, 1967); Richard Bauckham, *Tudor Apocalypse* (Abingdon, 1978). For a fuller discussion of the terminology employed in this paragraph and its application to the sixteenth century, see especially Bauckham's introduction and chap. 1 ("The medieval heritage").

Marjorie Reeves[19] and others have made us amply aware, in the Joachimist tradition and elsewhere; nevertheless it makes sense to claim, as Patterson, Bauckham, and Firth all do, that historicist exegesis experienced a revival in the sixteenth century. This revival entailed a shift in the apocalyptic chronology, especially in regard to the events of Revelation 20. That passage speaks of a thousand-year period in which Satan would be bound, then of a briefer period during which he would be set free for a short time. After that (or perhaps not; perhaps the millennium runs concurrently with the binding of Satan) will come the millennium, or thousand-year period during which the saints will come to life and rule with Christ. For Augustine, and for the ahistorical exegete generally, the millennium, or rule of the saints, was coterminous with the period of the binding of Satan: It was the period of the ascendancy of the church and the time in which he lived. For Joachim, the millennium was a future, but still historical, period that would follow the imminent unloosing of Satan. By and large, the sixteenth-century apocalyptic writers took the view (deriving from Wyclif's *De solutione Sathanae*) that Satan had already been unleashed and that Antichrist was embodied in the papacy – but they did not expect a future millennium, as some seventeenth-century writers were to do. These sixteenth-century Protestants were historicist in their interpretation of the apocalyptic prophecies, but not millenarian. Reginald Pole's handling of sacred chronology is very similar: There is no indication that he looks forward to a historical rule of the saints, and he sees his own period as one in which Satan had been recently released from his bonds; the mystery of iniquity is rapidly revealing itself, and lacks but little of the full revelation that will signal the defeat of Antichrist by the radiance of the Second Coming. Needless to say, the *dramatis personae* are quite different. For the Protestants the pope played a role like that Pole assigned to Henry, except that Protestants sometimes regarded the pope as Antichrist himself, rather than as a *precursor Antichristi*. The part of satanic Gospel, which Pole assigns to *Il Principe*, is sometimes played in Protestant mythology by papal decrees or canon law. But for Pole, as for them, the events of his own time were rapidly fulfilling biblical predictions of a time in which evil would fully manifest itself, and in which the true church would again suffer persecution, martyrdom, and division, before the Second Coming.

It is of special interest that one variety of Protestant apocalyptic

[19] See esp. Marjorie Reeves, *The Influence of Prophecy in the Later Middle Ages: A Study in Joachimism* (Oxford, 1969).

comes even closer to Pole's exact scheme. Pole was not unique in the sixteenth century in holding that the advent of Machiavelli marked a sacred epoch. Antonio D'Andrea has shown that a very similar view was presented in the 1577 preface to the Latin translation of Innocent Gentillet's *Contremachiavel.*[20] In this view, the new era began when John Wyclif and John Hus began to preach the Gospel in contemporary languages. The open preaching of the word of God was a blow to Satan's power, which he responded to by inspiring the soul-destroying doctrines of Machiavelli. It is possible that Pole's anti-Machiavellian campaign had an influence, direct or indirect, on this formulation, and there may even have been a family memory of Pole's strong views on Machiavelli in play, for Francis Hastings, Pole's grandnephew, was a member of the Gentillet circle and the Latin translation is dedicated to him. At this point, it is sufficient to note the convergence: There were other attempts in the sixteenth century to place Machiavelli in the framework of a revived historicist exegesis of apocalyptic prophecy.

Super omne quod dicitur deus: Machiavelli and deification

One of the traditional marks of Antichrist was his claim to divine status. Pole draws on three biblical texts in his association of Henry VIII with the self-deification of Antichrist. First, there was the "Lucifer" passage of Isaiah 14:13–14 (cf. *Apologia*, p. 158):

You said in your heart, "I will ascend to heaven; above the stars of God I will set my throne on high; I will sit on the mount of assembly in the far north; I will ascend above the heights of the clouds, I will make myself like the Most High."

The second text was the "son of perdition" passage of 2 Thessalonians 2, cited earlier: He will "exalt himself against every so-called god or object of worship, so that he takes his seat in the temple of God, proclaiming himself to be God." Since this passage in Thessalonians is based upon Daniel's description of the king symbolized by the "little horn" of the fourth beast of his vision (Daniel 11:36), Pole turned to the Book of Daniel for his third text. The "little horn" would be a "king of bold countenance, one who understands riddles . . . by his cunning he shall make deceit prosper under his hand, and in his own mind he shall magnify himself." He will "speak words against the Most High, and shall wear out the saints of the Most High, and shall think

---

[20] Antonio D'Andrea, "Machiavelli, Satan, and the Gospel," *Yearbook of Italian Studies* I (1971), 156–77, citing Innocent Gentillet, *Commentariorum de regno . . . adversus Nicolaum Machiavellum Florentinum* (Geneva, 1578), preface.

to change the times and the law" (Daniel 8:25; 7:25; pp. 156, 158, 168–9).

As apocalyptic identifications go, the association of Henry VIII with this composite God-challenging figure was not bad: Henry was arguably intelligent and arrogant, was certainly a northern king, had unquestionably made himself head of the church, and that could be thought of as a kind of deification. Indeed, John Jewel and others who applied these prophecies to the papacy pointed out that the pope's claim to be head of the church entailed invasion of divine prerogative.[21] For Pole, the godlike powers of the papacy were legitimate and Henry's usurpation of them was blasphemous. It was more difficult to make these passages fit Machiavelli. The secular outlook of *Il Principe* might well be thought uncongenial to divine pretensions, and indeed, Machiavelli's originality has often been thought to lie in his moving politics out of the sphere of the sacred altogether. For Pole, however, the secular world was part of a sacred universe, so that movement in thought away from sacred categories remained enclosed by those categories. Specifically, he holds that there is an implicit claim to godhead in the relativizing of good and evil in *Il Principe*, and that Machiavellian manipulation of religion, morality, or law entails a reversal of the roles of creature and Creator, and therefore fulfills the predicted arrogance of Antichrist.

The speech Cromwell makes to Henry VIII (pp. 118–23) is Pole's link between Machiavelli's text and biblical prophecy. Pole claims that this speech was the result of the satanic influence of Machiavelli on Cromwell. In it, Cromwell argues that the limitations placed on Henry's actions – indeed, on any prince's actions – derive from the undue influence of academic conceptions of statecraft, for scholars "argue that honesty has its foundation in nature, from which no one can decline in any way and not be considered wicked, whether he be prince or subject" (p. 119). But this idea has a leveling effect, for it binds prince and subject to the same standard. In fact, moral categories have no absolute sanction:

Experience of affairs, which is the better teacher, teaches that in fact the honest often changes. For if its foundation were fixed in nature, it would not vary so much among us, who live in nature, that what is called wicked among one nation would be called honest among another; what is called honest at one time be called wicked at another. . . . And if the definition of the honest is changed according to human will, whose will can more appropriately change it than that of princes, whose wishes ought to be held for laws? (p. 120)

[21] Bauckham, *Tudor Apocalypse*, chap. 5 ("The Antichrist").

The principle that the honest has no basis in nature has two practical consequences: Henry should declare himself head of the church (thus removing the moral authority that has fettered his desires) and should rule according to his will, which the people ought to accept as law.

Pole believed, then, that this speech was the result of the satanic influence of Machiavelli on Cromwell, and that in consequence of it Henry VIII himself became a disciple of Machiavelli. It is clear that Pole takes it to be, self-evidently, a restatement of the argument of *Il Principe*. In fact, however, it is much further removed from genuinely Machiavellian ideas than what Cromwell had said to Pole about *Il Principe* (pp. 135–6) and Pole's own summary (pp. 138–40) of the book – and even those are distortions. Indeed, Machiavelli does say, especially in the chapters Pole knew best, that the prince's conduct must violate moral norms; but this relativism is pragmatic, not philosophical. Machiavelli never claims that morality is an arbitrary human invention, only that it is sometimes necessary to act immorally to achieve political ends (*entrare nel male, necessitato*). Also, Machiavelli provides no direct support for a politics based upon the satisfaction of the private desires of princes. He is more interested in analyzing the conditions under which political power is acquired and maintained, and these conditions largely rule out the kind of arbitrariness proposed in Cromwell's speech. Thus, even if the speech were a verbatim account, it would not demonstrate a specifically Machiavellian influence on Henry VIII, as Pole thought it did. It is not, in any case, a verbatim transcript; Pole admits he was not present, but claims to know its substance (p. 123). He believed he had verified Cromwell's opinions, but reveals that he took the liberty of collecting together various things he knew Cromwell thought into one speech (p. 124). In recent years it has come to seem likely, on independent grounds, that Pole's account has some basis in fact; Cromwell may indeed have put before the king a plan that called for autonomy from Rome, and he may have risen in the king's service because of it.[22] But the connection with Machiavelli that the speech itself offers is too tenuous to permit the conclusion that Machiavelli was behind this plan or that Henry, in following it, became Machiavellian in any meaningful sense.

The significance of the speech for this inquiry is that its particular reading of *Il Principe*, distorted or not, permitted Pole to associate Machiavelli's teachings with the God-challenging subordination of law to will that was predicted of Antichrist. Antichrist would "seek to

[22] Geoffrey R. Elton, *Reform and Reformation: England 1509–1558* (Cambridge, Mass., 1977), pp. 136–7.

change the times and the law"; in Pole's opinion, no heretic or schismatic had ever gone so far as Machiavelli and Cromwell in undermining the basis of law and substituting human will for it (pp. 128, 141–3). Henry VIII's proceedings confirmed the principle, for in acting against internal opposition (especially against Pole's family), he had begun to manipulate statute law in brazen and unprecedented ways. It is precisely this manipulation of the laws of treason and *lèse-majesté* which Pole cites as the working of the "mystery of iniquity" (p. 155). The God-challenging character of such manipulation is also seen in Henry's plan to change the sacraments:

He who revokes these according to the prescriptions of his own will, so that they are changed, corrected or deleted in accordance with the decision of his will, is he not saying in his heart "I shall place my seat in the far north, I shall be like the Most High?" (p. 158)

In fact, Henry had claimed more than divine status:

But truly if we wish to observe how he has comported himself in his rule over his own subjects, is it not enough of that pride of his that he assumes the role of God, but he must also elevate himself, as the Apostle said the Antichrist would do, above all that is called God? (p. 158).

This final elevation – above God – is seen in contempt for law rather than in another aspect of Henry's bad behavior because God himself obeyed his own laws and kept the covenants he had made with Abraham and with the people of Israel. Therefore, to change the laws according to one's desires, or to rule in defiance of law, is to "arrogate to himself a power over all the creation of the Most High which is higher than that which the Most High himself demands," and thus goes beyond giving "open evidence of the working of Satan" (p. 159) to those acts predicted of Antichrist himself.

To deny the sacred character of law (moral or statute) is equivalent to asserting the sacredness of the king's will. This line of reasoning associated Machiavelli with the presumptions of Antichrist, and also made of him a supporter of the notions of sacred kingship that were being revived and applied to Henry VIII by Edward Fox, Richard Sampson, and Stephen Gardiner.[23] In fact, many of the arguments Pole uses in the *Apologia* against Henry's self-exaltation are anticipated in the *De Unitate*, in which Henry's corruption is traced not to Ma-

---

[23] Edward Fox, *De vera differentia regiae potestatis et ecclesiasticae* (London, 1534); Richard Sampson, *Oratio; qua docet hortatur admonet omnes potissimum Anglos, regiae dignitati cum primis ut obediant . . .* (London, n.d.) [cited as *Oratio de dignitate et potestate regia*]; Stephen Gardiner, *De vera obedientia* (London, 1535), also printed in Pierre Janelle, ed., *Obedience in Church and State: Three Political Tracts by Stephen Gardiner* (Cambridge, 1930).

chiavelli, but to the inflated conception of the sacredness of kings proposed by Sampson in his *Oratio de dignitate et potestate regia* (e.g., Sigs. Pivr, Viir).

Quasi prophetae personam sumens: Pole as prophet

The assimilation of Henry VIII to the biblical Antichrist is paralleled in the *Apologia* and in the *De Unitate* by Pole's identification with the prophets. In the *Apologia*, Pole urges the emperor to oppose Henry as well as the Turk, taking on himself the prophetic office of predicting defeat unless the internal threat to Christendom is taken as seriously as the external one:

If I seem to speak too confidently on this point, as if assuming the role of a prophet pronouncing with certainty on the outcome of battles, it is because God's very justice, set before my eyes, makes me to speak, and allots such a role to me for this time. (p. 167).

Pole's principal prophetic role in the *Apologia,* however, is as revealer of concealed truth. Concerning this role, he is full of self-reproach:

Now that I am resisting him I ought to fear only the reproach of having not resisted him strongly enough, of having opposed his impiety too laxly, since although for many years I had tangible evidence in hand to reveal his malicious impiety, by which he deceived many, I was like a guardian of his honor and a defender, rather than an opponent of his wicked opinions: I did not make public but kept hidden and concealed for the space of three years what could have damaged his reputation. (p. 160)

The three-year wait referred to here may be the period between the completion of the *De Unitate* and the *Apologia* (1536–9), whereas "many years" more likely refers to the time that had elapsed (nine years, perhaps) since Pole had recognized in Henry's policies the presence of the Machiavellian influence that his talk with Cromwell had prepared him to expect. He promised to make up in diligence what he has lacked in promptness and to conceal nothing of Henry's counsels and actions (p. 160). Despite this promise, however, Pole continued to delay, for the *De Unitate* was published without his consent, and the *Apologia,* which contains the full account of the roles of Cromwell and Machiavelli, saw print only in the eighteenth century. But whatever second thoughts may have led to further suppression of facts that could have injured Henry's reputation, at the time of the writing of the *Apologia* itself, Pole held the view that the time for full revelation had come.

We have seen that several Old Testament prophecies (Isaiah 14,

Daniel 7, 8) were central to Pole's association of Henry VIII and Antichrist. These prophets also provided a model for Pole. There is something of each of them in Pole's self-presentation – Isaiah's reluctance and his balancing of internal and external threats; Daniel's confrontation of his king and his faith in a God who was preeminently a revealer of secrets (2:28–30, 47). Pole also draws on Ezekiel 14 (pp. 149–50) in predicting Henry's downfall. But the most explicit identification Pole makes is with Moses and the Levites. Having revealed the king's secrets, like Daniel, Pole calls for Holy War against him, as Moses did against the worshippers of the golden calf, and, like the Levites who responded to the call, takes upon himself the sacrifices the battle requires. In a particularly elaborate allegory, Pole likens the golden ornaments of the Israelites to the spiritual ornaments – religion, piety, and faith – taken away by Machiavelli. When Moses found that his people had yielded to idolatry, he called for battle, asking those loyal to him to take the sword and go through the camp, killing their own brothers and friends (Exodus 32:27–9). The Levites answer the call, and Pole echoes Moses' blessing of them:

If the voice of the prophet said to those Levites: "Blessed be thou in the Lord who have consecrated your hands in the blood of your relations," how much greater blessing will they merit who . . . consecrate their hands in the blood of those who have visited such ignominious slaughter upon the people? (p. 154)

Then he himself becomes a Levite:

Those princes of tribes to whom I am sent, I, one of those Levites who have said in this cause to father and mother, "I know you not," and to my brothers, "I do not know you," will they listen to me the less when I propose the example of the Levites as an excellent and most pious model for their imitation, will they less obey the voice of Him who sent me because in all his letters to them that predator of the people calls me a rebel and a traitor? (p. 154).

Pole's offer to sacrifice himself for Henry's salvation ("If my death could, by virtue of Christ, work any change in his life, I could pray God for no greater favor on earth – may God himself be my witness! – than to be made a sacrifice for him"; p. 168) echoes Moses' offer to his own damnation ("Blot me, I pray thee, out of thy book which thou hast written" [Exodus 32:31]) on behalf of the Jews. This kind of offer, made likewise by Paul (Romans 9:3), was also part of the office of the prophet, who intercedes for the sinning people to the point of offering himself in their stead.[24]

---

[24] Pole's stance as a militant prophet, calling for a Holy War or crusade against the new

Pole's habit of identification with the prophets was already well developed in the *De Unitate,* where the precise form this identification takes is somewhat different. The difference between Pole's conception of his prophetic role in the *De Unitate* and his later formulation of that role in the *Apologia* is not great, but it helps to explain why he did not write down what he knew about Cromwell and Machiavelli until he composed the *Apologia,* and why he put off the publication of the *Apologia* once he had written it. Van Dyke's major argument against the historicity of Pole's account of Cromwell's Machiavellian reading was that Pole does not mention Machiavelli in the *De Unitate* and barely mentions Cromwell, even though the *De Unitate* deals with the same events in English history and is, like the *Apologia,* a scathing attack on the king. If Pole thought that Cromwell's Machiavellism was the inspiration for Henry's actions, why did he not say so there? A partial answer is found in Pole's conception of his prophetic mission and its changing exigencies.

In the *De Unitate,* as in the *Apologia,* Pole says that hidden matters have been revealed to him and that he must, in turn, reveal them to others. Christ gave him the order to write his book (Sig. Vvir), directly entrusted to him what might save Henry (Sig. Vviv); God himself guided the decision to send the finished book to the king (Sig. Aiir). God also revealed to Pole the king's intentions (e.g., in seeking a divorce):

Who could have informed me in what spirit you did this? Who indeed except God knew your heart? Even he, to whom God wished to reveal it knew, prince. And I say it was I to whom God revealed your heart in this matter. (Sig. Niiiv).

In the *Apologia,* though, this "revelation" of Henry's motives is tied to the discovery by Pole of Henry's "inmost counsels," which are Machiavellian. Here Pole disavows special knowledge almost as soon as he had claimed it: "God revealed it to me, but not really to me any more than to anyone else who took the trouble to find out the cause" (ibid.). Then, in a passage omitted from the Public Record Office manuscript, Pole derives Henry's motive from the facts of the case: If Henry's scruples about his marriage to his brother's widow were sincere, he would not have gone on to marry his mistress's sister!

And if the claim to special knowledge is more ambiguous here (see

doctrines, follows biblical models, of course. But it also remains within the terms of Machiavellian discourse, echoing the call for a new Moses in the final chapter of *Il Principe.* Machiavelli speaks of the liberation of Italy as a redemption and invokes the Mosaic emblems of divine favor: "el mare si è aperto, una nube vi ha scorto el cammino, la pietra ha versato acqua, qui è piovuto la manna . . ."

also the discussion of Christ's special commission to Pole at Sig. Vvir, ff., which turns out to consist in well-known truths of the faith, rather than the mysteries first hinted at), the call to revelation is more ambiguous as well. Pole tells us that his natural tendency since childhood was to conceal the sins of others or to find some means of correction privately (Sig. Bir); he would rather suffer unjust blame himself than censure others (Sig. Vvir). Even when he heard of the death of More and Fisher, he was silent for a month, dissimulating his reaction to the news. Then he received the call:

It was then that the words of the book of Isaiah seemed addressed no less to me than to the prophet: "Lift your voice like a trumpet," let it be heard, if possible, not only in this kingdom, but everywhere on earth where the name of Christ is venerated. (Sig. Svv)

Not the moment of the death of More and Fisher, but the moment at which, a month later, he read Isaiah 58:1 (probably in conjunction with his study of this prophet with Van Kempen) was the moment of prophetic call, and "he who had always kept silent" resolved to lift his voice. But when did he lift it? Both internal and external evidence suggests a far more complex intention than this simple call to speak out.[25] His intention to publish is suggested by a letter in which he defends its harshness of tone on the grounds that he wrote for Englishmen, not Athenians (*L.P.* X, 169 [no. 420]). He wrote to the king of Scots that he wanted it "to see the light" (*Epistolae*, I, 174), and we have seen that he promises to reveal what he had not made public for three years in the *Apologia* (p. 160; see also p. 75: "quae nunc edo"). But in a letter to the Privy Council (1537) in which he defends himself against the charge that he meant to defame the king, Pole claims that the book was written only for the king, and had been sent only to him and was not shown even to the pope: "never confessor desired to be more secret as I desired to be in that book."[26] The letter to Edward VI, Vergerio's preface to the 1555 edition, and the letter to Damian all give evidence for the view that Pole never approved of the actual publication of the book, tried to prevent it, and tried to limit the circulation of the printed edition when it appeared.[27] As we have seen, the treatise itself repeatedly speaks of Pole's personal aver-

[25] Cf. Dunn, "The development of the text," pp. 460–2; Egretier, *Défense*, pp. 24–5.
[26] *L.P.* XIII (1), 213 [no. 444]. Cf. the Latin version printed in *Epistolae*, I, pp. 179–87: "Ad eum certe solum misi; quocum ita egi, ut nemo umquam a confessionibus illi secretior esse potuisset" (p. 181). Pole also says that love for the king and respect for his honor kept him from publishing (p. 182).
[27] *Epistolae*, IV, p. 340; Pier Paolo Vergerio, ed., *Pro ecclesiasticae unitatis defensio* (Strasbourg, 1555); *Epistolae*, III, p. 39.

sion to publicity, yet insists on his intention to speak out. The best way of understanding these opposed intentions is to hypothesize that they represent a conditional intention to publish. One key to this intention comes at the beginning, when he says that the death of More and Fisher has set an example for him. If they have given their lives, surely he cannot, from a safe distance, fail to send what he has written to the king: "Therefore I shall never, with God himself guiding me, hesitate to send it, or even to testify publicly to these things, if the matter comes to that" (Sig. Aiir). Pole is ready to speak publicly – certainly, at this time prepared to condemn publicly the execution of More and Fisher, which the example of Isaiah had so powerfully prompted him to do – but that does not mean that he will instantly declare all he knows, either by publishing the *De Unitate* or by revealing the full extent of Henry's degeneration (Machiavellian influence, relation to Antichrist), which is only hinted at even in the *De Unitate*. Part of the reason for this reserve is that it gives the writer power over Henry, and keeps him guessing about what Pole will do with the finished treatise and about how much more information Pole has. At times Pole seems to be taunting the king, claiming revealed knowledge of his motives, then denying that he knows more than anyone else. But this taunting bears a serious relation to Pole's prophetic role itself: His reserve is not merely strategic, but charitable, for his function is to chastise the king (Sig. Yiiiv), to set his sins before his eyes (Sig. Yivr) so that he will repent; and obviously, if he did repent, there would be no need to publicize his sins. The complex use Pole makes of Isaiah 58 is most significant in this regard. Isaiah is the prophet with whom Pole most closely identifies his own mission in this treatise. Noëlle-Marie Egretier notes twenty-nine citations of this prophet as against seventeen for Psalms and seven each for Ezekiel, I Kings, and Genesis, the next most frequently cited Old Testament books. Pole was engaged in formal study of Isaiah at the time of composition and was inspired, as we have seen, by 58:1 in his own decision to speak out. But, as the treatise proceeds, Pole finds a deeper significance in that passage: At first, it seems an unconditional call for public revelation of the king's misdeeds; later, it is seen as sanctioning a more personal and private remonstrance:

What could I have done more pertinent to your salvation than to heed the example of Isaiah and the Jews (in whose acts your own are represented), in that passage where, by divine command, he condemns the people who come at him with questions, covered with sins. And this is his answer: "Cry aloud, without constraint, lift thy voice like a trumpet, *reveal to my people their sins*" [emphasis added]. It is that same command that I believe that I have received

directly from God in the interests of your salvation. . . . To that sinning nation
that demanded to know the divine precepts, Isaiah began by reminding them
of their sins before showing them the way to be delivered from them; and
as you have set me an identical question, I have used with you the same method
as that used by the prophet. (Sig. Yivr)

The trumpet voice, then, is to be used to call the king to repentance,
and not, or at least not yet, to call for his destruction.

This *conditional* character of Pole's obligation to reveal is also seen
in the final set of citations: Ezekiel 33:4–5, which warns that the blood
of the man who does not heed the trumpet will be upon his own head,
and Ezekiel 18:30, which promises safety to the penitent. In keeping
with the principle of conditional revelation, the example of the penitent
King David (Sig. Vvv, Xir) plays an important role in the *De Unitate*,
and Henry's resemblance to Antichrist is played down. The "Antichrist" passages of Daniel and Thessalonians are absent, and when
Pole uses Isaiah 14 in reference to Henry's blasphemous self-elevation,
he identifies the figure Isaiah addresses in that passage as the king
of Assyria rather than Antichrist. Pole has no intention of euphemizing
Henry's sins – indeed, he calls him head of the church of Satan (Sig.
Ovv) – but he does not want to lock him into the role of Antichrist
while there is hope that, like David, he might repent.[28]

This call to repentance in the *De Unitate* is more than a necessary
formality before condemnation; rather, it is an attempt to share with
the king the fruits of Pole's own religious experience. Both in its evo-
cation of the anguish of spiritual struggle[29] and in its proffering a
foretaste of the joys of heaven to the penitent (Sigs. Yiiv, Yvr, Ziiiv),
Pole's plea for the king's repentance is based on the example of his
own very recent and joyful experience of justification. This theme,
and this tone, are absent from the *Apologia*. A prophet might call for
Holy War in the end, but the call to repentance came first; he might

---

[28] The call to repentance and the example of David (as well as that of Solomon) also
appear in the "instructions" Pole sent to Henry with the treatise. These are calendared
in *L.P.* X, 403 [no. 974] and printed in Gilbert Burnet, *The History of the Reformation of
the Church of England* (Oxford, 1865), VI, pp. 172–6, from BL MS Cotton. Cleo. E.vi.,
fol. 334. Indeed, these instructions bear out the hypothesis of a conditional intention
to publish: e.g., "My full purpose and mind was, touching the whole book that never
no part thereof should a come abroad in any man's hands, afore his grace had seen
it" (p. 174); Pole's recollection of these instructions in *Apologia* (p. 75) was that he had
written to the king that he would suppress the book ("librum hunc me suppressurum")
while any hope of reform remained.
[29] See especially Pole's moving use of Isaiah 30:19–21; Sig. Xiiir: "He will surely be
gracious to you at the sound of your cry; when he hears it, he will answer you. And
though the Lord give you the bread of adversity and the water of affliction, yet your
Teacher will not hide himself any more."

reveal the king's secrets and call for his destruction, but first he would use what he knew to call the king back to God. The prophetic role included responsibility for the partial, gradual revelation of the truth. The Old Testament prophets provided a model of reserve as well as revelation, for they often keep back part of the truth, or spoke it in mysterious terms, or communicated it privately to disciples, "binding up the testimony" for future revelation.

Thus the *De Unitate* is framed as a private remonstrance, which may be made public if necessary. And even in its pages, only part of what Pole knows is told; the rest is presented in veiled terms. The most important example of this hinting at further revelation is to be found in Pole's account of Henry's actual fall into temptation. The dialectic of prophetic reserve is well illustrated by this passage, which must be cited at length:

Consider now, if you will, how God has guided the events that led to your dishonor. First he permitted Satan to approach you, to plant in your spirit the desire to augment your renown and the power of your kindgom. He persuaded you that it would come to pass if you claimed the sovereignty of all sovereignties on earth, which is the supreme headship of the church on earth. Now that was the best way to cast you down beneath all mortals on earth. But how did Satan persuade you of this? But why should we ask how it was done, since we have Sampson's book, which was Satan's instrument to persuade you. Does anything remain hidden that Sampson and the other instruments of Satan spoke in your ear, which they preferred not to write down? This, especially is hidden: how Satan took you up upon a high mountain and showed you, not all the kingdoms of the world, as he did to Christ . . . but rather all the property and land of the priests and promised to give them to you if you would publicly declare yourself supreme head of the church: you, who had hardly been the foot of the church before that! – and he succeeded. For it is written – says Satan in the person of Sampson – "Honor the king." This was the theological position of Satan, who then placed you on the pinnacle of the Temple. (Sig. Vivr)

This passage was central to Van Dyke's argument that Pole had not yet formed his views about Cromwell's Machiavellian temptation of Henry at the time of the writing of the *De Unitate,* for it was "psychologically very hard"[30] to believe that Pole could fail to mention Cromwell here if indeed he considered him the main temper. But this begs the larger question of the role of Sampson in the book. He was not Henry's closest advisor, nor was his book the most significant of the attempts to defend Henry VIII's supremacy. Christopher St. Germain, Edward Fox, and Stephen Gardiner had all written on the

[30] Van Dyke, *Renascence Portraits*, p. 411.

subject as well[31]: Yet Samspon is singled out by Pole, and much of the *De Unitate* is devoted to refuting him. It is conceivable that Pole knew so little about Henry's government that he thought Sampson a more important influence than Cromwell, yet Cromwell is never mentioned. Sampson's books bears no date but cannot be earlier than 1534, for the Privy Council commissioned it in December 1553.[32] Sampson plays the role of scapegoat in the treatise: If Henry should incline to repentance, Pole's focus on Sampson makes saving face easier, for counselors closer to the king are spared mention. The passage itself does not, on careful reading, give Sampson the leading role either. First, there are *other* instruments of Satan. Second, Sampson, or these others, may have spoken something in Henry VIII's ear that never got on paper. Here Van Dyke mistranslates "An vero aliquid latet, quod literis noluerunt mandare" as "Is anything hidden which Sampson and the other instruments of Satan said in thy ears, *since they have been willing to commit it to writing*"[33] implying that here Pole tells all he knows of the matter, but in fact the portion I have italicized asks whether there remains anything they did *not* write down, which anticipates a positive answer, and, in the portion of the text that follows, not cited by Van Dyke, gets that positive answer: Something does remain hidden ("how Satan took you up upon a high mountain"). The temptation itself is hidden. It becomes still harder to doubt that Pole is hinting at knowledge he had but chosen not to reveal here when one compares this passage with the description of Cromwell's plan for religious autonomy in the *Apologia:*

And with this speech, as upon the pinnacle of the temple or upon the highest mountain, he lifted him, whence he might behold all things subjected to the ecclesiastical power – all the monasteries of the kingdom, which were numerous and very rich, and all the bishoprics, then the entire patrimony of the Church, and added: "All this is yours if you will call yourself what you are in fact: the head of the Church." (p. 121)

It was this – the role of Cromwell, and through Cromwell of Machiavelli, in the formation of Henry VIII's religious policies – that remained hidden, though amply hinted at. The full position of the *Apologia* – Henry's presumption to divine honors by virtue of his moral relativism, his contempt for law and usurpation of papal prerogatives, his threat to Christian unity – is implicit in the *De Unitate;* but the

---

[31] Christopher St. Germain, *A Treatise Concernynge the Division Between the Spiritualtie and Temporaltie* (London, 1532?); see also n. 23, this chapter.
[32] Egretier, *Défense,* p. 22, citing BL MS Cotton. Cleo. E.vi., fol. 317.
[33] Van Dyke, *Renascence Portraits,* p. 411.

explicit identification with Antichrist is not made, and the role of Cromwell and Machiavelli is not mentioned directly. It was only when the attempt to bring Henry to repentance had failed, and Pole's role as prophet therefore shifted from Isaiah's call to repentance to Moses' call for Holy War, that the whole story was told, and even then only in a work whose publishing history testifies to continuing reticence and reserve on the part of its author.

There is no doubt that there was something in Pole's personality that drove him to these complexities of revelation and reserve, that his stance as concealer and revealer of his king's secrets had roots in his profound and troubling ambivalance toward the king who had stirred his anger as well as his gratitude since childhood. But the energies of this personal conflict took on archetypal significance for Pole at the time of his crisis or "conversion." He began to see himself as in some sense a prophet, and to relate his own spiritual struggle and the events of his time to the complex model of prophetic history. In the historicist typology Pole adopted, the prophet, like the historical process itself, reveals part of the truth and conceals the rest or expresses it cryptically. Though Pole longed for full disclosure, for the trumpet voice of Isaiah, he knew that the prophets themselves had "bound up the testimony," that their public role had often been ambiguous, the full import of their message being reserved for future revelation, when the times would be ripe.

Indeed, the entire typological tradition of exegesis, whether historicist or not, was based upon the notion that no prophet spoke only to contemporaries or could be fully understood by them, for the full significance of prophecy lay in its anticipations of Christ's life and doctrine and, beyond that, in its relation to the events of the Last Days. Then – in the radiance of the Second Coming and the revelation of the *mysterium iniquitatis* – all would be clear, but until then, that is to say, while historical time continued, prophecy retained its mystery, and the reflection of biblical truth in current events continued to be a source not only of illumination but of anguish as well. This Cardinal Pole keenly felt, for though he firmly believed he had been called by God to speak out against the English schism and the tyranny of Henry VIII, and had been entrusted with providentially revealed knowledge concerning the Machiavellian inspiration of these events, he received no revelation concerning when and how he should reveal what he knew, and he never solved the problem of the timing of his prophecy.

The trials of Pole's life, and the problems raised by the secular philosophy he thought responsible for those trials, drove him to agonized attention to the history of his own period. It was in contemporary events that he saw the processes of concealment and revelation, of damnation and salvation, being worked out. Biblical typology did not free him from but immersed him in the uncertainties of history. He felt himself to be a prophet in some sense, but he wavered between a metaphoric and a literal interpretation of his call. He knew he must speak out, but was never sure when to speak and how much to say. He himself believed that even these uncertainties had biblical sanction; that the prophets had been compelled to a reluctance and reserve like his; that indecision was inevitable while human time lasted.

Prophecy and Machiavellian discourse

Pole was the first major opponent of Machiavelli, yet to a certain extent his anti-Machiavellian writings participate in and derive their terms from the Machiavellian discourse they reject. Pole's reading of Machiavelli and his religious conversion experience were simultaneous and closely related processes. Recognizing in Machiavelli's works the emergence of unprecedented views, ones we would now call secular, Pole turned to medieval traditions of biblical typology to explain them, but his understanding of these traditions was shaped by the task of finding a place for Machiavelli in them. In its collision with the doctrines of Machiavelli and the English Reformation, Pole's religious faith took a historical or historicizing form as he tried to discover, even in the doubts, hesitations, and ambiguities of life in history, the working of divine purpose. It also became a faith in which, despite the negative judgment passed upon it, the emergence of a secular political theory is recognized as an event of the greatest moment. Pole rejected the doctrines of *Il Principe*, but at the same time attested to their importance by finding in their promulgation a sign of the beginning of a new era in the history of the world. He rejected the role of the secret Machiavellian counselor, which he thought was implied by *Il Principe* and lived out by Cromwell; yet his own role as prophet took its cue from the Machiavellian pattern he opposed, for in the *De Unitate* and the *Apologia* Pole became a purveyor of secret knowledge, a concealer and revealer of political arcana. The *De Unitate* and the *Apologia* exemplify a form of apocalyptic thought shaped by opposition to Machiavelli. Pole's themes (dissimulation, deception, the divorce of moral law from political effectiveness), as well as his mode of presentation (the secret book or discourse), mirror those of his adversary.

The principal idea by which Pole attempted to mediate between Machiavellian and biblical conceptions of politics was that of an ancient, secret, and mysterious political knowledge, which he refers to as arcana or *mysterium.* Machiavelli's doctrines and those of Pole himself were opposed as evil is to good. But both were modern expressions of ancient political arcana ultimately of supernatural origin. If *Il Principe* was a secret demonic text that could conceal or reveal the *mysterium iniquitatis* of Thessalonians, the *De Unitate* and the *Apologia* were counter-arcana, prophetic works whose authority was ultimately divine and whose publication history was meant to participate in the complexities of the occultation and revelation of divine truth.

Appendix: prophecy and fact

Study of Pole's prophetic typology has suggested that the absence of Cromwell and Machiavelli in the *De Unitate* and their appearance in the *Apologia* are to be explained on the basis of Pole's conception of prophecy: He would reveal what he knew in stages, as Scripture did. This answers one of Van Dyke's objections to the historicity of Pole's story of his meeting with Cromwell, which he explained as resulting from Pole's reading back into the events of 1528 conclusions about the demonic character of Cromwell and Machiavelli he had come to only in 1538. As his analysis continues to be influential, it needs to be addressed in fuller detail here. In summary, Van Dyke argued:[34]

1. Manuscripts of *Il Principe* were scarce, so Cromwell was unlikely to have known Machiavelli at this early date. In 1539 Lord Morley offered Cromwell a copy of the book as something as yet unknown to him.[35]

2. *Il Principe* does not deal with the question of the responsibilities of counselors toward princes, as the book recommended to Pole by Cromwell did. Castiglione's *Courtier* does deal with that subject, and was available in 1528.

3. If Pole had thought Cromwell demonic from 1528, he would not have continued to maintain polite relations with him for another ten years, nor would he have failed to mention his Machiavellian temptation of Henry in the *De Unitate,* which was finished in 1536; therefore:

4. Pole had neither read Machiavelli nor come to the conclusion that Cromwell played the role of demonic tempter to Henry VIII until after 1536. Some time after that, perhaps on a trip to Florence mentioned in the *Apologia,* Pole read *Il Principe,* and at about

---

[34] Ibid., pp. 377–418.
[35] Ibid., pp. 413–14. Text printed in Henry Ellis, *Original Letters Illustrative of English History,* ser. 3, III (London, 1846), pp. 63–7 [no. 278].

the same time (1538) Cromwell began the persecution of Pole's family. These two factors made him remember a conversation he had had with Cromwell ten years earlier and made him interpret it in the light of the wickedness he now perceived in Cromwell and in *Il Principe*.

Van Dyke believed that *some* book was actually offered to Pole by Cromwell: "The subject of the conversation and the offer to lend him the book are facts that would be apt to remain in a man's mind. There is not the smallest reason to accuse Pole of inventing them" (p. 400). But that book must have been *Il Corteggiano*, not *Il Principe*.

Manuscripts of *Il Principe* were in fact plentiful, however,[36] and Cromwell had lived in Florence, where the chances of hearing of this writer and acquiring a copy of his as yet unpublished work must have been better than in most other places. Besides, Lord Morley's letter does not show that Cromwell did not know Machiavelli, but only that Morley supposed he did not:

This book of Machiavell *De principe* is surely a very special good thing for your Lordship which are so nigh abouht our sovereign lord in counsel to look upon for many causes, as I suppose your self shall judge when ye have seen the same. (Henry Ellis, *Original Letters*, ser. 3, III, 66)

Morley certainly assumes that Cromwell will like the book when he does see it.

Il Corteggiano is a mild book in comparison with *Il Principe*, and there are no parallels in its publication history with the surreptitious treatment Cromwell gives the book he offers Pole. But *Il Principe* was, from the start, thought of as something to be kept secret or handled with caution. Bernardo Giunta, publisher of the 1532 edition (this was the second edition of *Il Principe*, appearing several months after the Blado edition of the same year), expected trouble and tried to ward it off in a defensive preface.[37] The contents were plagiarized, translated into Latin, and published with a careful palinode by Agostino Nifo even before the book itself was printed (*De regnandi peritia*, 1523),[38]

---

[36] Gerber, *Handschriften*, I, pp. 82–97; Pasquale Villari, *Niccolò Machiavelli e i suoi tempi* (Florence, 1877–82), II, pp. 405–8; William Gordon Zeeveld, *Foundations of Tudor Policy* (Cambridge, Mass., 1948), p. 77n., cites unpublished work of Garrett Mattingly showing that in the 1520s at least three Italian booksellers employed professional copyists to produce copies of the book.

[37] Niccolò Machiavelli, *Il Principe* (Florence, 1532), prefatory letter.

[38] Agostino Nifo, *De regnandi peritia* (Naples, 1523).

and the history of its influence in the sixteenth century and after offers many examples of the kind of surreptitious transmission Pole describes.[39]

It was a shocking book, and one that seemed to reveal secrets of getting and keeping power. Cromwell's treatment of it — keeping it secret but making it the basis of his advice to the king — is analogous to William Thomas's use of Machiavelli in his letters of political advice to Edward VI and to Stephen Gardiner's borrowings from it in his *Ragionamento*, which was intended to help Philip II retain power in England.[40] It is easy to see why Cromwell would not want to send it when he found Pole shocked by its ideas; but why would anyone need to keep *Il Corteggiano* secret?

Il Corteggiano is, as Van Dyke said, more explicitly a book of advice for counselors, whereas *Il Principe* addresses a prince. This is an important difference between these texts, but it does not strengthen Van Dyke's case. As the Morley letter shows, a book that tells a prince how to rule is also profitable for counselors to read, "a very special good thing for your lordship which are so nigh about our sovereign lord in counsel to look upon." In fact, a large fraction of the history of Machiavelli's influence concerns the use made of *Il Principe* by those who were not princes. In addition, Pole's memory of Cromwell's speech about the book includes a paraphrase of *Il Principe* 15 that contrasts the practical truths of experience (*verità effettuale*) with imaginary republics like those of Plato. There is nothing life this in *Il Corteggiano*, which can reasonably be thought of as belonging to the Platonic tradition rejected by Machiavelli and Cromwell. Pole might have put the words in Cromwell's mouth later, but there can be no question that the description as we have it fits *Il Principe* and does not fit *Il Corteggiano*.

Van Dyke is right in concluding that Pole's assessment of Cromwell underwent drastic revision and that Cromwell did not have in 1528

---

[39] Felix Raab, *The English Face of Machiavelli* (London, 1964), pp. 40–8. Peter S. Donaldson, ed., *A Machiavellian Treatise by Stephen Gardiner* (Cambridge, 1975); G. M. Bertini, "La fortuna di Machiavelli in Spagna," *Quaderni ibero-americani* (Turin, 1947), II, pp. 21–2, 25–6, discovered a proposal for an expurgated edition of Machiavelli's works, translated into Spanish and with the name of the author changed, made to the Inquisition by the Duke of Sessa's secretary in 1584; Dennis B. Woodfield's Oxford thesis, "Books surreptitiously printed in England before 1640 in contemporary foreign languages" (1964), published as *Surreptitious Printing in England, 1550–1640* (New York, 1973), deals at length with the London editions of Machiavelli's works published by John Wolfe under false imprint, 1584–8.

[40] Raab, *The English Face of Machiavelli*, pp. 40–8; Donaldson, *Machiavellian Treatise*. See also Chapter 2, this volume.

the mythic significance he was later to acquire. But Pole's crisis of obedience, and its resolution in biblical terms, may be taken as the catalyst that deepened the archetypal significance of Cromwell, as it did for all events and persons, in Pole's mind. It was in 1535, when Pole was studying Scripture and finding in it a key to his own experience, that Henry's descent into evil took on the apocalyptic character it has in the *Apologia*. Cromwell's role in this is not mentioned in the 1536 *De Unitate*, nor is *Il Principe* identified with the *mysterium iniquitatis* of Antichrist. But Pole still had hoped Henry would reform, and therefore adopted the rhetorical strategy of blaming as much as he could on Richard Sampson while at the same time making it clear that there were "other instruments of Satan" and affirming that the exact manner of Satan's temptation "remains hidden."

If one agrees with Van Dyke that Cromwell offered some book to Pole at that meeting in 1528, it is unreasonable to suppose that that book, whose identity Pole claims to have checked with Cromwell's associates, was anything other than Machiavelli's *Il Principe*. That does not mean, however, that Machiavelli's ideas were the inspiration for the supremacy, much less for the Henrician Reformation as a whole. Reading Machiavelli may have strengthened Cromwell's resolve to find bold solutions to the problems of church–state relations; *Il Principe* may be subtly present in the vigor and freedom from tradition of Cromwell's intellectual style; Machiavelli, who had a profound respect for law despite Pole's view to the contrary, may even have influenced Cromwell's persistent use of legislation to effect his reforms. But there were far more immediate influences on Cromwell – Marsiglio of Padua and conciliar theory, for example – and these can be shown to have directly influenced the legislation and official propaganda of the Cromwellian state.[41] The restoration to credibility of Pole's story about Cromwell makes it more probable that Machiavelli was known to one of Henry's counselors and therefore helps correct, as much recent research has done, the once common view that Machiavelli was unknown except by reputation in early Tudor England, though it does not connect him with any specific course of action or policy.

As to the spirit in which Cromwell recommended the book to Pole, A. G. Dickens, who must not be taken to share the view of the present author that the book in question actually was *Il Principe*, has written best:

[41] Elton, "The political creed of Thomas Cromwell"; Graham D. Nicholson, "The nature and function of historical argument in the Henrician Reformation" (unpublished Ph.D. thesis, Cambridge University 1977).

Concerning its broad tenor one need not feel totally skeptical, since it is easy to believe that Cromwell, in a characteristic mood of sardonic worldly wisdom, was guilty of baiting the complacent young humanist.[42]

Indeed, we may be reasonably certain that Cromwell's view of *Il Principe* was more wordly and less apocalyptic than that of Reginald Pole. Pole's attempt to come to terms with this radically secular thinker, in combination with other elements of the personal and religious crisis he experienced in 1535, led him to a prophetic, almost dualistic, vision of the history of his own time, as he came to see Henry VIII as a precursor of Antichrist and the Machiavellian texts as expressions of the *mysterium iniquitatis*. He met Machiavelli's challenge by reasserting sacred archetypes with new vigor, commitment, and literal-mindedness. But for Cromwell the sacred and the secular realms were not so uncompromisingly at odds. If this chapter has made it easier to believe that Cromwell offered Pole a copy of *Il Principe*, it remains improbable that Cromwell would have attached the same apocalyptic significance to this gesture as Pole had. Even if Cromwell did read Machiavelli and used him in framing advice to Henry, it is very unlikely that he ever thought of himself as a messenger of Satan.

[42] A. G. Dickens, *Thomas Cromwell and the English Reformation* (London, 1959), p. 77.

2

Bishop Gardiner, Machiavellian

Stephen Gardiner was born in the last years of the fifteenth century at Bury St. Edmonds.[1] After a brilliant academic career, in which he earned doctorates in both canon and civil law and drew praise from John Leland for reforming the study of law at Cambridge, he entered Wolsey's service in 1524, and from there was drawn into the service of the king, representing him in negotiations with Clement VII concerning the divorce in 1528. The following year he was appointed principal secretary and in 1531, after Wolsey's fall, was promoted to Wolsey's second See of Winchester. As a churchman, Gardiner's instincts were conservative, so that in the years 1532–4, as Henry's conflict with Rome deepened and his incursions upon the powers of the English church grew more serious, Gardiner fell into disfavor because of his resistance to change. But whereas Pole fled to exile and More and Fisher were executed, Gardiner capitulated entirely on the momentous issue of the king's supremacy and in 1535 published his *De vera obedientia,* a polished oration in favor of the claim to supreme headship over the church in England and a classic exposition of the doctrines of nonresistance and the sacredness of kings that then became and were to remain central tenets of official ideology throughout the sixteenth century. After Cromwell's fall, Gardiner was perhaps Henry's most influential minister and was closely associated with the turn toward orthodoxy in this last phase of Henry's reign, taking a large part in the framing of the Six Articles and in the composition of the "King's" Book. In the reign of Edward VI, he resisted the introduction of the Prayer Book and other departures from the Henrician religious settlement, and was ultimately deprived and imprisoned in the Tower (1548–53) for his failure to conform.

[1] James Arthur Muller, *Stephen Gardiner and the Tudor Reaction* (London, 1926), remains the standard biography. Gardiner's correspondence was also edited by Muller; see *The Letters of Stephen Gardiner* (Cambridge, 1933). Several of Gardiner's political works were printed in Pierre Janelle, ed., *Obedience in Church and State* (Cambridge, 1930).

Upon Mary's accession he was restored to his see and made lord chancellor, an office he held until his death in 1555. In this period he of course favored the reintroduction of papal authority, which was effected by the legatine mission to England of Cardinal Pole, so that the two most prominent surviving religious conservatives of Henry's time, one of whom had temporarily rejected papal supremacy, and the other of whom had gone into exile and had called for rebellion against his sovereign rather than do so, met again and were somewhat reconciled to one another by the success of their common cause and the needs of their common purposes.

Two more different temperaments would be difficult to imagine. Pole was a saintly man, never very worldly, whose great crisis brought out in him an almost heedless identification with biblical archetypes of sacrifice and martyrdom and led to his abandoning his family to the wrath of the king whose religious policies his conscience rejected.[2] He was a man of great integrity who often failed to find middle ground on which to compromise – not only with Henry but also with the church that had become his refuge in exile. He held with great persistence to his own religious experience, which seemed to require an affirmation of something very much like the "faith alone" doctrine of the reformers, and at the end of his life he was actually summoned to Rome to answer heresy charges, though he did not live long enough to comply. Gardiner was a worldly prelate, rigid like Pole in most religious matters, but his rigidity arose not so much from the intensity of personal religious experience as from his sense of intellectual superiority and his convictions concerning the political implications of religious innovation. He had compromised or dissembled on the main issue, though Janelle may have been right to say that the claims of the papacy were never very important to him.[3] He may sincerely have come to believe that royal supremacy was the only guarantor of religious orthodoxy and then, when history proved this view wrong, reverted on political grounds to papalism. There is much to support such a view, especially in the sermon "De somno surgere," which he preached on the occasion of England's return to allegiance to Rome, for there he welcomes the restoration but makes it plain that the long wait had been a necessary one. There had been several occasions on which Henry VIII had considered and almost acceded to the idea of returning to the papal fold; but in each case, as Gardiner tells it, "the

---

[2] See Chapter 1, this volume
[3] Janelle, *Obedience*, p. lix.

time was not yet," for there were weighty political considerations that required delay.[4] Here we have a real difference between Gardiner and the papal legate who listened to this sermon at the moment of England's symbolic return to catholicism. For Pole the claims of the papacy were absolute; there could never be a time when prudential or political considerations outweighed them. For Gardiner the political element, even in religious matters, was most important, and there were times when the exigencies of human history required that obedience even to divine commands be deferred.

The difference thus suggested is nowhere clearer than in what we have come to know about the attitude of the two men toward Machiavelli. The previous chapter examined the close relationship between the religious crisis of Pole's early life, the events of the English schism, and the ways in which Pole used his reading of Machiavelli to find a place for himself – albeit a somewhat inflated place – in those events. For Gardiner, too, the break with Rome was a turning point, and he chose to remain loyal to the king and to contribute powerfully to the ideology of sacred kingship being prepared in support of the king's supremacy over the church. There is no evidence that he was influenced by Machiavelli in his about-face, or in any of the positions he took during Henry's reign, though the term "Machiavellian" has hovered around his name, as it has around the names of most of the astute politicians of the sixteenth century, from that time to this. But we know now that, like Pole, he did make a thorough study of Machiavelli somewhat later in his career, and that when he did, he attempted to fuse his beliefs about sacred kingship, as he first shaped them in the 1530s, with a thoroughly (and literally) Machiavellian interpretation of English history and politics. The new evidence we have about Gardiner's reading of Machiavelli comes from a treatise he wrote during Mary's reign, which survives in an Italian translation entitled *Ragionamento dell'advenimento delli inglesi et normanni in Britannia*,[5] prepared as a manual of advice for Philip II, and showing how

---

[4] Janelle, *Obedience*, p. lvii; Muller, *Gardiner*, pp. 264–6. The three principal contemporary accounts of the sermon, which agree very closely in most details, are in John Foxe, *Acts and Monuments*, ed. George Townsend (London, 1843–49), VI, p. 577; *The Chronicle of Queen Jane and Two Years of Queen Mary*, ed. J. G. Nichols (London, 1850), p. 161; *Concio reveren. d. stephani, episcopi vintonien. angliae cancelarii* (Rome, 1555; repr. in *Epistolae Poli*, ed. A. M. Quirini [Brussels, 1757], V, pp. 293–9).
[5] This treatise survives in two extant manuscripts, Escorial MS I.III.17 and Besançon [Bibliothèque Publique de Besançon] MS 1169. See my edition and translation, *A Machiavellian Treatise by Stephen Gardiner* (Cambridge, 1975). Doubts about Gardiner's authorship were expressed in a review by Dermot Fenlon in *Historical Journal* XIX (1976), 1019–23, and by Sidney Anglo in "Crypto-Machiavellism in early Tudor England: The problem of the *Ragionamento dell'advenimento delli inglesi, et normanni in Britannia*," *Ren-*

Philip could secure his hold over England by heeding the lessons of English history and following strategic advice derived rather directly, though without credit being given, from *Il Principe* and the *Discorsi*. Analysis of this work reveals that whereas Pole regarded Machiavelli's "amoral" teachings, especially those of *Principe* 18, as the biblically predicted secret of Antichrist, Gardiner quotes exactly those passages that Pole and the other critics of Machiavelli thought most amoral, and, almost in the manner Pole claimed Cromwell had done, made these teachings the basis of a private manual of advice for Philip. Where Pole saw Machiavelli as a threat to Christendom and as the cause of schism, Gardiner made acceptance of Machiavellian politics the foundation of a strategy for installing a permanent Catholic dynasty in England. Where Pole saw utter contradiction between the office of a Christian monarch, ruling by law, and the supposed lawlessness of Machiavelli's prince, Gardiner attempted to reconcile Machiavelli with his own long-held views concerning the sacred character of royal authority and its subordination to law. And where Pole saw the new polity of Machiavelli, Cromwell, and Henry VIII as a grim parody of divine example, a rejection and usurpation of divine prerogative, Gardiner's Machiavellian prince is, in surprising ways, an imitator of God, mirroring both the mercy and the necessary severity of the divine attributes. Yet, as opposed as Gardiner's and Pole's reactions to Machiavelli were, they were linked by a common theme: For both men, Machiavelli's writings provided a glimpse into the arcana of statecraft. For both, Machiavellism was essentially a secret doctrine, with close associations, for better or worse, with the mysterious potencies of sacred kingship.

Secret Machiavellian treatises and Tudor rulers

Part of the story of Machiavelli's association with the *arcana imperii* concerns the ways in which his works were so often treated in a secretive or surreptitious manner. *Il Principe* circulated in manuscript for nearly two decades before it was published in 1532, and since it appeared after Machiavelli's death in 1527, it was not clear whether he himself had wished to make it public.[6] Large portions of it were

aissance and Reformation/Renaissance et Réforme n.s. II [o.s. XIV] (1978), 182–93. I presented further evidence in my edition of the description of England that Gardiner's translator appended to the *Ragionamento:* "George Rainsford's 'Ritratto d'Inghilterra' (1556)," *Camden Miscellany XXVII* (London, 1979), pp. 49–111; see esp. pp. 59–64 and in "Bishop Gardiner, Machiavellian," *Historical Journal* XXIII (1980), 1–16. The present discussion draws on and expands some of this earlier published work.

[6] See Chapter 1, n. 30, this volume.

borrowed by Agostino Nifo and used in the *De regnandi peritia* (Naples, 1523), with no credit given to the actual author. Lucio Paolo Rosello's *Ritratto del vero governo* of 1552 borrowed from both Nifo and Machiavelli, and was in turn used for some portions of Gardiner's treatise, as Sidney Anglo has shown, all without Machiavelli being mentioned.[7] Translations of Machiavelli's works appeared under pseudonyms; editions of his work, like those of John Wolfe of London, to be discussed at length in the following chapter, appeared under false imprint. In several different instances, plans were made for the preparation of expurgated editions to be issued under a name other than Machiavelli's.[8] The story is a long one, much of it chronicled in Adolph Gerber's work on sixteenth- and seventeenth-century editions and translations of Machiavelli. Some of this pattern of covert or surreptitious transmission may be attributed to ordinary sixteenth-century attitudes toward what we now think of as literary property: It simply was very common to borrow literally without saying so. Much of it, especially after 1559, when Machiavelli's works were placed on the first papal Index to be printed, is attributable to the need to avoid censorship. Some, even before the official condemnation, may be seen as a defensive reaction to anticipated trouble over ideas that could be dangerous; even Giunta, the publisher of one of the two 1532 editions of *Il Principe*, saw fit to defend his author against possible attack from malicious critics.[9] Some seems to have been due, as in the case of William Thomas (to be discussed), to the desire to profit by deception, passing off Machiavelli's powerful political ideas as one's own advice on issues of state. But whether the motives were prudential, religious, or careerist, the widespread tendency to present Machiavelli's texts or ideas in some form of disguise, and the caution and secrecy with which the transmission of his thought often proceeded, contributed to his reputation as the purveyor of a secret doctrine.

We have seen that Pole regarded *Il Principe* in this way: It was the secret ideology behind the Henrician state, and had been privily transmitted to the king by Cromwell, so that Henry was acting under the influence of a book he perhaps hadn't even read. Further, Machiavelli's doctrine was a revelation of the ancient mystery of iniquity of Thessalonians, and its appearance on the scene marked the turning of an era of sacred history, signaling the temporary ascendance of Antichrist before the Last Days. There are surely mythic pressures to

---

[7] Lucio Paolo Rosello, *Ritratto del vero governo* (Venice, 1552). See Anglo, "Crypto-Machiavellism."
[8] See Chapter 1, n. 33, this volume.
[9] Niccolò Machiavelli, *Il Principe* (Florence, 1532), prefatory letter.

be discerned in Pole's account of Cromwell's secret use of *Il Principe*, and the truth of the matter is still difficult to assess, but it is interesting that the myth that is operating in Pole's *Apologia* (*Il Principe* as the basis of secret advice to the reigning monarch) became fact not only in the succeeding reign, but in the one after that, for William Thomas made Machiavelli the basis of his secret advice to Edward VI, and Stephen Gardiner's *Ragionamento* followed the same pattern, drawing on Machiavelli for advice to Philip of Spain, Mary's consort.

The early life of William Thomas is obscure. What we know for certain about him begins in the 1540s, when we find him in the service of Sir Anthony Browne,[10] who was also a close friend of Gardiner's.[11] Under the pressure of gambling debts, Thomas embezzled some money from Browne and was forced to flee to Italy. After several years there he made some sort of settlement with the English agent at Venice, and tried to ingratiate himself with the king by publicly defending Henry VIII's controversial reign in Bologna, Padua, and Rome. He also set to work on a *History of Italy* (1549) and an *Italian Grammar* (1550), the latter an immensely popular and often reprinted work. He returned to England in 1549, quite well known for his travels and language studies, and was appointed clerk of the Privy Council. In this capacity he made himself "a sort of political instructor to the young king, who appears to have narrowly watched the proceedings of his council, and without the knowledge of his members, sought Thomas's opinion on their policy and on the principles of government generally."[12] The form his instruction took is made clear by a letter of his to the young king, in which he offered to write essays on any of eighty-five topics concerning statecraft, at the king's pleasure.[13] The topics represented the fruit, so he says, of his study of "divers authors," but, as Weissberger pointed out long ago, there was really one author who had inspired his choice of topics: "his eighty five questions, in fact, might serve as chapter headings for the *Discorsi*."[14] This does not put the matter strongly enough. Most of them in fact *are* chapter headings from the *Discorsi*, and all of them treat of matters discussed there or in *Il Principe*. A few examples must suffice here, though the

---

[10] E. R. Adair, "William Thomas: A forgotten clerk of the Privy Council," *Tudor Studies*, ed. R. W. Seton-Watson (London, 1924), pp. 133–60. See also Daniel Lleufer Thomas in *DNB*, s.v. "Thomas, William," and Margie Mae Hankinson, "William Thomas: Italianate Englishman" (unpublished Ph.D. dissertation, Columbia University, 1967).
[11] Muller, *Gardiner*, pp. 141–2.
[12] *DNB*.
[13] J. Strype, *Ecclesiastical Memorials* (Oxford, 1822), II, Pt. 1, pp. 157–61.
[14] L. Arnold Weissberger, "Machiavelli and Tudor England," *Political Science Quarterly* XLII (1927), 593.

whole list can in fact be correlated with chapter headings or leading ideas from Machiavelli:

Whether is wiser and most constant, the multitude or the prince? (cf. *Disc.* I:58)

Whether religion beside the honor of God, be not also the greatest stay of civil order; and whether the unity thereof be not to be preserved with the sword and rigor? (cf. *Disc.* I:12)

Whether they be not often deceived, that think with humility to overcome pride? (*Disc.* II:14)

Whether it be not necessary for him that would have continually good fortune to vary with the time? (*Disc.* III:9)

Whether money be the substance of war, or not? (*Disc.* II:10)

Whether the country ought not always to be defended, the quarrel being right or wrong? (*Disc.* III:41).

Weissberger thought that Thomas's use of Machiavelli was limited to the *Discorsi*, but this is not so. There are topics that could have been drawn from either *Il Principe* or the *Discorsi*, as, for example, the topics dealing with mercenaries, with cruelty and kindness, and with virtue and fortune. And several of his topics are chapter headings of *Il Principe*:

How flatterers are to be known and despised. (Ch. 23)

How a prince ought to govern himself to attain reputation. (Ch. 21)

With this list, Thomas sent a letter in which he suggested that the king keep their relationship secret:

It becometh a prince for his wisdom to be had in admiration, as well as of his chiefest counsellors, as of his other subjects. And since nothing serveth more to that, than to keep the principal things of wisdom secret, till occasion requireth the utterance, I would wish them to be kept secret referring it nevertheless to your Majesty's good will and pleasure.[15]

The king accepted the plan. Thomas became clerk of the Privy Council and began to write. The treatises he actually composed were fairly conventional, however. The first treatise, in fact, bears no relation to Machiavelli at all, for Edward requested an essay not on Thomas's list – one on reform of the coinage. A letter containing Thomas's response to this request is extant, and is interesting for our purposes because it shows how the treatises Thomas prepared were kept secret – they were sent under seal in the pouch containing the minutes of Privy

---

[15] Strype, *Ecclesiastical Memorials*, II, Pt. 1, p. 161.

Council meetings – and it reveals exactly how Thomas regarded his own role as a private political instructor: He wanted the king to pretend that the material Thomas prepared for his perusal was the fruit of the king's own research:

Albeit that I think myself both unmeet and unable to give any judgment in so great and weighty a matter, without the counsel and advice of others, yet since it is your highness' pleasure to have it secret (which I do much commend) I therefore am the bolder to enterprise the declaration of my fantasy: trusting that upon this ground better devices and better effect may ensue than my head alone can contrive. And because Mr. Throgmorton is absent, I have delivered it thus sealed to Mr. Fitzwilliams, to deliver unto your Majesty as it were a thing from the Council, assuring your highness that no creature living is or shall be privy either to this or to any of the rest through me. Which I do keep so secret to this end, that your Majesty may utter these matters as of your own study; whereby it shall have the greater credit with your Council.[16]

An attempt at reforming the coinage was in fact made, and the young king was influential in the process, and apparently did, as Thomas recommended, keep the fact that he had received an essay on the subject from Thomas a secret.

What Thomas kept secret, or at any rate concealed, even from the king, was the extent of his own reliance on Machiavelli – not in this treatise on the coinage, but in the rest of the treatises he was to prepare for the king. Machiavelli is referred to several times in them, but not in a manner that indicates the extent of the debt. For example, in the treatise "Whether it be expedient to vary with time,"[17] he seems to make Machiavelli the author of a rather conventional simile comparing politics to music ("Truly as the musician useth sometime a flat, and sometime a long, to make his song perfect; so saith Machiavegli, ought man to frame his proceeding unto his time"). But the actual indebtedness to Machiavelli is far more extensive: The comparison Thomas makes between Fabius and Scipio comes from *Discorsi* III:9, from which the title of the treatise itself is drawn, and Thomas uses Machiavelli's comparison between the force of the lion and the wiles of the fox (*Prin.* 18) in making the point that different strategies are appropriate at different times. As others have noticed,[18] there is something of a contrast between the daring role Thomas carved out for himself as a secret political instructor to Edward, drawing on Machiavelli for advice to a reigning king, and the intellectual timidity of the actual treatises

[16] Adair, "William Thomas," p. 142, citing BL MS Cotton. Vesp. D XVIII, fols. 28–9.
[17] Strype, *Ecclesiastical Memorials*, II, Pt. 2, pp. 365–72.
[18] See Felix Raab, *The English Face of Machiavelli* (London, 1964), pp. 40–8.

prepared. The Machiavelli we find in Thomas is toned down, qualified, sometimes so tamed as to make one wonder why Thomas had recourse to him at all. Thus, in the essay under discussion, Thomas denies that the principle of varying one's conduct that he is espousing conflicts with the moral virtues:

I mean not, that any man should vary in amity, turn from virtue to vice, or to alter in any such thing as requireth constancy; but touching the other public or private doings, I think nothing more necessary than to vary with the time.

Thomas's lion and his fox are domesticated creatures. One suspects, on the evidence of the boldness with which he began, and from the daring that characterized much of his life as we know it, that he originally had more interesting plans for this project than the finished treatises display. In any case, the relationship with Edward did not last very long; after six essays were completed, he petitioned the king for foreign employment. Upon Mary's accession, he naturally lost his post; he then joined Wyatt's rebellion and was executed in 1554. Bale credits him with a plot to kill Bishop Gardiner, and Sir Nicholas Arnold, who turned state's evidence, claimed that Thomas was the deviser of a plot to have John Fitzwilliams (the same Fitzwilliams who acted as courier between Thomas and Edward VI) kill the queen.[19]

What is most important for our purposes is the similarity between Pole's story of Cromwell's Machiavellian advice and what Thomas actually did. For Pole and Thomas (and Cromwell too, to the extent that Pole may be believed on this, which may not be very far), the ideas of Machiavelli and the role of secret royal advisor had a close affinity, and an ambitious courtier could use Machiavelli (particularly if he kept his source a secret) to rise in the king's service.

Gardiner was already the holder of high office when he wrote the *Ragionamento,* but he too made Machiavellian ideas the basis for secret advice to an actual ruler, Philip of Spain, Mary's consort. Gardiner's original is lost, and the text of this work that survives is an Italian translation by George Rainsford, dedicated to Philip and dated (after Gardiner's death in November 1555) March 16, 1556–7.[20] One of the surviving manuscripts is in the Escorial, where it came by Philip's gift in 1574.[21] This is obviously the presentation copy. The other manuscript is in the Granvelle papers at Besançon, having belonged to An-

[19] *DNB* and John Bale, *Scriptorum illustrium maioris Brytanniae* (Basel, 1557–9), II, p. 110.
[20] Donaldson, *Machiavellian Treatise,* p. 45.
[21] Escorial MS. See *Catologo de los libros de su Magestad* in the Escorial Library. See also Jole Ruggieri, "Manoscritti italiani nella Biblioteca dell'Escuriale," *La Bibliofilia* XXXII (1930), 422–3; XXXIII (1931), 148.

toine Perrenot de Granvelle, Bishop of Arras and chief diplomatic minister to Charles V.[22] The translator clearly regarded the treatise as a useful contribution to Philip's education about England, and appended his own "Ritratto d'Ingliterra," so that, as he says, "nothing might be lacking in this little book that might contribute to an understanding of the laws, procedures, customs, nature and humor of the people of Britain."[23] But the treatise itself was obviously intended for Philip's use, for it ends with an elaborate encomium to him, and the political questions it takes up are those specially relevant to a prince in his position – a new prince, who needs to respect the laws and customs of his new possession while dealing severely with possible rivals.[24]

Most historians have regarded Gardiner as a foe of the Spanish match: It was he who had backed Edward Courtenay as a consort, who appears to have been behind the Commons's insubordinate demand that Mary marry an Englishman, and, once the choice of Philip was inevitable, it was he who insisted that severe restrictions on Philip's power be included in the treaty. In its final form, the treaty barred the Habsburgs from succession unless Mary had a child; Philip was not allowed to bring large numbers of Spaniards to England; he was to be attended by Englishmen; business was to be conducted in English, not Spanish; he was not to take the Queen or her treasure out of the realm; England was not to be drawn into war with France; and Philip was to make no changes in English laws or procedures.[25]

The *Ragionamento* addresses itself to such a situation. It is about what happens when a foreign dynasty comes to England, and in the analysis of the reigns of Vortigerius, Hengest, William the Conqueror, King Canute, and others, the implicit argument is that foreign princes who made such large concessions as those envisioned by the marriage treaty were successful, whereas those who attempted to rule in disregard of English law and custom failed. Further, lest the relevance of the lessons of history be missed, Philip himself was included as the latest in a series of foreign sovereigns, and his reign was welcomed as the start of a golden age of peace and good religion. The treatise : in the form of a dialogue between Alphonso, a traveler who has

---

[22] *Catalogue général des manuscrits des Bibliothèques Publiques de France – Départments*, Vol. 32, Besançon, ed. Auguste Castan (Paris, 1897), I, p. 823.
[23] Donaldson, *Machiavellian Treatise*, pp. 45, 103. See n. 5, this chapter, for the published text of the "Ritratto."
[24] Donaldson, *Machiavellian Treatise*, introduction, pp. 23–39.
[25] See E. H. Harbison, *Rival Ambassadors at the Court of Queen Mary* (Princeton, N.J., 1940), esp. chaps. 3 and 4.

come to the court of Philip in search of political wisdom, and Stephano,
clearly modeled on Gardiner himself, a high official in that court, who
answers his questions. Alphonso is specifically interested in the great
alterations (Ital.: *mutationi*) that have occurred in England's past. It
turns out that this word refers not to just any change in government,
but specifically to those times when foreign dynasties came to power
in England. Stephano lists these: first the coming of Brutus the Trojan,
then Caesar, then the British kings, the Anglo-Saxons, the Danes, the
Normans – and finally Philip of Spain:

[William the Conqueror's] successors ruled securely until the death of Edward
VI. Since he had no bodily heir the kingdom passed to his sister Mary, who
with the consent of the lords and in accordance with the procedures of the
kingdom took for husband and king Philip, son of the Emperor Charles V,
for the common good of the kingdom and for the good . . . of all Christendom.
(pp. 50–1, 108)

Note that in Gardiner's schema, the year 1554 marks a new period,
just as 1066 did. He ignores the beginning of the Tudor dynasty in
1485 and other such transitions from one native dynasty to another,
and places Philip's coming in the context of those more momentous
occasions on which the rule of England passed to a foreign line. The
conclusion of the treatise returns to this theme and is even stronger
on this point, emphasizing that "William subjugated the realm of England and left it in trust to his successors until the coming of the powerful and most merciful Philip." Philip's accession was not a "change
or alteration in the kingdom, but legitimate succession, confirmed by
all orders, for the restoration of religion, the honor of the kingdom
and benefit of the people" (pp. 97, 149–50). Mary is left rather pointedly out of account, and the treatise concludes, after these words, with
a flowery tribute to the noble blood of the House of Austria. The
reign of Philip and Mary is presented as the beginning of the Habsburg
dynasty in England. All this, of course, is in striking contrast to the
marriage treaty. Stephano minimizes Mary's role and completely ignores the fact that the treaty had made Habsburg succession contingent
upon the birth of a child to Philip and Mary.[26]

Thus, we have a Gardiner who favored, rather than opposed, the
consolidation of Habsburg power, at least after Philip actually came
to England. However, he did so with reservations. Almost all of those
limiting provisions of the marriage treaty that Gardiner had insisted
upon reappear in the *Ragionamento:* The foreign ruler must respect

[26] Thomas Rymer, ed., *Foedera*, 2nd. ed. (London, 1728), XV, pp. 377ff.; Harbison,
Rival Ambassadors, p. 101.

English law; he must keep his own countrymen out of office and refrain from bringing in soldiers or settlers, for new subjects, particularly
English ones, have to be conciliated. Thus the restrictions insisted upon
by Gardiner in the treaty are here presented as part of a complex
strategy in which the English retain a large measure of independence
and the new dynasty is assured of long continuance in power.[27] That
such was in fact Gardiner's strategy seems clear when we review the
record. His stubbornness in regard to the treaty now appears not as
an effort to keep Philip out – he couldn't have achieved that in any
case – but as an attempt to ensure maximum independence for England under a regime that he welcomed as the guarantor of religious
orthodoxy. The old view – essentially that of E. H. Harbison – according to which Gardiner was the leader of an anti-Spanish faction,
in competition with the pro-Spanish faction of Paget, needs revision.
This new evidence helps us make better sense of Gardiner's various
activities at the time. For example, it helps explain why it was Gardiner
who researched Philip's independent claim to the English throne
through the Lancastrian line[28] and why we find his name associated
with a movement in Mary's third Parliament to have Philip crowned.[29]
But though the *Ragionamento* may help to make sense of certain aspects
of Gardiner's public career at this time, it seems quite impossible that
the treatise itself was ever intended to be made public. The translator
prepared the Italian version for Philip's use, and though he does not
say whether Gardiner asked him to make this translation (it is possible
that the treatise was found among Gardiner's papers after his death,
and that Gardiner himself made no plans for its circulation), Philip
himself is the audience the book was intended for by its author. Not
only are its Machiavellian borrowings and its exempla from English
history designed especially for a prince in Philip's position, but the
work ends with unreserved praise of Philip, who was chosen by divine
providence "by honorable means of holy matrimony to rule over the
powerful realm of England as a most pious father." He is "without
dispute the arbiter of peace and war of all Christendom" (pp. 98–9,
150–1).

Because the treatise does present Philip and not Mary as the ruler
of England, because it borrows, as we shall see, some of the most
"amoral" passages from Machiavelli, and, worse, does so in support
of a Machiavellian reinterpretation of the terms of the marriage treaty

[27] See also Donaldson, *Machiavellian Treatise*, pp. 23–39.
[28] *Calendar of State Papers, Spanish* (London, 1862–1954), XII, p. 242.
[29] Ibid., XIII, p. 125.

in accord with Habsburg dynastic interests, the possibility that the work was intended for publication may be regarded as highly improbable. The goal of making Philip agreeable to his new subjects proved impossible in any case, but the printing of a book like this by the chancellor would have made things far worse, and it may be presumed that the gift of the two manuscripts – one to Philip and the other to Granvelle – would have been consonant with Gardiner's own intentions, and that the *Ragionamento* was not intended for public consumption, but was conceived as a private, secret manual of counsel.

As with Thomas, Gardiner's Machiavellian treatise conceals its debt to Machiavelli, in fact even more so than with Thomas, for Machiavelli is not only not mentioned, but the reader is sometimes actually misled: The story of Camillus's castigation of the treachery of the Faliscan schoolmaster is attributed to Livy, but Gardiner quotes from Machiavelli's adaptation, not from the original (*Machiavellian Treatise*, pp. 91, 144 and note). Paul the Deacon is cited as a source in the discussion of wars of necessity and given credit for a remark that in fact occurs in Sallust's *Jugurtha* as quoted in *Discorsi* II:8. It is this Machiavellian passage, not Paul or Sallust, that Gardiner is actually following (pp. 58, 115 and note). One cannot tell whether this was done out of a desire to seem more original than the actual reliance of the work on Machiavelli would have warranted, or because Machiavelli had by this time (he had already been attacked privately by Pole and in print by Osorio and Politi) come to be regarded as something of a tainted source. In any case we have with Gardiner, as with William Thomas and the Thomas Cromwell of Pole's *Apologia*, an example of the tendency to regard Machiavelli as a potent source of advice for rulers, but one best handled in a secretive manner.

The details of Gardiner's use of Machiavelli as the basis for a manual of counsel for Philip of Spain must now concern us.

The "matrimonial" new prince

In the treatise, the proposition that new dynasties are made strong by respecting native rights is developed by examples from English history, and these examples are fit into a scheme borrowed from Machiavelli's analysis of the new prince and the principles that govern his relations with his new possessions. Before examining Gardiner's borrowings in detail, it is useful to examine the overall scheme. Machiavelli had divided princes into hereditary ones and new ones – and it was the new ones who had to use amorally problematic, "Machia-

vellian" methods. For the hereditary prince, it is sufficient to make
no changes in the laws and customs (*Prin.* 1, 2). But which was Philip?
Oddly, Machiavelli had not included Philip's situation among the cases
he discussed. Philip was a hereditary prince in the sense that his accession was according to the established procedures of England, but he
was a new prince in the sense that he was foreign, he was resented
by his new subjects, and he intended eventually to rule in fact and
pass the kingdom on to his heirs despite the restrictions of the treaty.
Of this intention there is no doubt: The marriage was conceived from
the start by the Habsburgs as a way of bringing England under the
rule of that dynasty, and Philip actually foreswore in secret the limitations of the treaty as soon as he had signed them.[30] As we have
seen, Gardiner assumes in the treatise that Philip's coming is the start
of permanent Habsburg rule. Gardiner has to carve out his own niche
for a prince like Philip from Machiavelli's categories. First, thinking
of Machiavelli's distinction between hereditary and new states, and
the distinction between gained through conquest or other exercise of
virtù and those gained through fortune, Gardiner places princes like
Philip with those who must pursue a mild course; adding to Machiavelli's categories the specific case of the prince who has come to power
through marriage:

He who has gained a realm or a province by force of arms has one way to
hold it, and he who has gained one through favor of friends, hereditary laws,
or by *matrimony* must take a different course to keep his state. The basis of
this latter course should be mercy, affability and generosity. (p. 145, emphasis
added)

But there are exceptions to his recommendation, and in making them,
Gardiner quotes from *Principe* 3 on "mixed" principalities, states that
are neither entirely new nor entirely hereditary. If such states are
similar in language and customs to the original possession of the prince,
then the only addition the prince must make to the strategy for hereditary princes (mild rule, respect for the established ways) is to make
himself safe from those of royal blood.[31] But when the new possession
differs in language and custom, it is a great help for the prince to go

[30] Ibid., XII, p. 5.
[31] "Le difficulte non sono grande di mantenere un regno per un principe nuove, quale
per via d'amicitia è intrato, quando egli è sicuro di quelli del sangue reale" (p. 93). Cf.
Prin. 3: "questi stati, quali acquistandosi si aggiungono a uno stato antiquo di quello
che acquista, o e' sono della medesima provincia e della medesima lingua, o non sono.
Quando e' sieno, è facilità grande a tenerli . . . a possederli securamente basta avere
spenta la linea del principe che li dominava."

and live there.[32] Thus England is, for Philip, a mixed principality – partly like a hereditary state and partly like a new one – and it must be ruled according to the overall strategy Machiavelli had proposed for such states when they differ in language from the original possessions of the prince. Mildness is recommended, except to those of royal blood, who must be eliminated, and residence in the new state is essential.

Military independence and territorial integrity

Consideration toward new subjects means, first of all, keeping one's own countrymen out, whether as settlers, office seekers, or auxiliary military forces. Gardiner approaches this issue by analyzing the Anglo-Saxon migrations. The historical record (Gardiner uses Polydore Vergil's *Anglica historia* as his regular source for English history) did not make it clear whether the Angles and Saxons had come to Britain because of famine in Germany, or whether they were called in by the British king Vortigerius, who asked for the help of stronger men than he could control and made things worse by marrying the daughter of their chief and appointing Saxons to high office.[33] In either case, the relationship between the foreign nationals and the natives could not be controlled, and British folly led to Saxon domination. Both possibilities are explored with the help of Machiavelli. First, if the Saxons came as soldiers called in by Vortigerius, the case falls under Machiavelli's principle that mercenary or auxiliary forces are never to be trusted. Gardiner quotes *Principe* 12 on the poor character of such troops (the solidiers brought in by Vortigerius would technically have been auxiliary rather than mercenary forces, since they remained under the command of their own officers. Gardiner ignores Machiavelli's distinction, and thus makes Machiavelli's harshest words about mercenaries apply to auxiliaries as well). They are rapacious, insolent, ambitious, disobedient, and undisciplined. They have no fear of God or faith toward men and are motivated only by money, an insufficient inducement to risk life in one's service.[34] Gardiner, following his

[32] "Poi gli è un grand adiuto, quando il principe andasse ad habitarne" (p. 93). Cf. *Prin.* 3: "E uno de' maggiori remedii e più vivi sarebbe che la persona di chi acquista vi andassi ad abitare." Also: "Pure che non alterasse lor leggi, ne li agravasse con nuovi essationi o datii, egli in breve tempo venerà antico nel principato" (p. 93); cf. *Prin.* 3 "[debbe avere dua respetti . . .] l'altro, di non alterare nè loro legge nè loro dazii; talmente che in brevissimo tempo diventa, con loro principato antiquo, tutto uno corpo."

[33] Donaldson, *Machiavellian Treatise*, introduction, pp. 21–3; text, pp. 51–64, 108–19; Polydore Vergil, *Anglicae historiae libri XXVI* (Basel, 1534), pp. 52–4.

[34] "Perche i sono rapaci, ambitiosi, superbi, disobedienti. Alcuni ne sono instrutti (pel

source, cites the example of the Venetians, who lost in one day what they had acquired in many centuries through reliance on mercenaries, as well as other Machiavellian exempla: the Carthaginians, the emperors of Constantinople, and the Milanese, all of whom made ruinous bargains with mercenaries (*Prin.* 12, 13; *Ragionamento*, p. 56). To the Machiavellian instances, Gardiner adds his own observations on the mercenaries who fought for Francis I, then for Henry VIII, then for Henry II; on the cowardice and treachery of the mercenaries who fought for Edward VI during the risings of 1549; and, of course, on Vortigerius and his Saxons. The danger presented by these troops was worsened by two factors: Vortigerius allowed them to share the honors and offices of the kingdom (p. 56), and he allowed them to enter in great numbers. His sharing of honors and offices with them is discussed at length later in the treatise, in conjunction with Gardiner's section on insult, together with the similar offenses of Edward II and King John (see the later discussion in this section). The arrival of multitudes of Saxons is analyzed at this point in the treatise in conjunction with *Discorsi* II:8. In this chapter, Machiavelli contrasted wars begun by princes with those caused by movements of entire peoples in the face of natural disaster. The latter kind – wars involving the migration of entire populations – are the most destructive of all, for princes are satisfied with dominion and tribute, whereas the movement of peoples leads to life-and-death competition for land and the other necessities of life. When one people drives out another in this way, the very name of the country is often lost – as Maurusia became Judaea after the Hebrew conquest, Transalpine Gaul became France, Pannonia became Hungary, and Britain became England. Gardiner quotes nearly the entire chapter in this case, with minor changes, as, for example, the omission of Britain from Machiavelli's list of countries that lost their names, since, in his context, its listing would have been redundant. There is one rather significant change made in the quoted material, and it brings us back to the contemporary relevance of all this to Marian politics and to English fears of Spanish domination. When the number of invaders is very large, they usually overrun a

lungo uso) nella disciplina militare, ma pochi osservino l'ordini d'essa. Tengino poco timore verso Iddio, et meno rispetto a li huomini. . . . Et tutto l'amore che portino à colui che servino, depende solamente di quel poco stipendio che egli donne, il qual non sarai mai tanto che li basta di vivere . . . ne tanto che basta che moriranno per causa sua" (pp. 54–5).

Cf. *Prin.* 12: "Perchè le sono disunite, ambiziose, sanza disciplina, infidele . . . non timore di Dio, non fede con gli uomini . . . la cagione di questo è che le non hanno altro amore nè altra cagione che le tenga in campo, che uno poco di stipendio; il quale non è sufficiente a fare che voglino morire per te."

country at the first opportunity, but when the number is small, they have to begin by occupying a small area and making friends.[35] That tells us why the English would not have wanted the Spanish to come in; it shows that their fears were not frivolous, but rested upon the precedent of all those nations that had lost their names and their land, either by trusting auxiliary forces or by foolishly admitting settlers. But why would Philip, whose aim was in fact to conquer England, want to heed those fears? In the discussion of the reigns of King Canute and King Stephen (pp. 132–3), Gardiner presents two contrary examples to show that the wise foreign-born ruler ought to keep his own countrymen out. According to Gardiner, who oddly departs from Polydore in these two cases, perhaps to supply exempla where the facts of history lacked them, Canute brought in great numbers of Danes and advanced them to positions of importance in England. At his death, Gardiner says, there was a great slaughter of Danes throughout the land, in revenge for the contempt in which the native population had been held. The interlocutors in the dialogue, who sometimes disagree, both emphatically defend the killing: Neither reason nor human nature can tolerate the supplanting of native talent by unworthy foreigners (p. 133).

King Stephen's course was wiser, in Gardiner's telling: Though he was duke of Normandy and French by birth, he kept his dominions separate, appointing Englishmen to office in England and Normans in Normandy. Because of this, there was a "continual fraternal love" (p. 133) between the two peoples. Here we are close to the language of the marriage treaty between Philip and Mary, which envisioned an "entire and sincere fraternity" (*Statutes of the Realm*, IV, p. 224) between

---

[35] "Ma quando il nomero che si parti d'una provintia non è grande che non ponno al primo impeto usar tanta violenza conviene loro con arte occupare qualche luogo, et mantenersi per via d'amicitia et confederati come fece nostro Hengesto . . ." (p. 60).

Cf. *Disc.* II:8: "Ma quando quegli che sono costretti abbandonare la loro patria non sono molti, non sono sì pericolosi come quelli popoli di che si è ragionato; perchè non possono usare tanta violenza, ma conviene loro con arte occupare qualche luogo, e, occupatolo, mantenervisi per via d'amici di confederati."

Gardiner omits Machiavelli's phrase "non sono sì pericolosi" and insists, using Machiavelli's own example of the conquest of Latium by Aeneas, that foreign settlers always present a danger, whether their initial numbers are small or great. Gardiner adjusts Machiavelli here because of the contemporary parallel. His bringing together Machiavelli's analysis of the dangers of mercenaries and the dangers of settlers bears upon the contemporary situation in England, and refers particularly to the exclusion of Spanish soldiers and Spanish settlers by the terms of the marriage treaty (Rymer, *Foedera*, XV, pp. 377–81. English version in *Statutes of the Realm*, IV, pp. 222–6). In order to show that English resistance to the Spanish presence is based upon sound historical and political principles, the qualifying phrase Machiavelli had used needed to be left out: Foreigners are dangerous in any numbers.

England and Spain if precisely this principle were adhered to. And, Gardiner warns, the prince who does otherwise will end up like Canute – and here the warning becomes bold indeed, referring directly to Philip's Italian policies – unless he is continually in arms, like the Spanish in Naples.

The corollary to Gardiner's rejection of the presence of foreigners is, as in Machiavelli, an emphasis on military self-sufficiency. If foreigners are not to be asked in, the native forces must be adequate. This means that the prince must be learned in the art of war (p. 118; *Prin.* 14) and his subjects must be armed and trained, "for there is nothing so weak and infirm as a principality founded on the arms of another" (p. 118).[36] Alphonso raises serious objections to the idea of a militia, however, arguing that the English common people have been so rebellious throughout their history that to arm them would be dangerous. Also, peasants who have been in the army seldom return peacefully to the land; they are a corrupting influence, and their discontent can lead to sedition. Alphonso points out that many wise princes in England had restricted acquaintance with military discipline, limiting public assembly and forbidding instruction in the use of the harquebus or crossbow. Stephano's answer is that knowledge is never the cause of evil – and if military science is used ill, it is the fault of the prince, who ought to be able to command his people in war and return them to peaceful occupations in an orderly way. Henry VIII's trust in the people and his use of native forces in his victories at Thérouanne and Tournai shows that English common people can be trusted as soldiers if the ruler knows his business. He also defends the English people from their reputation for revolt, arguing that the famous revolts in England's past were due to mismanagement of the people by the prince or were caused by faction among the nobility (pp. 118–23).

Thus Gardiner found in *Il Principe* and the *Discorsi* powerful support for the idea that a new prince of Philip's type ought to permit his new subjects a large degree of military self-sufficiency. England's case was not Italy's. England already enjoyed self-rule and already had a militia, but Machiavelli had much to offer concerning this issue, and Gardiner, a perceptive reader of his source, made use of both *Il Principe* and

[36] "Et quanto al mancare armi proprii di suoi soggetti, affermo che nessuno regno o principato è sicuro anzi tutto suggeto a le colpe di fortuna non havendo virtu in tempo di necessità, che lo puole diffendere. L'era l'opinione de i savii, che non è cosa si debole et infirmo come il principato fondato sopra "armi d'altrui" (p. 61).

Cf. *Prin.* 13: "Concludo, adunque, che sanza avere arme proprie, nessuno principato è securo; anzi è tutto obligato alla fortuna, non avendo virtù che nelle avversità con fede lo difenda. E fu sempre l'opinione e sentenzia degli uomini savi 'quod nihil sit tam infirmum aut instabile quam fama potentiae non sua vi nixa.' "

the *Discorsi* to show that such self-sufficiency would not necessarily conflict with the interests of the new prince.

The new prince under the law: respect for the rights of the governed

Gardiner's purposes led him to find more passages in Machiavelli in which respect for the rights and laws of new subjects is advised than one might have supposed possible. To study Gardiner's borrowings on these subjects is to be reminded that, although Machiavelli often shows the prince how he can get his way, he generally, at the same time, points out the limits of princely will – limits set by the laws, values, and institutions of the communities over which the prince rules. There is far more balance between the prince and the people, even in *Il Principe*, than we sometimes remember. The *Ragionamento* contains a long section on the dangers of insult, probably because Philip of Spain was not careful of the feelings or rights of others. In fact his tactlessness in his relations with Mary and with England, sometimes moved his father to anger and desperation.[37] He failed to write to Mary in his own hand until months after their marriage had been celebrated by proxy; he signed himself "Philippus Rex" in letters to the English Privy Council before he had even arrived in England;[38] and fears were common on both sides of the alliance that his personal failings would endanger the match. That is perhaps why Gardiner goes to such pains to stress respect and the dangers of insult in the treatise. Vortigerius's elevation of Saxons to office was insulting to men of merit in the kingdom (pp. 110–11, 117–18), as was Canute's similar offense (pp. 132–3). But perhaps the most insulting of English kings was Edward II, who promoted his minions – first Gaveston, then the Spensers – to high office in contempt of the able and serious men of the realm. For all his distaste for rebellion, Gardiner's sympathies in this story are clearly with the great lords, who "held the honor and safety of their country dear" (p. 127) and first warned, and then saw to the death of, the contemptuous sovereign. This example from English history leads to one from Machiavelli (p. 128; *Disc.* II:26) that concerns the seige of Amida by the Persian captain Cobades. Growing tired of the long siege, Cobades began to withdraw his forces – but the vituperation heaped upon his army by the natives on the walls so enraged him that he returned to the siege, took the

[37] See Harbison, *Rival Ambassadors*, p. 184.
[38] Ibid., p. 188.

city, and sacked it. Insult can take various forms: Greedy and avaricious kings are guilty of it when they show contempt for the property rights of subjects, and several English kings (Rufus, John, and Richard II) were guilty of this (pp. 130–2). As in other cases, Gardiner uses both major works of Machiavelli in saying that injury to property is remembered longer even than injury to persons.[39] Perhaps the worst form of disrespect of his subjects that the prince can show is scorn for the law. Laws were instituted for the safety and well-being of princes, as well as of peoples. When there is no law, people revolt and princes become tyrants: "there is no worse example in a kingdom than to make a law and not observe it, and so much the worse when it is not observed by him who made it" (*Ragionamento,* p. 130; *Disc.* I:45). James III of Scotland broke his own laws, saying that he was king to give laws to others, not to accept them from anyone. (Note the similarity of this formulation to Pole's account of Cromwell's idea of royal will; see Chapter 1.) King John of England also held the laws in contempt, and for this he was driven from the throne. Here Gardiner, who in fact locates nearly every passage in Machiavelli where the point is made, quotes *Discorsi* III:5 on respect for law:

Princes should know that they begin to lose their state at that hour when they begin to break the laws and change ancient customs and usages under which men have lived for a long time . . . for it is much easier to be loved by the good than by the bad; better to obey the laws than command them. (pp. 130–1)[40]

---

[39] "L'huomo dismentiga facile l'ingiurie fatte contra suo padre o contra suo fratello, perche non furono li sempre necessarii, ma la necessita delli bene venne ogni giorno, et pero ogni giorno si ricordi deli beni tolti" (p. 76).
  "Gli huomini sdimenticano più presto la morte del padre che la perdita del patrimonio" (*Prin.* 17).
  "Le cose che hanno in sè utilità, quando l'uomo n'è privo, non le dimentica mai, ed ogni minima necessità te ne fa ricordare; e perchè le necessità vengono ogni giorno, tu te ne ricordi ogni giorno" (*Disc.* III:23).
[40] "Sapino donque i principe, che à quel hora commicianno à perdere lor stato, quando essi commincianno à romper le leggi et mutare quelli modi et costumi, quali sono antiche, sotto le quale gli huomini lungo tempo hanno vivuti. Et poi privati che sono del stato diventassino mai tanto prudenti, di cognoscere con quanta faciltà i regni si tengino da coloro che saviamente si consiglianno dorebbe molto piu loro tal perdita, et à magiore pena se condamnerebbono se stessi che si d'altri fussino condemnati. Perche egli è molto piu facile d'esser amati delli boni, che delli cattivi; meglior obedire à le leggi, che commandarle: perche l'uno e pieno di pericolo, l'altro di sicurtà" (p. 76).
  "Sappino adunque i principi, come a quella ora ei cominciano a perdere lo stato che cominciano a rompere le leggi, e quelli modi e quelle consuetudini che sono antiche, e sotto le quali lungo tempo gli uomini sono vivuti. E se, privati che ei sono dello stato, ei diventassono mai tanto prudenti che ei conoscessono con quanta faciltà i principati

Gardiner, a lawyer, had always believed this and had often said it. Here he alters Machiavelli slightly in a way that makes the passage echo his own formulation of the same issue in one of his letters. This is the addition: "[It is] better to obey the laws than command them, *since the one is full of danger, and the other is safe*" ("meglior obedire à le leggi, che commandarle: perche l'uno e pieno di pericolo, l'altro di sicurtà" [*Ragionamento*, pp. 76, 131]). The stress falls upon political consequences rather than moral imperatives. We find the same sequence of ideas in a letter Gardiner wrote to Somerset during Edward's reign, defending himself from the accusation that he advised Henry VIII to rule by proclamation. According to Gardiner, it was Cromwell who had raised the issue of rule by fiat, taunting Gardiner, the civil lawyer, with the principle "quod principi placuit legibus habet vigorem":

The Lord Cromwell had once put in the king's our late sovereign lord's head to take upon him to have his will and pleasure regarded for a law; for that, he said, was to be a very king. And thereupon I was called for at Hampton Court. And as the Lord Cromwell was very stout, "Come on, my Lord of Winchester," quoth he (for that conceit he had, whatsoever he talked with me, he knew ever as much as I, Greek or Latin and all), "answer the King here," quoth he, "but speak plainly and directly, and shrink not, man! Is not that," quoth he, "that pleaseth the king a law? Have ye not there in the civil law," quoth he, "quod principi placuit and so forth?"

When the king himself requested a response, Gardiner answered that he

had read in deed of kings that had their will always received for a law, but, I told him, the form of his reign, to make the laws his will, was more sure and quiet. "And by this form of government ye be established," quoth I, "and it is agreeable with the nature of your people. If ye begin a new manner of policy, how it will frame, no man can tell; and how this frameth, ye can tell; and I would never advise your Grace to leave a certain for an uncertain."[41]

Thus there is a parallel between Gardiner's adaptation of Machiavelli's words about respect for law and the advice he gave to Somerset in 1547 and claimed to have given Henry VIII earlier. In all three cases, respect for law is advised because disrespect leads to danger. Gardiner, who had spoken on this issue several times earlier in his career, found

si tenghino da coloro che saviamente si consigliano; dorebbe molto più loro tale perdita, ed a maggiore pena si condannerebbono, che da altri fossono condannati. Perchè egli è molto più facile essere amato dai buoni che dai cattivi, ed ubedire alle leggi che volere comandare loro" (*Disc.* III:5).
[41] Muller, *Letters*, p. 399.

just those places in Machiavelli where respect for law was stressed (most readers of Machiavelli miss them) and even added a few words to his source so that the Machiavelli quotation would agree entirely with his long-held views.

"The laws" in such a passage means statute law, as opposed to royal prerogative. The relation between the two could be quite complex – and we shall see that Gardiner, in this treatise, allows the prince wide latitude indeed in getting around particular laws, but public respect for the statutes was part of Gardiner's attitude from early on. Perhaps at the time of the interview Gardiner had in fact taken the side of the prerogative, and not, as in his version, the side of statute. He admits that rumor had him playing the part he assigned to Cromwell ("Cromwell turned the cat in the pan afore company"), and we do not know which minister gave Henry such advice. Pole's account in the *Apologia* supports Gardiner and lays the blame for the proposal that Henry rule by will on Cromwell. On that side, too, is the preamble of the Statute of Proclamations – though the act, as we have it, as well as Cromwell's entire practice, show a more constitutional side. Probably, as W. H. Dunham put it, the "rule of law" and royal power were, paradoxically, both held to be binding, by Cromwell, by Gardiner, and by many others, so that the stories tend to get confused in the later telling.[42] But we cannot doubt that statute law was important to Gardiner and that he never publicly spoke in favor of its abrogation. Under Edward, it became the cornerstone of his resistance to religious change, for he refused to conform to Edwardian reforms on the authority of the Henrician statutes and claimed that, even under Henry, the best common lawyers had assured him (to his surprise) that statute law was so far binding, even upon the king's immediate servants, that following the king's express command was no defense against a charge of *praemunire*. And, under Mary, there is an interesting episode reported by Fleetwood, the London recorder in 1575, that shows Gardiner in much the same light as he presented himself. As in the meeting with Henry at Hampton Court, so in this case someone had proposed that Mary dispense with statute and rule by proclamation. The argument was that the laws of England were binding upon the kings of England but not upon the queens, and that Mary ruled, not as a king ruled, but as a conqueror, and was not bound by the laws of her predecessors. It was Gardiner who rejected this proposal as preposterous

[42] W. H. Dunham, "Regal power and the rule of law: A Tudor paradox," *Journal of British Studies* III (1964), 24–56.

and who, as in his version of the Hampton Court interview, insisted upon rule by statute.[43]

The point of view taken in regard to contempt for the law in the *Ragionamento* is also illuminated by an earlier work of Gardiner's on the subject – a treatise composed in controversy with Alexander Alesius and Martin Bucer at the time of the diet of Regensburg and bearing the title "Contemptum humanae legis iusta authoritate latae gravius et severius vindicandum quam divinae legis qualemconque trangressionem" ("The contempt of human law, made by rightful authority, is to be punished more heavily and more seriously than any transgression of the divine law").[44] In this work, Gardiner opposes leniency toward those who violate minor religious obligations imposed by civil authority, especially those who claim "Gospel freedom" to ignore fast days and the like. Gardiner's position is that such regulations, promulgated by human authority, must be protected by more grave sanctions than those provided for violations of the divine law because these human laws, minor though they be, test respect for the principle of authority; and although the source of regulation is human, the principle of obedience to human law is an obligation to God. The contempt of human laws thus implies contempt of God himself, and therefore constitutes the crime of injury of the divine majesty. But are not transgressions of divine laws more serious than transgressions of human laws? Here Gardiner distinguishes between contempt and mere transgression unaccompanied by contempt, and holds that mere breach of divine law, through human weakness, is less serious than the intentional flouting of civil authority. This is a curiously paradoxical form of the authentically biblical notion that obedience to established authority is obedience to God. The idea is far from absurd, yet there is a touch of Gardiner's personal arrogance in maintaining it in this extreme form, especially as it argues for the death penalty for minor infractions. The argument unfolds like this: Princes ought not to allow divine laws to be condemned, but neither should they be too severe in punishing infractions; offenses against divine law ought to be left to God's vengeance and the church's correction, for otherwise the Christian religion would seem to be maintained by constraint of princes rather than by mutual charity. The kinds of offenses that require severe punishment are those that "tend to the tearing asunder of the body of the church and to the overthrow of human society" –

---

[43] Ibid., p. 45, citing BL Harley MS 6234, fols. 20r–23v.
[44] Text in Janelle, *Obedience*, pp. 174–212.

like murder and heresy; as well as those minor regulations of the prince that test respect for authority:

If that the prince, having regard for the glory of God and the maintenance of the Church, forbid some otherwise indifferent thing, for example the eating of flesh on a certain day, when enacting a penalty he will not have in view the thing ordained, which considered in itself is of very small moment, but the maintenance of peace, quiet and obedience . . . so that for the protection of his dominion, and establishing of his authority, the following words may have force: who has not obeyed his prince, let him die the death. (pp. 179–81)

The reformers were fond of citing biblical verses against "human traditions" and against those who substituted "the commandments of men" for the word of God. For Gardiner "human law is confirmed by divine authority" (p. 203).

Thus the principle of obedience, which holds human society together, is at the same time the most important divine command. And the claim of exemption from human law because of Gospel freedom is a crime against God as well as a threat to civil order: In fact, Gardiner believed that if his own views on the seriousness of contempt for law were not followed, monarchy and hierarchy would collapse.

These opinions are repeated in the criticism of Catherine Parr's religious views reported by Foxe ("the religion by the Queen so stiffly maintained did . . . disallow and dissolve the policy and politic government of princes"),[45] and in his remonstrances against religious reform under Edward,[46] and even find an echo in Gardiner's position on the pronunciation of Greek. Writing to the vice-chancellor of Cambridge, he says that contempt is a serious matter in any affair, but especially serious in relation to things of least importance – "in re levissima gravissimus."[47]

Let us keep these opinions of Gardiner's, especially the rule that contempt in minor matters can be more serious than transgression without contempt in major ones, in mind while examining the position on contempt for law taken in the *Ragionamento*. We have seen that Gardiner, with Machiavellian support, believed that respect for law was crucial, especially for a new prince attempting to make his power secure. But Gardiner's legalism, like that of Machiavelli himself, is of a restricted, arguably cynical, kind. For neither author argues that the

[45] Foxe, *Acts and Monuments*, V, p. 556.
[46] Muller, *Letters*, pp. 286ff, 308, 318–19.
[47] Ibid., p. 137.

prince's conduct must always be within the law. In fact, the reverse is often suggested, as when Gardiner condemns Richard II and Henry VI for allowing their rivals to live, in keeping with Machiavelli's words about eliminating rivals, even though killing them would clearly have been illegal,[48] and when Gardiner holds it to Henry VIII's credit (in a story not otherwise attested) that he had certain gentlemen hung at their own gates, apparently without process of law, upon the complaint of poor suitors claiming that the gentry had used the risings in the North of 1536 as an excuse for oppressing the poor (*Machiavellian Treatise*, pp. 147–8). What is at issue is not whether the prince always stays within the law, but whether he appears to respect it and maintains its integrity as a social institution. The important political sin is public contempt for law. Thus, Gardiner offers several examples of kings who scorned the law, and he selects not those monarchs who were famous for crime, like Nero or Caligula or Richard III, but rather ones who were morally less reprehensible but politically more foolish, men who lost power by showing contempt for law in public: Vortigerius, Rufus, John, and James III of Scotland (pp. 129–30). Like Machiavelli, Gardiner leaves the moral question to one side: Princes need to respect law because it is politically advisable to do so. Comparing this Machiavellian attitude toward law and its social function to Gardiner's opinions in *Contemptum humanae legis,* one is struck by the congruence of the religious argument and the Machiavellian one. Both treatises place great stress upon outward conformity and the maintaining of appearances, and both place relatively little emphasis on transgression of the law, which can be tolerated so long as the principle of obedience and the social fabric are not threatened. Transgression of the law, in the case of eliminating those of royal blood, can even be a good thing if it keeps a man in power and prevents the social collapse attendant upon a struggle for succession.

Cruelty, kindness, and the elimination of rivals

William the Conqueror was a foreign prince who ruthlessly suppressed the native population of England and succeeded in passing his new possession on to his heirs. Consideration of his methods leads the interlocutors into an extended discussion of the relative merits of cruelty and kindness that draws heavily on Machiavelli, on Paolo Giovio's *Commentario de le cose de' Turchi* (Rome, 1535; English translation by

[48] Donaldson, *Machiavellian Treatise,* p. 141. Eventually, as Gardiner notes, Henry VII "was finally forced to protect himself against young innocent Edward" (p. 139), Reginald Pole's uncle (see Chapter 1, this volume).

Peter Ashton: *A Shorte Treatise upon the Turkes Chronicles,* 1546), and on Lucio Paolo Rosello's *Ritratto del vero governo del principe dall'essempio vivo del gran Cosimo de'Medici* (Venice, 1552).[49] The material from Turkish history has the effect of exaggerating or drawing out to its logical conclusions Machiavelli's preference for harsh methods, whereas the material derived from Rosello has, for the most part, a moderating effect on the discussion, as does Gardiner's use of passages from the *Discorsi* in which Machiavelli himself seems to soften positions taken in *Il Principe.* The effect of the section as a whole (pp. 137–47) is to suggest that a new foreign prince in Philip's position will need to avail himself of at least some of the grimmer tactics Machiavelli had discussed and recent Turkish history had exemplified. Philip is not directly mentioned, but it is made clear that the "matrimonial" new prince must, while conciliating his subjects, make himself safe from those of the royal blood by whatever means necessary.

Since the title of the *Ragionamento* tells us that the work concerns the coming of the English and the Normans to Britain, William the Conqueror must have an important place in the dialogue; but the way in which he is introduced into the conversation is significant, for his methods seem to contradict the principle, previously established and directly relevant to the marriage treaty between Philip and Mary, that foreign princes ought to keep their own nationals out of the way if they want to rule effectively in England:

Stephen wanted Englishmen in England and Normans in Normandy, and by this means there was a continual fraternal love between the English and Normans, and he, though he was French (the name of which is hated by the English), ruled until his natural death.

And the prince who does otherwise will find those dangers that the aforesaid Canute found, unless he is continually in arms like the Spaniard in Milan and Naples, and he will end as the Danes in England. After the Danes, the Normans, led by William, a spirited and powerful man, seized their opportunity,

[49] In his review article on my edition of the *Ragionamento* (see n. 5, this chapter), Sydney Anglo demonstrated that a small portion of the Machiavellian material used by Gardiner in the treatise actually came more directly from Lucio Paolo Rosello's *Ritratto del vero governo,* published in 1552, and that Rosello himself sometimes went directly to Machiavelli, but more often took his Machiavellian passages at second hand from Agostino Nifo's *De regnandi peritia,* a work that translates large portions of *Il Principe* into Latin without attribution, which appeared in 1523, some nine years before *Il Principe* itself was published. Thus, some of Gardiner's "Machiavellian" passages are second- or even thirdhand. However, this discovery ought not to change our assessment of the Machiavellian inspiration of the passages in question, for Gardiner sometimes makes use of *both* Rosello and the Machiavellian original, showing his awareness of the ultimate source of the material he uses. See n. 56, this chapter.

conquered the kingdom, and sought to extinguish the name of the English as the Danes had tried to do but with a stronger hand. (pp. 133–4)

The Danes were slaughtered by the aggrieved English, but William, whose rule was even harsher, succeeded, and his example, perhaps, invalidates that of the conciliatory King Stephen. After several pages devoted to the *virtù* William displayed in taking the opportunities afforded by the discord between King Harold and his brother Tostig, the discussion returns to William's policies as king. He built fortresses, extinguished the royal line, deprived the natives of dignities and offices, which he gave to the Normans, scorned the nobility, taxed the people, and, as the English grew ever more alienated from him, forbade them the use of arms and established a curfew (pp. 137–8).

Both Stephano and Alphonso agree that William's behavior was prudent, if cruel, because a new prince must eliminate rivals, and also because there is a kind of irreversibility in harsh methods. People don't forget the wrongs a new prince has done them, and therefore he cannot easily moderate his conduct after his initial conquest (p. 138). The general principle is stated in *Principe* 17: "For a new prince above all it is impossible not to earn a reputation for cruelty since new states are full of dangers." The principle of eliminating rivals is amplified by quotations from this chapter[50] and from *Discorsi* III:4.[51] From *Discorsi* III:4 is also derived the principle that new benefits do not cancel old injuries.[52]

But though William's prudence is agreed upon, the morality of what he did (and therefore the morality of the Machiavellian texts that in-

---

[50] "Quel principe nuovo (non parlo deli hereditarii) che lascierà vivo o in libertà colui al qual la provincia per qualche giure puole venire nodrisse la serpente in senno proprio, come fece Luigi re di Francia il quale per l'ambitione deli venitiani era fatto solo arbitrio d'Italia, et signor de la tertia parte di quella, vi misse un compagno nel regno di Napoli, il re di Spagna, accioche li malcontenti del suo governo havesserò dove ricorre à lamentarsi, et mediante lui vendicarne lor odii" (p. 85; cf. pp. 138–9).

"El re Luigi fu messo in Italia dalla ambizione de' Veneziani . . . feciono signore, el re del terzo di Italia . . . [Luigi] per volere il regno di Napoli, lo divise con il re di Spagna; e dove lui era, prima arbitro d'Italia, e' vi misse uno compagno, a ciò che gli ambiziosi di quella provincia e malcontenti di lui avessino dove ricorrere" (*Prin.* 3).

[51] "Per tanto dico, che colui che fara altramente troverà mille pericoli, et se stesso sempre in una continua paura, la quale è peggiore che la istessa morte, et sempre in pericolo di perder lo stato, et la vita mentre che coloro vivano, i quali sono stati spogliati o defraudati di quello" (p. 85; cf. pp. 138–9).

"Si può avvertire ogni principe, che non viva mai sicuro del suo principato, finchè vivono coloro che ne sono spogliati" (*Disc.* III:4).

[52] "Perche non si cancellò mai un simili ingiuria vechia con la liberalita ò clementia nuova" (p. 84; cf. p. 138); cf. *Disc.* III:4: "Mai le ingiurie vecchie furono cancellate da' beneficii nuovi."

form the discussion) is questioned: "This," Alphonso says of William's elimination of those who could harm him, "is a more common practice among all princes than divine law permits." Stephano's answer, though it is not the only answer the treatise provides for the problems raised by the conflicts between Machiavelli's text and ordinary morality, is a very clear statement of the principle of separation between moral and political questions: "Our purpose at present is not to show what a prince is permitted to do and what he is not permitted to do, but only to show by what ways and means a prince can maintain or lose his state" (p. 138). Stephano is thus embracing what would later be called "reason of state,"[53] and he does so in response to the moral problems implicit in the Machiavellian texts that the dialogue here relies upon. Elsewhere, as we shall see, this tendency to separate moral and political questions is balanced by various attempts to suggest that the "amoral" aspects of Machiavellian politics may be thought of as a special prerogative of kingly office.

Stephano's application of these principles to English cases shows the same tendency to separate the question of effectiveness from the question of moral virtue. Henry VII was plagued by the threat of revolt until he finally executed "young innocent Edward" (Cardinal Pole's maternal uncle), and Richard III could not obtain the throne until he had "quenched the royal line" by murdering his nephews. Such an action was "tyrannically ordered," to be sure, but kings like these knew "how to protect themselves against those who could hurt them" (p. 139). Drawing on Giovio, Stephano continues with an account of Sultan Selym's murder of his father, two brothers, and five nephews (pp. 139–41).

Stephano uses Machiavellian texts to resolve the moral issues raised by other Machiavellian texts. When Alphonso remarks that Stephano's English examples of the murder of rivals have been placed in the proper context, such conduct being more Turkish than Christian, Stephano replies with a paraphrase of Machiavelli's comment on Philip of Macedon's cruelty:[54] Not only does cruelty sometimes work better

---

[53] Quentin Skinner relates the *Ragionamento* to this tradition in *The Foundations of Modern Political Thought* (Cambridge, 1978), I, pp. 252–3.

[54] "Io non li lodo, anzi dico che sarebbe meglior per i christiani vivere privati, che con tanta crudelà di regnare. Ma questo e un giogo di sicuro che puol farlo, et non vuole fidarsi di coloro iquali per adrio ponno offenderlo" (p. 87; cf. p. 140).

"Sono questi modi crudelissimi, e nimici d'ogni vivere, non solamente cristiano, ma umano; e debbegli qualunque uomo fuggire, e volere piuttosto vivere privato, che re con tanta rovina degli uomini; nondimeno, colui che non vuole pigliare quella prima via del bene, quando si voglia mantenere conviene che entri in questo male" (*Disc.* I:26).

than compassion, but it can also be defended as an evil more tolerable than the alternative, which is anarchy.[55]

At this point in the text, material from Rosello's *Ritratto* begins to alternate with quotations from Machiavelli and references to English history. The first use of Rosello concerns other princes who, like William, made effective use of harsh methods. Cambyses spared no one when he won a victory, and neither did Sulla (p. 142; *Ritratto* 14v). Stephano then adds his own examples – Attila and Tamerlan: "such men did not seek to be loved: it was enough for them simply to be feared." This passage, like the discussion of the "Turkish honor" of the murderous Selym, has the effect of reminding the reader of the close relation between cruel methods and tyranny. Machiavelli had avoided explicit discussion of tyranny in *Il Principe*. The reason Gardiner brings it to the surface here is not that he wants to be more Machiavellian than Machiavelli, recommending that the methods of Attila be imitated in the England of Philip and Mary, nor is it that he wants to undermine the Machiavellian texts by associating them with famous tyrants. Rather, he wants to emphasize both the necessity for severity when circumstances require it and the moral cost: "Where mercy is effective, he is more than severe who will practice the contrary" (p. 141). Bringing Selym, Cambyses, Sulla, Attila, and Tamerlan into the discussion lends urgency to the question of how far their methods, or those of William, are really necessary in the England of 1554–5, how far the position of Philip resembles or does not resemble that of these tyrannical conquerors. In fact, Gardiner may have got the idea of using Turkish history in this way from Rosello, for, though Rosello does not offer an account of Selym's career, as Gardiner does, he does make the point, borrowed by Gardiner, that there are differences in circumstances, and especially differences in political constitutions, that make the extreme methods of the Turks inapplicable in Christian countries. In some places and among some peoples, cruelty is required; without it the Turkish empire would have fallen, and this is so because all authority resides in the monarch, and he can execute

[55] "Per tanto non si dee currare un principe della infamia di crudele di tenere i subditi in ufficio et uniti, perche con pochi essempi sara piu pietoso che quelli, iquali per non fare morire uno lascino sequire tumolti o altri disordini onde nascino occisioni et rapine lequale offendono l'universale, et l'essecutione del principe fatto offende solamente un particolare" (p. 88; cf. p. 141).
"Debbe, pertanto, uno principe non si curare della infamia di crudele, per tenere li subditi suoi uniti e in fede; perche con pochissimi esempli, sarà più pietoso che quelli e' quali, per troppa pietà, lasciono seguire e' disordini, di che ne nasca occisioni o rapine; perchè queste sogliono offendere una universalità intera, e quelle esecuzioni che vengono dal principe offendono uno particulare" (*Prin.* 17).

whom he pleases at whim (p. 143; *Ritratto,* fol. 15). But for Gardiner, echoing Rosello, the reason for extending the Machiavellian treatment of cruelty so that it includes the Turk is finally for purposes of contrast: In Christian countries, princes share power with their lords and cannot act so arbitrarily.

Questo non avviene tra' Christiani, perche i Prencipi partecipano in tal modo con loro baroni lo stato, che di quelli le signorie sono hereditarie. (*Ritratto,* fol. 15v)

Ma si un principe di Francia o d'Ingliterra procedesse in tal maniera, si roinarebbe incontinente . . . i baroni in Ingliterra et Francia participanno del stato co'l re, et i hanno privilegii et authorita grandissima co'l popolo talche non si puole intieramente usare tal severità, ne con la crudeltà manegiarli. (*Ragionamento,* p. 91; cf. p. 144)

Stephano is more emphatic than Rosello about this, stressing the authority of the barons in England according to ancient laws and warning that, if a wholly Turkish regime were attempted, "the barons would lead the people against him" (p. 144).

Most of the other passages borrowed from Rosello likewise have the effect of moderating the more extreme implications of the Machiavellian texts with which they are intermixed, and upon which Rosello had probably designed them to comment. Gardiner quotes a long passage from *Principe* 17, in which Machiavelli holds that, if one must choose between being feared and being loved, it is safer to be feared, so long as one abstains from seizing the property of one's subjects and thus avoids being hated as well as feared. Men are apt to remember, as Machiavelli's well-known remark here quoted by Gardiner has it, the loss of a patrimony rather than the death of a father (p. 142). Also from *Principe* 17 comes the comparison between the excessive clemency of Scipio and the necessary severity of Hannibal (pp. 142–3). These passages are taken directly from Machiavelli. After quoting them, however, Gardiner switches to Rosello, pointing out that Scipio defeated Hannibal in the end and that Alexander, Cyrus, and Caesar (like the most successful English kings, the Gardiner text adds) preferred mercy (pp. 143, 144; *Ritratto* fols. 17, 14v). In fact, mercy must predominate in the character of the ruler; otherwise he will not resemble God, whose image he bears (p. 145; *Ritratto* fol. 15v). Gardiner also draws on the *Discorsi* for a long passage on the kindness of Camillus (p. 144; *Disc.* III:20) in this section, setting a "mercy" text from the *Discorsi* against a "severity" text from *Il Principe.* Thus, Gardiner quotes at length Machiavelli's controversial preference for fear over love, for harsh methods over merciful ones, but then turns to Rosello and to other places in Machiavelli's works for a contrasting point of view.

However, the harsh teachings of *Il Principe* have not been quoted merely to be rejected as inapplicable to England or unusable by a Christian prince. One aspect in particular of the discussion of harsh tactics in *Principe* 17 is endorsed by both speakers in the dialogue, in words borrowed from Rosello (this is the one instance where Gardiner uses Rosello in a way that underlines rather than moderates Machiavelli's point) and applied to an English instance: Innocent individuals may be made to suffer for the common peace, as Edward Courtenay had to do.[56] The example is a significant one, for Courtenay, who had been imprisoned in the Tower from 1538 to 1553 for being the son of the executed Marquis of Exeter, had been a friend of Gardiner's during the latter's own imprisonment in the Edwardian years, and Gardiner had at one time favored a match between Courtenay and Mary.[57] Gardiner, even while emphasizing his innocence, regarded his fate as a proper application of the principles of *Principe* 17.

The more crucial contemporary instance of a person who presented a danger to the state, though innocent, was that of Elizabeth, and the

[56] When Machiavelli discusses the necessary execution of individuals, the "pochissimi esempli" whose "esecuzione" is less harmful to the state than the disorders and rapine that might result from their being left alive, he does not make absolutely clear whether such victims of public necessity are guilty or not; what is important is that such actions can be publicly justified: "E quando pure li bisognasse procedere contro il sangue di alcuno, farlo quando vi sia iustificazione conveniente e causa manifesta" (*Prin.* 17).

Stephano in Gardiner's dialogue agrees: "Pero vorei havendo giustificatione conveniente, che egli procedesse contra il sangue, con ogni rigore" (p. 89).

It is Alphonso who, making use of Rosello's clarification of the point, insists that a prince can proceed even without a manifest cause: "Diciate havendo egli causa puole procedere contra il sangue, io credo che quella non è crudeltà alcuna ma giusticia. Anzi il principe puole punire chi e sospetto colpevole, in alcuni casi, quantunque non provato manifestamente, come i parenti ò figlioli di ribelli come fece Henrico con Cortineo, ilqual per la colpa imputata al padre venne, innocente, prigionato. Questo il principe puole giustamente fare, havendo locchio alla pace commune deli subditi piu che al privato commodo o particolar vendetta" (p. 89).

Compare: "Anzi per comune parere de' savi, il Prencipe può punire chi non è colpevole, come sarebbe cacciare in essilio alcuni di famiglie sospette, overo i figliuoli de' rebelli; havendo tuttavia l'occhio alla commune pace" (Rosello, *Ritratto*, fol. 15r).

As Sidney Anglo points out, Rosello's text itself is often derivative, as here, from Nifo's *De regnandi peritia*. Gardiner shows no awareness of that added complexity, but is aware that "Rosello reads, for much of the time, like a commentary upon Machiavelli's *Il Principe*" (Anglo, "Crypto-Machiavellism,"190). Indeed, Gardiner not only draws on Rosello in preference to Machiavelli in certain places, as Anglo recognized, but also shows his awareness of Rosello's text *as* a commentary by setting material from Rosello alongside the Machiavellian original. His procedure is thus very similar to Rosello's own, for Rosello sometimes follows Nifo's adaptation of Machiavelli and sometimes refers directly to the Machiavellian texts.

[57] *Spanish Calendar*, XI, pp. 338–9; Donaldson, *Machiavellian Treatise*, p. 24.

position the *Ragionamento* takes on the question of necessary cruelty may shed some light on what has appeared to be a wavering on Gardiner's part in regard to her fate. After the Wyatt rebellion, there was strong feeling at court, particularly on the part of Simon Renard, the imperial ambassador, that Elizabeth ought to be executed. We find Gardiner opposing this with some vigor, and at the same time saying privately that he had no hope of seeing the kingdom in peace while she lived. To complicate the picture, he made efforts to have her formally disinherited and declared illegitimate.[58] We have seen that the *Ragionamento* displays ambivalence concerning Machiavelli's apparent approval of the execution of the innocent for reasons of state, on the one hand associating such behavior with Turks and tyrants and on the other holding out the possibility that such methods might have their place in the governance of England. What decides the question, in theoretical terms at least, is the kind of prince Philip is, and, as we have seen, Gardiner takes some care to carve out a special niche for the prince who, like Philip, is part "new" prince in the Machiavellian sense and part hereditary. The strategy of the "matrimonial" prince must combine the severity of the conqueror with the mildness of the long-established ruler, and must do so in a specific way:

He who has gained a realm or a province by force of arms has one way to hold it, and he who has gained one through favor of friends, hereditary laws or by matrimony must take a different course to keep his state. The basis of this latter course would be mercy, affability and generosity . . . for truly it is not very difficult for a new prince who has come in by way of friendship to hold his kingdom, when he is safe from those of the royal blood. (pp. 145–6; cf. *Prin.* 3)

With the *Ragionamento* in mind, one can see how Gardiner could refuse to bend the law to allow Elizabeth's execution, and at the same time favor her death, perhaps by nonjudicial means. John Foxe reports several stories of Gardiner's plots against Elizabeth. Once, Foxe says, Gardiner sent a death warrant to the Tower, which was not put into effect because of irregularities in its form, and on another occasion Gardiner sent his servant James Bassett to Woodstock with a score of men, who would have killed the princess but for the providential absence of the keeper and the refusal of his deputy to admit the party.[59] The *Ragionamento* doesn't prove such stories true, but it does show that, if Gardiner was its author, he had come, at some point in Mary's reign, to believe that the solution to problems of this kind lay in Ma-

---

[58] *Spanish Calendar*, XI, p. 335; XII, pp. 125–6, 167, 200.
[59] Foxe, *Acts and Monuments*, VII, p. 592; VIII, p. 618.

chiavelli's principle that rivals must be eliminated, and the special ap-
plicability of this principle to the case of the matrimonial new prince.
Perhaps he hoped that Philip, thus properly instructed as to the political principles involved, would see to its application himself. In any
case, the *Ragionamento*'s lengthy discussion of cruelty and kindness
focuses in the end on the need for even the matrimonial prince, whose
overall policy must be conciliatory, to adopt a Machiavellian severity
in regard to eliminating rivals to the throne, and can hardly have been
composed without Elizabeth in mind.

Entrare nel male

With the debate on cruelty and kindness, we have come to material
that is Machiavellian in the stereotyped sense. Rightly or wrongly, what
was often thought most distinctive about Machiavelli's political thought,
in the sixteenth century as well as in later centuries, was its preference
for political effectiveness over the claims of morality or religion. Much
of the material Gardiner borrowed does not fit that conventional image
of Machiavelli: respect for law, the folly of insult, and the need for
states to rely on their own arms. These are genuinely Machiavellian
themes, but they are not centrally related to the vexing issue of political
morality. There are several other morally neutral adaptations of Machiavellian texts in Gardiner's volume: the discussion of reputation
(pp. 109, 148–9; *Disc.* III:34; *Prin.* 19); the passage on the folly of
trusting the word of exiles anxious to draw one into wars designed
to get them home (pp. 136–7; *Disc.* II:31); the dangers of faction (pp.
134–5; *Prin.* 12, 13). These passages, like the others, keep the contemporary situation, and especially Philip's special problems, in mind.
Philip was a young prince, who had yet to establish his *virtù* indepen-
dently of his illustrious father; he was beset, in the winter of 1554–
5, with pressure from Italian exiles asking for renewal of war (with
Gardiner opposing their influence); and faction, as Gardiner saw it,
was as it always had been, a major problem in ruling England. All
these motifs for which corroboration was sought in Machiavelli entail
no radical departure from moral virtue. The discussion of severity
may be thought to raise moral issues that are not adequately resolved.
But here Gardiner had Rosello behind him as well as Machiavelli.
Rosello, like Nifo before him, had been willing to follow Machiavelli's
views on the utility of harsh methods fairly closely, so long as it was
granted that mercy ought to prevail over severity *where possible*. But
Rosello and Nifo avoid the explicit, head-on confrontation between
political and moral principles that Machiavelli's *Principe* insists upon,

indeed delights in, and which gave rise, perhaps more than any other single factor, to Machiavelli's reputation as an amoral or unchristian author.

But Gardiner does follow Machiavelli into these morally problematic areas. After praising Henry VIII's affability, Stephano mentions greatness, force and gravity of spirit, and irrevocability of judgment as other qualities that gain repute for a prince and make his state secure. He should also endeavor to seem compassionate, kind, affable, merciful, generous, and observant of trust. But, as Machiavelli had said of an approximately similar list of virtues, praiseworthy as they are, it is sufficient for the prince to avoid those vices that would cost him his state.[60] The change from *condizioni umane* in Machiavelli to *conditioni delli principi* in Gardiner is significant: If there is any approach to a moral argument in favor of the use of immoral methods in *Il Principe,* it is that human nature, being bad, requires them. Gardiner, like many writers who followed,[61] justifies the same tactics in terms of the special nature of kings or the special privileges of kingship. Stephano continues, adding material from *Principe* 18. Machiavelli's chapter is here rearranged considerably, but the whole passage is composed of short bits from this one chapter:

As for being held merciful, generous and observant of faith, I commend them most highly, provided that to observe them does not bring more danger than good. The contrary of these are sometimes of great help to the man who uses them, particularly when he works them in artfully. Pope Alexander VI was in his time the great master of this art, hiding an ambitious endeavor with a veil of piety, and without doubt such deception was often of greater use than the simple truth: for he who deals honestly with the wicked and the crafty will fail as did Henry VI. A new prince especially cannot observe all the things by which men are held good, even if he wants to, since it is often necessary, to maintain his state, to act contrary to mercy, religion and faith. Therefore his character must be such that he can change what he does like the wind according to the variety of fortune while what he says seems full of faith,

---

[60] "Queste qualitade sono massime lodevole, ma alquanto duro per un principe d'osservare. *Steph:* E ben vero neanche le conditioni delli principi non consenti intieramente d'osservarle, et pure quando l'osservasse sempre, sarebbe à lui piu damnose che utile, pero egli è assai s'el principe è tanto prudente, ch'il sapia schifare la infamia delle contrarie, quando è sforzato d'usarle, et fugire quelli vitii, i quali torrebono il sato" (p. 96).

"E io so che ciascuna confesserà che sarebbe laudibilissima cosa in uno principe trovarsi, di tutte le soprascritte qualità, ma perchè le non si possono avere nè interamente osservate, per le condizioni umane che non lo consentono, gli è necessario essere tanto prudente che sappia fuggire l'infamia di quelli vizii che li torrebbano lo stato" (*Prin.* 15).

[61] See Chapters 4–6 this volume.

mercy and charity, for these semblances gain him great reputation with the
multitude, and a people marks more the effects of the eyes and of the tongue
than those of the hand. (p. 149)[62]

Gardiner shifts the famous animal metaphor of *Principe* 18 so that it
applies not to princes themselves, but to those with whom they have
to deal ("Colui che procederà realmente con i volpi et huomini tristi
se roinera come Henrico sesto"). The lion is omitted, and it is the fact
that *other* men behave like foxes that justifies the prince's recourse to
immoral methods. Gardiner also omits Machiavelli's singling out of
religion as the quality most useful to simulate. These modifications
soften the impact of the original only very slightly; the *Ragionamento*
borrows, in Machiavelli's own language, the essential argument of
Principe 18: Moral virtues are sometimes a hindrance to effective rule;
the vices are often more useful in keeping one's state, especially when
cloaked with the false appearance of piety. The passages Gardiner
quotes were among those most offensive to Machiavelli's critics. Reginald Pole, as we have seen, cited the same passages as evidence that
Machiavelli had been inspired by Satan, and *Principe* 18 was also the
focus of attacks on Machiavelli by Osorio (1542) and Politi (1552).[63]
If Gardiner knew of the clerical opposition to Machiavelli that was
soon to result in the placing of his works on the first papal Index, he
chose to ignore it. His quite complete endorsement of Machiavelli's
ideas on the political utility of vice is deliberate, for the *Ragionamento*
assembles passages on the topic from two different chapters of *Il Principe* and runs them together into a single continuous quotation.

The positioning of these remarks in the treatise must also be mentioned. These lengthy borrowings are not only the last bits of Machiavelli to be used in the *Ragionamento,* but constitute a kind of conclusion and summary, closing the main body of the treatise and directly
preceding the final remarks on the greatness of Philip: "Now nothing
remains for me to say on this subject, having shown how William subjugated the realm of England left it in trust to his successors until the
coming of the powerful and most merciful Philip, son of the emperor
Charles V. This I do not call change or alteration in the kingdom,
but legitimate succession" (p. 149). That the leading ideas of Machiavelli's most controversial chapter constitute the final section of Gar-

---

[62] Gardiner has here rearranged the sequence of a number of passages from *Prin.* 18.
See Donaldson, *A Machiavellian Treatise,* p. 149 and note.
[63] Hieronymus Osorius, *De nobilitate christiana* (Lisbon, 1542), fols. 98–9; Ambrosius
Catharinus [Lancelotto Politi], *De libris christiano detestandis, et a christianismo penitus
eliminandis* [printed as cols. 339–44 of the "disputationes" appended to the author's
Ennarationes in quinque priora capita libri Geneseos] (Rome, 1551–2).

diner's dialogue on dynastic transitions in England, and of the implicit advice the dialogue offered Philip of Spain, suggests that Gardiner regarded Machiavelli's moral teachings, and not merely his advice on political tactics, as essential. The new prince in England needed to learn not only the appropriate strategies for ruling his new subjects, but also a moral attitude, or, if one prefers, an amoral attitude. For Gardiner as for Machiavelli, political life could not be made entirely consistent with traditional teachings concerning the moral virtues, and the *Ragionamento* recognized this principle by quoting amply from *Principe* 18 in its own conclusion.

Secular politics and sacral kingship

Gardiner was aware, however, of the potential contradiction between the ethical suppleness advocated in chapter 18 of *Il Principe* and the moral implications of the beliefs he had long held concerning the sacred character of kingly office. One of the ways the treatise addresses itself to this contradiction is by simply accepting it – that is, by suggesting that politics must be regarded with a kind of double vision, that the facts of political life must be recognized for what they are, whether or not they can be made to accord with the sacred ideals of kingship. To the objection that the conduct of William the Conqueror violated divine law, Stephano had replied:

Our purpose at present is not to show what a prince is permitted to do and what he is not permitted to do, but only to show by what ways and means a prince can maintain or lose his state. (p. 138)

The *Ragionamento* recognized – to use a Machiavellian phrase that Gardiner does not adopt – that the effective truth or *verità effettuale* will often differ from the moral perfection of imaginary republics, and therefore addresses itself to what princes must do to keep their states, and to what subjects will in fact do when they are not properly managed.

It is in the context of this tendency to view the facts of secular politics as a proper subject of inquiry, standing apart from moral or religious questions, that one must understand Gardiner's apparently quite uncharacteristic treatment of rebellion in the treatise. In the *De vera obedientia* of 1535, Gardiner had powerfully championed the doctrine of nonresistance to royal authority, even in cases where the king was wicked or an infidel. Yet his interest in warning Philip against oppressive policies likely to lead to revolt, as well as his Machiavellian perspective, led him to present rebellion in a light that seems almost

favorable in the pages of the *Ragionamento*. The English slaughter of
their Danish masters is defended (pp. 132–3); the barons of England
are said to have the right to lead the people against a ruler who tried
to institute a Turkish form of absolutism (p. 144); and, in the extended
discussion of the revolts that had taken place in English history (pp.
121–6), Stephano defends the English people against their international reputation for rebelliousness by arguing that in the Great Rebellion of 1382, in Jack Cade's rebellion against Henry VI, and in the
risings in 1549, bad government had inevitably led to revolt. Rebellions
occur when factious nobles set a bad example or when a prince levies
excessive taxes, fails to redress grievances, or is known to be cruel:
"Generally the faults of the people are caused by the negligence, lack
of prudence, or by the bad example of the prince who governs them"
(pp. 124–5).

Stephano claims not to be excusing the rebels (p. 123), merely
pointing out political realities, but the accounts given of the risings
against the various kings often adopt the point of view of the oppressed
or abused populace. Richard II's taxes "created such hatred among
the people against the king that they said openly that if they allowed
the shepherd to shear the sheep so many times a year he would shortly
skin them too; and therefore they decided not to pay such an extraordinary tax and made this Straw their leader" (p. 124); the in-
solence of the nobles who managed the realm for the young Edward
VI was "insupportable to all good men" (loc. cit.); and, in a passage
that applies to Vortigerius and Edward II, Stephano says that "when
good men have their prince for an enemy . . . not only will they defend
themselves, but they will also take the offensive" (p. 126). The stress
falls here on the naturalness and the predictable character of such
responses to bad government and on the responsibility of the prince
for avoiding such occasions for revolt.

All this is very unlike the Gardiner of the *De vera*, and Alphonso's
question to Stephano makes it clear that the author is aware of how
sympathetically he has treated the rebels: "Then you consider it permissible for the people to rise against their prince for any cause at
all?" (p. 125). Stephano's reply to this challenge shows that Gardiner
had not forgotten his earlier writing on the sacredness of king; in fact,
this is the part of the treatise in which nearly every aspect of his earlier
kingship doctrine is summarized and recapitulated. The first section
of this reply sets forth the doctrine that the rule of kings is sacred
and providential, and that kings enjoy divinely sanctioned preeminence
over all other men:

Steph: I do not think it is permissible, rather I affirm it to be damnable, for he is the minister of God ordained to such office to govern the people committed to his charge not by chance, as others affirm, but by the providence of God; and therefore nothing is dearer to God than the prince, and this is shown by the extraordinary gifts given them. Have you ever read that God has added years or days to anyone's life except a king's? Take the example of Hezekiah: he ought to have died of natural causes, but God prolonged his life fifteen years beyond its natural span. Thus you may see that the Omnipotent, in token of their preeminence on earth, assigns kings an archangel, a prince of the angels, to guard them until death. Therefore the great King Solomon said that the hearts of princes are in the hands of God, implying that God has a greater concern for them than for other, private men. (p. 125)

Then follows a statement of the principles of obedience and nonresistance, presented as a logical consequence of the sacred preeminence of the king:

And thus all ought to honor and obey them for their sacred ministry, which is also confirmed by the words of King David when it was told him that his enemy King Saul was sleeping and he could kill him without danger. "God forbid," he replied, "that I should lay violent hands upon the Lord's anointed." These examples show that God does not want violence done to his ministers, for as Paul said those who resist them disobey also the commandment of God. (And in another passage in Ephesians he said: "Obey princes in fear, not as you would please men merely but as you should please God, knowing that each will receive mercy for the good he has done whether he is a slave or free.") (p. 125)

The opening of the discussion of sacred kingship, with its rejection of chance and its assertion of providence, discloses a significant divergence from Machiavelli. The author of the treatise accepts Machiavelli as an authority on strategy, and even, as we have seen, follows his principle of the necessity of using methods that are not virtuous, but he does not accept the belief that political life is therefore under the rule of fortune. The scriptural proofs of providential kingship are interesting on several counts. In the *De vera*, Gardiner, as here, had given special emphasis to King Hezekiah in arguing that kings have no earthly superior.[64] But the point of establishing Hezekiah's preeminence, as is made clear in the discussion of his reign (pp. 103–18), is to establish the right of kings to govern the church and exercise

---

[64] "Ut ad probandum supremam principum potestatem, atque authoritatem unius Ezechiae exemplum divina historia testatum, ac nobis commendatum merito suffecisset." The *De vera obedientia* was first published in London in 1535. I cite Janelle's text, *Obedience in Church and State*, p. 130.

supreme authority over the priesthood. Like Henry VIII, Hezekiah recognized no priestly or papal superior. The issue of royal preeminence had to be cast in somewhat different terms in a time of Catholic restoration, when Philip of Spain was the king in question. Later in the treatise, the language of Stephano's speech on sacred kingship is echoed and applied specifically to Philip. He was "not advanced by chance, or crime, like many other princes, but brought forth in this age in justice by the highest divine providence" (p. 150). Like Hezekiah, he is the restorer of the true faith (p. 149). But part of that restoration included a return to papal supremacy, so when Hezekiah is used as the biblical exemplar of the preeminence of kings, it is his extended life span, a mark of divine favor toward his person, and not his supremacy that receives attention. Also, in the *Ragionamento,* God has a greater concern for kings than for private men. Though a great deal in the passage echoes Gardiner's antipapal polemics of twenty years earlier, when Gardiner had first expounded the doctrine of the supremacy of kings, supremacy is thought of in the present context as political supremacy over private individuals; the potential conflict between royal supremacy and papal power is not addressed.

In other respects, Stephano's conception of kingship as expressed here is that of the *De vera,* the tract "Si sedes illa" composed in defense of Fisher's execution, and the "Contemptum humanae legis," which Gardiner wrote in controversy with Martin Bucer. A central passage of the *De vera,* for example, holds that kings are "vicegerents" of God, "representors of his image" who excel over all other men and are owed obedience as to God himself, for God's sake. Resistance to them is resistance to God, as Paul had said.[65] Romans 13:2 (Vulg.: "Qui resistit potestati Dei ordinationi resistit") is the main text on nonresistance in this passage, as in the *Ragionamento,* but because it did not refer explicitly to kings, it is supplemented in both passages by citation of Proverbs and by another passage in Paul (Titus 3 in the *De vera,* Ephesians 6 in the *Ragionamento*) where obedience to the *princeps* is enjoined. The *Ragionamento's* citation of Ephesians 6:5–6 also makes

[65] "Tanquam vicaria potestate obedientiam exacturos, quam illis nos pari cum fructu praestaremus propter deum ac si deo ipsi immediate, id quicquid esset honoris exhiberemus. Quo certe in loco principes posuit, quos tanquam ipsius imaginem mortalibus referentes, summo, supremoque loco voluit haberi, eosque inter reliquas omnes humanas creaturas praecellere, ut scribit divus Petrus. Seque authore eosdem principes regnare, ut proverbia sacra testantur, Per me, inquit deus, reges regnant. Adeo quidem ut secundum Paulum quisquis potestati resistit, dei ordinationi resistit: qui Paulus quod hic generaliter locutus, Tito explicans mandavit, ut admoneret universos suis principibus obedire" (*De vera,* fol. 9; Janelle, *Obedience,* p. 88).

a point identical to the *De vera*'s insistence that princes are to be obeyed "propter deum" and not as a service or honor to men.

Because kings bear the image of God, obedience to them is a religious obligation, and disobedience or rebellion a religious offense. This idea is central to the *De vera* (see also pp. 78, 80, 90) and to the "Contemptum humanae legis."[66] Because the doctrine of obedience derives from such a conception of kingship, in which kings stand "in the place of" God, it is the office, and not the character of individual rulers, that matters; even tyrants have been providentially chosen to occupy that place, and they must be obeyed, however grievous their commands. The *De vera* holds that even an infidel king bears the image of God (p. 96), that a bad prince may be given to a bad people (p. 114), that there are no scriptural limits to obedience to princes, and that the people should endure harsh rule ("imperia quantumvis gravia") for the sake of God, not inquiring into the justice of the king's commands (pp. 98–100). The "Contemptum humanae legis" teaches similar lessons: "Ungentle masters" are to be obeyed for God's sake; mild princes manifest God's clemency, severe ones His call to penitence.[67] These ideas are repeated in the *Ragionamento:*

If the prince performs his duty to his subjects they have continual cause to thank God for his singular gift, which is the most excellent favor God can give a people. If he does otherwise we have to realize that he is ordained for the sins of the people, for many passages of Holy Scripture show that such is the punishment God sends a people (and truly he cannot send one greater). Therefore we ought to endure it with all humility and patience, and as Saint Augustine says, reverently kiss the rod that beats us because it comes from above, which means nothing else but that however princes stray from a true course, led either by evil advice or by their appetites, nonetheless the people are always obliged to obey them and not seek to take the sword from the hand of him to whom God has given it, but to leave vengeance to Him (for " 'vengeance is mine,' says the Lord"). Thus it is never permissible in any circumstances to take arms against a prince, even if he is a tyrant. (pp. 125–6)

The beliefs that God has given the sword of vengeance only to kings and that only God can execute vengeance upon them may be found

---

[66] E.g., p. 174: "Qui hominem potestate preditum spernat, non hominem spernat, sed Deum"; cf. I Thess. 4:8, p. 176: "In pace obediat principi propter deum . . . neque iis mandatis hominis frustra colitur"; and related passages, pp. 184, 200.

[67] "Neque animi christiani argumentum est, subditum de principis sui legibus, severae ne sint an remisse, esse sollicitum. Iussa ille capessat et faciat, et dominis etiam discolis obediat propter Deum. Si principem tamen mitem, agnoscat in Principe Dei clementiam, sin severum, disciplinam misericordiae Domini interpretetur, invitantis populum ad poenitentiam" (Janelle, *Obedience*, p. 176).

throughout the literature we have been discussing (e.g., "Si sedes illa," pp. 60–2; *De vera,* p. 100; "Contemptum humanae legis," pp. 174, 178, 182).

Stephano's digression on sacred kingship has been necessary to clear him from Alphonso's charge that he favors rebellion. He denies the charge: In the sphere of moral obligation, the duty of obedience is absolute and rebellion is never justified. But, as he points out in concluding his remarks, the prince needs to be concerned with what people actually will do, as well as with what they ought to do: "It is never permissible in any circumstances to take arms against a prince, even if he is a tyrant," but as men do many prohibited things on the impulse of the moment, princes need to "attend carefully to their office, so as not to give them occasion to rebel" (p. 126).

And, though Stephano here speaks of the prince setting an example of virtue, the treatise as a whole makes it perfectly clear that the prince's attention to his office must, like the conduct of his subjects, be regarded from the point of view of political cause and effect, as well as that of moral prescription: "Our purpose at present is not to show what a prince is permitted to do and what he is not permitted to do, but only to show by what ways and means a prince can maintain or lose his state" (p. 138). Thus there is a tendency to separate moral and political questions in the *Ragionamento;* the moral standard for both prince and people remains anchored in the theory of absolute obedience to sacred kings, and this theory appears in the treatise in a form closely modeled upon Gardiner's own Henrician polemics on the subject. But that standard is not and cannot be upheld in actual political life, as Stephano, the man of long experience, has come to know. Here knowledge of the reasons people actually do rebel, together with the methods (Machiavellian in inspiration and entailing the use of morally flawed techniques) by which princes may prevent them from rebelling, is essential.

There is no evidence that Gardiner read Machiavelli during Henry's reign or drew on Machiavelli when he formulated his position on kingship in the mid-1530s, though of course he, like nearly every other Tudor statesman, has been accused of Machiavellianism in the broad sense from time to time. What we can observe in the early work, however, is a theory of kingship in which the secular and sacral aspects of the office were related in a way that provided a model for Gardiner's later attempt to reconcile Machiavelli and sacred kingship. The attempt to work out a defense of Henry VIII's claim to supreme headship of the Church of England led Gardiner to argue not only that kings are providentially chosen, sacred beings but also, paradoxically, that the religious significance of their rule and the basis of their claim to preeminence over priests and popes lay precisely in the secular character of their office. As we have seen, Gardiner consistently interpreted Romans 13:2, I Thessalonians 4:8, and other pauline passages concerning the obligation of obedience to power as applying to kings. Kings are those supreme earthly powers, instituted by God, to whom the Christian owed obedience even when their commands were harsh or unjust. Obedience to earthly authority, undertaken in the right spirit, is obedience to God himself, and in fact, the more unjust the authority, the more religious value obedience has, for

if we suffer buffeting justly for our faults (as Saint Peter saith), what gramercy is it to us? – for that is exhibited into the laws and not unto god. (*De vera*, p. 81)[68]

In this view, the Passion of Christ revealed the *mysterium* of political subjection:

This secret will of God being, by his unsearchable device, hidden from the beginning is now in the end of the world revealed unto us by our Christ the slain sacrifice and ransom of mankind who in appeasing the most justly deserved wrath of God hath declared the wholesome doctrine of obedience in his deeds and hath suffered for us, leaving us an ensample that we should follow his footsteps. (p. 77)[69]

It is the office of a king to bear the sword and to represent to men the wrath of God to which Christ submitted. It cannot be the office of an ordinary Christian, still less of a priest, bishop, or pope, for Christ is their model. Gardiner asks how any syllable of the New Testament can be thought to support the earthly authority of the pope, since Christ "sought not an earthly kingdom." The office of the vicar of Christ is not to rule,

but to be in subjection, not to command princes but to acknowledge himself to be under their power and commandment, not only when they command things indifferent and easily to be done, but also when they command things not indifferent so they be not wicked: in checks, in scourgings and beatings

---

[68] "Si debitam legibus poenam, ut habet divus Petrus, luentes colaphizati patiamur, quae nobis gratia? Legibus etenim hoc exhibetur, non deo" (*De vera*, p. 80).
[69] "Cuius certe divinae voluntatis mysterium a seculis inscrutabili dei consilio absconditum, revelavit nobis in fine temporum noster Christus, humani generis hostia, et piamentum, qui iustissimam dei iram placando, doctrinam obedientiae factis aedidit salutarem, et pro nobis passus est, nobis relinquens exemplum, ut sequamur vestigia eius" (pp. 76–78).

unto death, yea, even to the death of the cross. Indeed, these are Christ's footsteps and this is the majesty of rule bearing in Christ. (pp. 131, 133)[70]

Since Christ never sought authority among men, he cannot have given it to the bishop of Rome to use as his vicar (p. 132). There is a contrast here, sustained throughout the treatise, between the imitation of Christ, commanded to all Christians, and especially to priests and bishops, and the royal *imitatio dei*. It is the king alone who may stand in the place of god in the exercise of earthly power, and he can do this because he is secular and not religious, because he is not so stringently bound to the example of Christ's humility as the clergy are.

A similar logic informs the "Contemptum humanae legis," where, paradoxically, Gardiner argues that the contempt of human laws, the laws of the prince, should be punished more severely than transgression of divine laws. Partly this is because sins against divine law will be amply punished in the afterlife anyway, whereas contempt for human law threatens public peace and order, and thus the conditions necessary for the pursuit of a Christian life by others. There are many whom "the dread of God does not restrain, yet regard for man holds them in check," because human nature stands in awe of present and corporeal things. Therefore

the contempt of human law was more severely to be avenged than that of divine laws, not because God is smaller than man, nor because human laws are to be set before those of God, but because it is in the interests of public peace that men who ignore God and do not acknowledge his majesty, should at any rate stand in awe of the power of man. (p. 191)[71]

This is a Machiavellian idea as well: "Where the fear of God is wanting, it comes about that either a kingdom is ruined, or that it is kept going by the fear of a prince, which makes up for the lack of religion" (*Disc.* I:11). If men will not obey God, whom they cannot see, they may at

---

[70] "Idem Christus tam aperte sit, et verbis et factis protestatus, non terrenum se regnum quaesisse. . . . Cuius profecto vices sunt, si quis eas bona cum fide obire velit, non praeesse, sed subesse, non principibus imperare, sed eorum potestatem, atque imperium agnoscere. Idque non solum cum aequa imperent, et facile obeunda, sed iniqua etiam modo impia non sint, in conviciis, in plagis, in verberibus usque ad mortem quidem crucis. Haec sunt certa Christi vestigia, atque adeo haec in Christo dominandi maiestas" (pp. 130–2).

[71] "Multos esse, quos quum timor Dei non cohibeat, hominum tamen reverentia contineat . . . quod ita fert humana natura, quae praesentia magis et corporea et timet et veretur. Secundum quem loquendi modum etiam dicere possem contemptum humanarum legum quam divinarum severius vindicandum, non quod Deus homine minor sit, aut humanae leges divinis preferantur. Sed quod expediat publicae tranquillitati, homines qui Deum ignorant, et illius maiestatem non agnoscunt, hominum saltem potestatem formidare" (p. 190).

least obey his mortal and visible representatives. In fact, it is because the king is human, because he stands in the place of God without being divine himself, that obedience to his commands is such an important test of respect for God's majesty:

Therefore it must be observed that contempt of human laws implies injury offered to the majesty of God, in so far as he deemed it necessary that man should obey to man; and that every soul should be subjected to the higher powers; to such an extent that whoso despiseth a man endowed with power, despiseth not man, but God. Who does not love his brother, whom he sees, how can he love God whom he does not see? Now he does not love who does not acknowledge the authority of his superior, but injures it through contempt: which, while he does, he also offends most grievously the divine majesty. (p. 175)[72]

The divine command that men obey other men thus provides a way of regarding human law as a part of the divine law:

I do not, for myself, oppose man to God, nor human things to divine, but I compare the different parts of divine law between themselves, and call human law that which man proclaims by the authority of God, which itself to that extent is also divine. (p. 185)[73]

As in the *De vera*, the secular, human character of kingship paradoxically makes it not less but more sacred, for human law rests upon the principle of obedience and requires no ecclesiastical sanction.

In these treatises, Gardiner is quite far, most of the time, from the radical secularism of Machiavelli, in which the prince is no longer under the obligation to follow the moral virtues if the circumstances require him to depart from them. When Gardiner speaks of the responsibilities of kingship in these early works, it is always in the context of the traditional assumption that good government is government in accordance with Christian virtue (e.g., pp. 104–6, 110–12). But there are aspects of his solution of the problem of the relation between the secular and sacred realms that could be extended in a Machiavellian direction. Kingly power is, for Gardiner, independent of ecclesiastical

[72] "Itaque animadvertendum est, contemptum legum humanarum ad divinae Maiestatis iniuriam pertinere, quatenus voluit hominem homini parere oportere: et sublimioribus potestatibus omnem animam subiectam esse debere. Adeo ut qui hominem potestate preditum spernat, non hominem spernat sed Deum: et qui fratrem quem videt non diligit, Deum quem non videt, quomodo potest diligere? Non diligit autem qui superioris auctoritatem non agnoscit, sed violat per contemptum, quod dum facit, etiam divinam Maiestatem gravissime offendit" (p. 174).
[73] "Ego non oppono hominem Deo, nec humana Divinis, sed Divinae legis partes inter se confero, et humanam legem dico, quam divina authoritate homo fert, quae et ipsa eatenus etiam divina est" (p. 184).

validation. The king imitates the harsh justice of God rather than the humility of of Christ. He is expected to act in accordance with virtue, but must be obeyed even when he is unjust. The principle of royal *imitatio dei*, as it appears in these treatises, is already one in which severity and rigor dominate (see esp. pp. 30ff, 182). In the *Ragiona-mento*, the independence of princely power from clerical power is taken a step further, and under Machiavelli's influence the prince's conduct is held to be free of the moral law in certain respects. In addition, the severity of kingly rule, sanctioned in the earlier period by analogy with the rigors of divine justice, is elaborated in directly Machiavellian ways, and comes to include the detention and execution of rivals to the throne and of the innocent relatives of rivals to the throne, or even of persons who might possibly prove a threat at a later time. Yet there is an attempt to regard even such tactics as an aspect of royal imitation of God, so that the principle of *imitatio dei* is invoked in reference to some of the most morally problematic aspects of Machiavelli's teachings.

Indeed, the principle of analogy between human rule and divine was so basic to the political assumptions of the West that it was inevitable that early readers of Machiavelli, who did not have access to a radically secular view of the world, should, if they thought he was right in what he said about political life, attempt to apply the principle of *imitatio dei* to his advice to princes, and when Gardiner invokes this principle, he does so in language borrowed from Rosello. Not only so, but the passage in question is one Rosello adapted from Nifo's *De regnandi peritia* of 1523; the process of reconciling Machiavelli and *imitatio dei* had commenced even before *Il Principe* itself was published.

To begin with Nifo. The *De regnandi peritia* follows *Il Principe* so closely that it has long been regarded as a plagiarism, which by modern standards it is. It is a more systematic work than Machiavelli's, however, and makes an attempt to moderate or soften many of the positions of the original. One such attempt comes in the discussion of the relative merits of cruelty and kindness, based upon *Principe* 17: Cruelty is useful, but too much of it may make a prince uncautious, and it is not always preferable to mercy as a strategy. But the main reasons to temper its use derive from the God/king analogy: God is more merciful than just, and so therefore ought the king to be.[74] Rosello follows Nifo closely, though he places the issue in a more specifically biblical context

---

[74] "Temperanda est igitur crudelitas, atque clementia, ita tam ut mansuetudo semper praecellat. Hinc misericors et iustus dominus a sacris viris deus dicitur: in quo animadvertendum misericordiam iustitiae praeponi" (*De regnandi*, 4:3).

("sacris viris" becomes "scrittura sacra"),[75] and the attempt to coordinate Machiavelli on cruelty and kindness, fear and love is pursued somewhat further, as he relates Machiavelli's praise of princes who manage to be feared without being also hated to the severe justice of God, which likewise does not lead to hatred (fol. 17v). Gardiner's use of the *imitatio dei* motif in the context of a discussion of cruelty and kindness based on Machiavelli derives directly from Rosello,[76] though he does not follow blindly. As we have seen, Gardiner has Machiavelli's text itself continuously in mind in this section, as well as Rosello's adaptation of it, and in addition has focused the discussion of cruelty and kindness upon specifics of English history, and specifics with a bearing on present problems. His invocation of the principle of *imitatio dei* here is part of a discussion whose conclusion is that princes whose careers resemble that of Philip of Spain must be generally merciful, but they must eliminate those of royal blood and others who might threaten their maintenance of power, even if such persons are innocent.

What we have in this use of *imitatio dei* by Nifo, Rosello, and Gardiner is a slight but extremely significant shift in the formulation of one of the central motifs of sacred kingship directly in response to Machiavelli's text. The idea that the ruler imitates the justice of the gods when he is severe, and their mercy when he is clement, is a recurrent feature of most Western, and indeed many non-Western, variants of the belief in the sacredness of kings, and can be found in the Pythagorean kingship fragments collected by Stobaeus, in Philo, in the Letter of Aristeas, and in countless medieval political texts.[77] But in all these texts, the polarity in the divine attributes more exactly mirrors the doubleness of the conduct of the prince: Fear and love, mercy and strict justice are the usual terms. Nifo, Rosello, and Gardiner all use

---

[75] "La clementia dee vincere la crudeltà, altramente il Prencipe non si rassomiglierebbe à Dio, di cui egli e imagine viva, poi che veggiamo quanta pietà usa Dio verso di noi peccatori, le cui colpe ci rendono degni della morte eterna, e come giova à buoni e cattivi senza promettersi da noi guiderdone alcuno: La scrittura sacra chiama Iddio misericordioso, e giusto, mettendo pur avanti la misericordia alla giustitia" (fol 15v).

[76] "La clementia debbe vincere la crudelta, altremente il principe non rassimigliara a Dio, di cui e il vivo imagine. La scrittura sancta chiamo Iddio misericordioso et giusto mettendo innanzi la misericodia" (p. 92).

[77] See E. R. Goodenough, "The political philosophy of Hellenistic kingship," *Yale Classical Studies* I (1928), 55–102, esp. pp. 67–73 and 75ff, and the same author's *The Politics of Philo Judaeus* (New Haven, Conn., 1938), pp. 90–100; Moses Hadas ed. and trans. *Aristaeus to Philocrates (Letter of Aristaeus)* (New York, 1951), pp. 173–81, 191. The Pythagorean kingship fragments anthologized by Stobaeus were printed with a facing Latin translation in *Aristotelis politicorum libri octo . . . Pythagoreorum veterum fragmenta politica a Io. Spondanus conversa et emendata* (Basel, 1582).

the term cruelty (*crudelitas, crudeltà*) for the harsh side of princely governance, and they do so because Machiavelli does. It is a well-known feature of Machiavelli's style, and of more than his style, that he eschews the use of euphemistic terminology, and when he speaks of the hard choices a prince must make, he speaks of them in a value-laden vocabulary. Leo Strauss believed that Machiavelli's formulation of such questions as the relation of fear to love and cruelty to kindness were meant to recall traditional descriptions of the divine attributes, so that when Machiavelli departs from traditional terminology and describes the prince as cruel and amoral, he blasphemously intends his readers to question the nature of the God whose imitator such a prince is.[78] When, for example, Machiavelli characterizes the methods of Philip of Macedon as inimical to every civilized way of life, and then quotes the words of the Magnificat to describe these methods (*Disc.* I:26), the implication is that God himself is a tyrant. Strauss's view of Machiavelli's intentions has not found wide acceptance and appears to rest on unwarranted assumptions concerning the status of Machiavelli's work as a continuous commentary on traditional Western political values. But whatever Machiavelli himself intended, the fact that the preference for mercy over severity was so often sanctioned by analogy to the divine nature made his own reversal of this traditional argument potentially a questioning of the divine nature. That Nifo, Rosello, and Gardiner all relate Machiavelli's discussion of whether it is better to be feared or loved to the polarity of the divine attributes shows, at any rate, that some interpreters of Machiavelli in the sixteenth century could not divorce their reading of Machiavelli from their commitment to this central principle of sacred kingship. They do not take God to be a tyrant, but in their attempt to justify the harsher aspects of Machiavelli's theories by analogy to the divine nature, they press the principle of analogy to, and perhaps beyond, its limits. The principle of analogy either had to be abandoned or radically revised, for otherwise one would be required to find an analog in the divine nature not only for the rigor that is under discussion here, but for all of the politically useful vices Machiavelli discusses in *Principe* 15 and 18, and which Gardiner, following Machiavelli, also endorses in the *Ragionamento*.

In fact, there is an attempt to find an analog to the full text of *Il Principe* in the divine nature in the work of Louis Machon, to be discussed in Chapter 6. With the writers under discussion here, the attempt to apply the principle of *imitatio* is not so systematic; nevertheless, none of them can wholly abandon either Machiavelli's text or the

---

[78] Leo Strauss, *Thoughts on Machiavelli* (Glencoe, Ill., 1958), pp. 49, 156–7.

principles of sacred kingship it would seem to negate, and their Machiavellian prince is, in some respects, an imitator of God.

Another way in which the treatise registers its double allegiance – to Machiavelli as well as to the doctrines of sacred kingship of Gardiner's earlier career – is by presenting its teachings, so largely dependent upon Machiavelli, as a kind of mysterious secret teaching. The treatise begins with Stephano asking the traveler Alphonso why he has come to England, and it turns out that he is a seeker after a kind of wisdom very much like the hermetic wisdom of the ancient sages:

The desire for knowledge even made the divine Plato (whose teaching resounded with such great stir in the Academy of Athens that it was said openly that if God had to speak with a human tongue He could not employ one more learned or more eloquent) travel to Egypt, Calabria and Apulia to find Archytas of Tarentum: he preferred to journey and be this man's disciple than to stay in his own country and be the master of so many others. Apollonius of Tyana went wandering all his life, seeking knowledge wherever it fled from the world. He went first among the Persians, passed the Caucasian Mountains, penetrated the territory of the Albani, the Scythians, the Masagetae, and the most rich kingdoms of India; then finally he reached the Brahmans, and heard the deep secrets of the birth of the great Iarchas who sat on a golden throne teaching divine philosophy. From there he returned to Alexandria and thence to Ethiopia to learn from the gymnosophists and to see that most famous altar of the sun in the arena where they taught their deep mysteries. Therefore do not be amazed, illustrious sir, if I, consumed by this desire to learn the sciences and to understand and see the customs, laws, and procedures of various peoples have placed my life in such dangers. Furrowing the implacable sea, crossing harsh mountains in Europe as well as in regions of Africa and Asia I have at last arrived with great contentment of mind at the most splendid court of Philip, King of England. (pp. 105–6)

Plato, the Brahmans, the gymnosophists, Apollonius of Tyana – these men were all repositories of the so-called *prisca theologia,* or ancient hermetic wisdom. Gardiner here draws on Philostratus's *Vita Apolonii,*[79] and specifically on the preface to an edition of that text that had appeared in 1555. Most of the details of Apollonius's travels are given in the form in which they are found in Rhinuccino's preface – but for the detail of the secrets of the birth of King Iarchas he had to go to the text itself (pp. 165–9). The secret was that Iarchas was divine, that he was an incarnation of the holy River Ganges, and that he had the power to make the crops grow and the seasons change. The ancient mysteries and the divinity of kings intersect in Iarchas, so that by

[79] *Philostrati Lemnii senioris historiae de vita Apollonii Tyanei* (Paris, 1555).

choosing this particular version of the quest for secret knowledge, Gardiner suggests that Alphonso's inquiry into English history and politics is analogous to Apollonius of Tyana's penetration of the arcana of divine kings with magic powers.

Perhaps Gardiner partly believed that kingship brought extraordinary powers with it; we have noted his remarks on Hezekiah's supernaturally extended life span and on royal tutelary angels. He also believed, or pretended to believe, in the magical healing powers of royal cramp-rings.[80] But whatever Gardiner really thought about these matters, Alphonso's invocation of the hermetic tradition directs the reader to regard what follows as secret knowledge. The Machiavellian counsel of the *Ragionamento* is therefore presented as the esoteric side of the ideology of sacred kingship. The political arcana Alphonso discovers in England (and Gardiner conveys to his royal reader) reveals how the authority of kings, divine in origin and sacred in character, must be sustained by methods derived from *Il Principe* and the *Discorsi*.

Thus the *Ragionamento* connects Machiavelli with mystery of state in several ways:

1. It uses Machiavellian texts as the basis of a secret manual of counsel for a reigning king, while suppressing entirely its reliance on those texts. In this regard, Gardiner's treatise conforms to the pattern seen in William Thomas' treatises prepared for Edward VI and in Thomas Cromwell's alleged reliance on *Il Principe* in the advice he gave to Henry VIII.
2. Further, the content of political advice that the *Ragionamento* offers entails a stark opposition between outward appearances and hidden intentions. Outward respect for law is set beside the necessity of executing rivals to the throne; respect for English customs is countered by the goal of extending Habsburg rule beyond the life of Philip; the doctrine of obedience is juxtaposed to the inevitability of rebellion. If the counsel offered in the *Ragionamento* were put into practice, England would appear to be governed by its own laws in accordance with the marriage treaty, and the doctrine of sacred kingship would remain its official ideology; but the hidden principles animating the conduct of government would be the interests of the Habsburg dynasty and the political ethics of Machiavelli.
3. Finally, the exposition of these contradictions in the treatise is

---

[80] Muller, *Letters*, p. 259.

framed by the fiction of Alphonso's quest for secret knowledge, which implies that the Machiavellian strategies of the *Ragionamento* somehow participate in an ancient and sacred mystery of kingship.

Machiavellism, in the *Ragionamento dell'advenimento delli inglesi et normanni in Britannia, is* the mystery of state Alphonso has traveled to England to discover.

3

John Wolfe, Machiavelli, and the republican arcana in sixteenth-century England

The association of Machiavelli with the myth of the *arcana imperii*, or mysteries of state, belongs, on one level, to the history of political thought and is part of the story of how Machiavelli's ideas were received, transformed, and restated. On another level, it belongs to the history of political discourse, more broadly conceived, and concerns the ways in which attempts to use or oppose Machiavelli's ideas altered patterns in the production of political texts and restructured roles in that production. To read Machiavelli as if he dealt with the *arcana imperii* entailed changes in the meaning of what it was to write and publish a political text, changes in how authors of such texts thought of themselves, their activity, and their audience. Texts in this tradition are not merely about the arcana: Very often they *are* arcana, secret or private works meant to be kept from public view. These texts, following Machiavelli, counsel rulers to dissimulate their intentions and conceal the modes by which they exercise their power, and the writers of these texts often conceal their own relation to their work, their intentions, and their sources. Machiavellian authorship participates in the occultation it describes. The Machiavellian arcana of William Thomas and Stephen Gardiner illustrate this principle, and the political writings of Reginald Pole offer a more complex instance, in which an anti-Machiavellian becomes a purveyor of counter-arcana, creating his own partly secret text, and endowing it with a numinous, prophetic authority to counter the satanic power of the Machiavellian *mysterium*.

This chapter explores another kind of association between Machiavelli and the arcana, another kind of secret text, and another role made possible by the confluence of Machiavelli's texts and the idea of secret political writing. We are concerned here with the idea that Machiavelli's works had a hidden republican or antityrranical meaning, and with the relation of that idea to the career of John Wolfe, the London printer who produced surreptitious editions of several of Machiavelli's major texts in the 1580s.

John Wolfe's career had several phases. After learning his craft in Italy, he became something of political activist in the printing trade in London, printing books in violation of patent rights and fomenting disorder among unemployed and journeymen printers. His enemies called this activity "Machiavellian." As part of the resolution of the dissension in the printing industry, Wolfe became a member of the Stationers' Company and held the office of beadle of the company, in which position he helped to discipline his former allies and played a role in the suppression of dissident religious printing as well. During this phase of his career, he was one of the most active and successful printers in the city, produced his surreptitious editions of Machiavelli, and pioneered the use of false imprints for foreign propaganda, producing false letters of news to be distributed abroad in support of government aims. He was also involved in the Essex affair, to the extent that he arranged for the printing and dedication of John Hayward's *Henry IV,* which the government found seditious enough to send its author to prison for three years.[1] In the following pages, his political activity, his surreptitious printing, and his association with Machiavelli will be described in somewhat fuller detail. Wolfe was not a royal counselor or a political "author" in the conventional sense. But if, like his adversaries in the Staioners' Company, we refer to him as a Machiavellian printer, it is to suggest that the various roles he played in his trade participated in and were made possible by the discursive practices that are the subject of this study. The salient features of his career, diverse as they were, constitute an episode in the history of the association between Machiavelli and the political arcana.

Machiavelli and the republican arcana

The particular form of the connection between Machiavelli and the arcana of politics relevant to John Wolfe's career as a printer is the myth or belief that Machiavelli's works embodied a secret antityrranical or republican intention. This belief is recorded in Pole's *Apologia* and appears in the preface to Wolfe's edition of *Il Principe* and *I Discorsi.* Pole was neither a republican nor a defender of Machiavelli, so it is especially interesting that his *Apologia ad Carolum Quintum* (1539), the

---

[1] On Wolfe's life see Harry R. Hoppe, "John Wolfe, printer and publisher, 1579–1601," *The Library,* ser. 4, XIV (1933), 241–88, and Hoppe's unpublished M.A. thesis of the same title, University of London, 1933; Dennis B. Woodfield, *Surreptitious Printing in England, 1550–1640* (New York, 1973); pp. 5–13, 95–102, 109–17. Woodfield's book is a revision of the author's Oxford D. Phil. thesis of 1964, "Books surreptitiously printed in England before 1640 in contemporary foreign languages."

first statement of the myth of the satanic Machiavelli, should also be the source, or at least the first instance, of the notion that *Il Principe* was written with the secret intention of hastening the fall of the Medici.

Pole offers the story as something he had heard in Florence. When challenged to explain the immorality of Machiavelli's book, his fellow citizens claimed that Machiavelli's own response to detractors had been to explain that

> he had not followed his own judgment in that book, but that of the man to whom he wrote, whom he knew to be of a tyrannical nature, putting in things could not but greatly please such a person, but which, if they were put into practice, would make his reign brief, as experience taught and as he himself well knew, along with all others who had written of the institution of a prince or king by force. This he greatly hoped, for he burned inwardly with hatred for the prince to whom he wrote, and hoped for nothing else from his book than that, by writing to a tyrant what would please a tyrant, he might bring about the tyrant's speedy overthrow by his own act.[2]

Pole's treatise was not published until the eighteenth century, but his views had some circulation during his lifetime; appear to have influenced other writers, particularly Osorio and Politi; and may have influenced the Calvinist perception of Machiavelli as a tool of Satan a generation later.[3] Pole did not accept the view of the Florentines that Machiavelli wrote with a hidden antityrannical purpose ("thus they say, to excuse Machiavelli's blindness of spirit"), but the story became well known at a later date. In 1578, Matteo Toscano refers to it in the *Peplus Italiae:*

> It is well to remember what he [Machiavelli] responded to his critics in his own name: for he affirmed that the princes who were then oppressing Italy tyrannically imbued with his wicked precepts, had become worse by his teaching and that punishment for their crimes would crush them all the sooner for that, for when they had fully immersed themselves in vice, they would speedily and deservedly provoke spirited anger.[4]

The same view of the purpose of the prince is expressed in André Rossant's *Les meurs, humeurs et comportemens de Henry de Valois.* Rossant adds that the people of Florence, moved to revolt by the Medicis' following of Machiavelli's precepts, would "free themselves from his yoke

---

[2] Angelo M. Quirini, ed., *Epistolarum Reginaldi Poli* . . . (Brescià, 1744–57), I, p. 152.
[3] There are many similarities between Pole's views and the preface of the Latin translation of Innocent Gentillet's *Contremachiavel* (Geneva, 1577). The case for a direct link depends upon these and upon Pole's family ties with the English Calvinists. I plan to discuss this in a separate article.
[4] Paris, 1578, p. 52

and take up again their ancient liberty."[5] Thomas Fitzherbert's *First Part of a Treatise Concerning Policy and Religion* retails the story in a form similar to that reported by Pole.[6] All these authors know the claim that Machiavelli was really a republican and that the purpose of *Il Principe* was to exacerbate the Medici tyranny to provoke opposition. Gaspar Scioppius's "Machiavellica" of 1619 expresses a similar view, but with the emphasis placed not upon the excessive behavior *Il Principe* might provoke in the tyrant, but rather upon the revelation to the people of the *arcana tyrannorum*.[7]

Alberico Gentili, the brilliant international jurist who lived in England and was a professor of law at Oxford, gives the idea of a hidden republican intention in *Il Principe* a similar inflection, focusing not so much on the "spirited anger" the Medici rule would provoke, but rather on what benefit readers who were not princes would derive from a book describing the methods of princely tyrants:

He was a eulogist of democracy, and its most spirited champion. Born, educated and attaining to honors under a democratic form of government, he was the supreme foe of tyranny. And so, naturally, he did not favor the tyrant. It was not his purpose to instruct the tyrant, but by revealing his secret counsels *[arcanis eius palam factis]*, to strip him bare, and expose him to the suffering nations. Do we not know that there have been many princes such as he describes? That is the reason why princes of that type object to the survival and publication of his works. The purpose of this shrewdest of men was to instruct the nations under pretext of instructing the prince, and he adopted this pretext that there might be some hope that he would be tolerated as an educator and teacher by those who held the tiller of government.[8]

Gentili and Scioppius regard the people, and not the prince, as the real audience for the work, and regard its republican intention as taking effect through a disclosing of arcana. Gentili does not refer this defense to Machiavelli himself, and perhaps did not know the

---

[5] Paris, 1589, p. 11: "Or Machiavel pour dire ce que j'en scay en passant, estoit un secretaire de Florence, le quel reprit d'un sien amy que son livre estoit pour rendre un prince tyran, fait ceste response que vrayment il l'avoit fait a ceste intention, a fin que le Duc de Florence, usant de ce qui est parti en iceluy, tombast en telle indignation de son peuple, que estant occasion par ce de revolter contre iceluy, il se fit quitte de son joug et reprint sa premiere liberté."

[6] Douai, 1606, p. 412. See Sydney Anglo, "More Machiavellian than Machiavel," in A. J. Smith, ed., *John Donne: Essays in Celebration* (London, 1972), p. 380.

[7] "Revera autem et recte consilium eorum fuit, detegendis Tyrannorum arcanis eos populis invisos reddere, et tyrannidem impedire." MS Vatican. Lat. 13669, p. 99, as cited by Mario D'Addio, *Il pensiero politico di Gaspare Scioppio e il machiavellismo del seicento* (Milan, 1962), pp. 444–5n.

[8] *De legationibus libri tres*, tr. Gordon L. Laing (New York, 1924), II, p. 156. The passage appears in the first edition (London, 1585), Sig. Oiii.

story of Machiavelli's reply to his critics. The passage in the *De Legationibus* constitutes, in its context, an apology for Gentili's recommendation of the *Discorsi* as a model for imitation, and so it is possible that Gentili's view derives merely from reading that work, with its more obvious republican tendencies, and trying to reconcile it with the apparent monarchism of *Il Principe*, rather than from contact with views like those of Pole. At any rate, the publication of the *De Legationibus* in London in 1585 made available in England a view of Machiavelli that held him to be a republican, an unmasker of princely arcana, and that made the question of publication central: Unpublished, Machiavelli's works might be read as a manual for tyranny; published, they could "instruct the nations."

The "Palermo" edition of *Il Principe* and *I Discorsi*

The *De Legationibus* had been printed by Thomas Vautrollier, but Alberico Gentili's usual publisher, beginning with the *De juris belli* in 1582 and the *Lectiones* and *Epistolae* in 1583, was John Wolfe,[9] who also printed five works of Machiavelli between 1584 and 1588. The first of these was a composite volume containing both *Il Principe* and *I Discorsi* in Italian. This was not only the first English printing of the full Italian text of these works, but also the first example of surreptitious printing in England, for the volume bore the fictitious imprint "Palermo" and falsely offered itself as the work of the heirs of Antoniello degli Antonielli.[10] In a preface by "the printer," an interpre-

---

[9] See A. W. Pollard and G. R. Redgrave, eds., *A Short-title Catalog of Books Printed in England, Scotland, and Ireland and of English Books Printed Abroad 1475–1640*, 2nd ed. (London, 1976–86), Nos. 11733, 11735, 11736, 11738, 11739, and 11740.

[10] Protestants in the reign of Mary had used fictitious imprints for books published abroad, as for example the "Roan" edition of Gardiner's *De vera obedientia* (1553), but Wolfe's Machiavelli editions, followed closely by his editions of Aretino, were the first false editions actually printed in England. See H. R. Plomer, "The Protestant press in England in the reign of Queen Mary," *The Library*, ser. 3, I (1910), 54–72; Woodfield, *Surreptitious Printing*, passim. Wolfe was first identified as the printer of the "Palermo" Machiavelli by Alfred Pollard. See Salvatore Bongi, "Un aneddoto di bibliografia machiavellesca," *Archivio storico italiano*, ser. 5, XIX (1897), 126–35. See also A. Gerber, "All of the five fictitious Italian editions of writings of Machiavelli and three of Pietro Aretino printed by John Wolfe of London (1584–1588)," *Modern Language Notes* XXII (1907), 2–6, 129–35, 201–6; Harry Sellers, "Italian books printed in England before 1640," *The Library*, ser. 4, V (1924), 105–28. The editions of Machiavelli Wolfe printed, with their imprints, are as follows: (1) *Il Prencipe*. Palermo, appresso gli heredi di Antoniello degli Antonielli, 1584 (STC 17167); (2) *I Discorsi*. Palermo, appresso gli heredi di Antoniello degli Antonielli, 1584 (1 and 2 are always bound together); (3) *Historie Fiorentine*. In Piacenza apresso gli heredi di Gabriel Giolito, 1587 (STC 17161); (4) *Libro dell'arte della guerra*. In Palermo appresso Antoniello degli Antonielli, 1587 (STC 16163); (5) *Lasino doro*. In Roma, MDLXXXVIII (STC 17158).

tation of Machiavelli's intentions very similar to that of Alberico Gentili is set forth, according to which what seemed to be a manual for tyranny is defended as a treatise on good government.[11] According to Gentili, Machiavelli's text concealed its meaning. Wolfe's editions concealed the facts of their origin.

John Wolfe was born about 1547 in Sussex and indentured to John Day, the printer, in 1562. He may have been the son of Thomas Wolffe, fishmonger, of St. Nicholas, Cole Abbey. He is referred to as a fishmonger in the records of the Stationers' Company, and since his trade was printing, membership in the Fishmonger's Company must have been a matter of patrimony rather than apprenticeship. It seems quite likely that he was of a Sussex family, for we know he was a retainer of George Goring of Hurstpierpoint and Ovingdean, Sussex, his patron and supporter in the struggles between the insurgent printers and the company in 1582–3,[12] and there is a Wolfe family, including several men named John, going back to the sixteenth century in neighboring Ashington.[13] Wolfe went to Italy sometime after 1569, when his apprenticeship to Day would have ended, and stayed long enough to gain a thorough acquaintance with Italian printing. He may have studied printing with the Giunti in Florence, for he later used the Giunti lily as an ornament, and with Giolito.[14] He was still in Florence in 1576, because there are two "rappresentazioni" published in Florence "ad instanzia di Giovanni Vuolfio, inglese" dated that year.[15] He must have returned to England by 1579, when his first license to print a book in England is recorded in the Stationers' Register.[16] He began to print Italian books in England in 1581 with Petruccio Ubaldini's *La vita di Carlo Magno*. In the preface, Ubaldini states that the book is the first Italian text printed in England and praises the study and diligence of the printer, who has made it possible for Italian books to be printed as successfully in England as in Italy itself.[17]

The surreptitious Machiavelli editions were thus prepared by a well-trained English printer with Italian experience and appear near the

[11] Wolfe's preface and Gentili's are compared in detail below.

[12] See Cyril B. Judge, *Elizabethan Book Pirates* (Cambridge, Mass., 1934), p. 33.

[13] Mark Antony Lower, *A Compendious History of Sussex* (London, 1870), I, p. 23.

[14] Gerber "Fictitious Italian editions," 131, and R. B. McKerrow, *A Dictionary of Printers and Booksellers in England, Scotland and Ireland, and of Foreign Printers of English Books 1557–1640* (London, 1910), p. 297. On the Giunta connection see also Woodfield, *Surreptitious Printing*, p. 6.

[15] Gerber, "Fictitious Italian editions," 130.

[16] *Coheleth, seu concio Salamonis.* See Edward Arber, ed., *A Transcript of the Register of the Company of Stationers of London, Between 1554–1640 A.D.* (London, 1875), II, p. 353.

[17] Sig. A2v. This is not accurate, as there was an Italian translation of Cranmer's catechism printed by Mierdman in 1553; see Sellers, "Italian books," 105–7.

beginning of his successful career in publishing Italian language books. Why were they issued under false imprint? Dennis Woodfield's Oxford dissertation on surreptitious printing, which is otherwise a valuable study of this aspect of English publishing and sheds a great deal of light on many aspects of Wolfe's career, emphasizes the financial motive to the exclusion of all others.[18] English printing had a bad reputation, and literature printed in foreign vernaculars in England fell into an odd and relatively unsupervised category in regard to licensing. Especially in the political category, normally so sensitive a subject in Tudor times, the ambiguity of the regulations created the possibility of printing vernacular political texts banned elsewhere, if one could avoid (as false imprints did) the consequences of England's reputation for unreliable printing. Elizabeth's injunctions of 1559 required all books dealing with "matters of religion, or policy, or governance, that hath been printed either on this side the seas, or on the other side," to be licensed, but works in classical languages and other languages commonly used in the school were exempted.[19] Political literature in Italian thus fell into an ambiguous category, and in 1580, when a plan was drawn up for the licensing of "light" literature, foreign language texts were not included.[20] Under these conditions, according to Woodfield, Wolfe decided to print foreign books on the Index for distribution both in England and at the Frankfurt book fairs for profit, and issued them under false imprint to sell them more readily. In support of this interpretation, Woodfield cites Giordano Bruno's testimony before the Inquisition to the effect that his own books published in England were falsely imprinted in order to increase their sales.[21]

Although it is plausible that false imprinting could increase sales, Bruno's peril may also have been a factor in his testimony. We cannot be sure that Wolfe was only interested in sales either. Both Machiavelli's bad reputation and the special sensitivity of the government concerning books dealing with "policy" and statecraft are well known. When Wolfe undertook the publication of the most controversial of all sixteenth-century books on statecraft, he sought no license for it, though he had secured one for Ubaldini's biography of Charlemagne, also in Italian, and he issued it under false imprint. The sale of books at the Frankfurt fair provides one context for these facts and the history of the transmission of Machiavelli's texts another. As we have

---

[18] Woodfield, *Surreptitious Printing*, pp. 8–9; cf. thesis, pp. 24, 39ff.
[19] Arber, *Transcripts*, I, pp. xxviii–xxxix.
[20] Ibid., II, pp. 751–3.
[21] Woodfield, *Surreptitious Printing*, p. 20; cf. thesis, p. 70; see Vincenzo Spampanato, ed., *Documenti della vita di Giordano Bruno* (Florence, 1933), p. 91.

seen, from the 1520s on, Machiavelli's two major works had been issued in all sorts of disguises: Nifo had plagiarized *Il Principe,* and Thomas and Gardiner had drawn upon Machiavelli for private advice to their sovereigns. To explain the caution and secretiveness with which Machiavelli was handled solely on the basis of personal advantage is unduly limiting.

Wolfe's own motives, insofar as we can know them, are best assessed on the basis of the letter from the printer to the reader published as a preface to the combined volume of *Il Principe* and *I Discorsi* issued in 1584. This letter has interesting similarities with the Gentili passage and suggests that the printer did not regard Machiavelli only as the author of profitable texts. The epistle from "lo stampatore al benigno lettore" begins by decrying the habit, common in recent times, of forming opinions on subjects one knows nothing about. In this way, the printer himself had formed an unfavorable opinion of Machiavelli years before, and would never have read his works unless they had been recommended by "a very wise man, and one profound in political matters" who praised Machiavelli, smiled at the excesses of his detractors, and assured the printer that the devil himself could never be so black as Machiavelli had been made out to be. This man gave the printer a copy of "the book" (it is not clear whether *Il Principe* or *I Discorsi* is meant, or both), and the printer read it several times:

The more I read, the more it pleased me, and to speak truly, every hour I discovered new doctrine in it, new sharpness of wit, and new methods for learning the true way of drawing some utility from the profitable reading of histories, and, in brief, I realized that I had learned more from this book in one day about the government of the world, than I had in all my past life, from all the histories I had read. I learned exactly what difference there was between a just prince and a tyrant, between government by many good men and government by a few bad ones [*dal governo di molti buoni, a quello di pochi malvagi*], and between a well-regulated commonwealth and a confused and licentious multitude.[22]

Both Gentili and Wolfe take as their task the correction of current impressions of Machiavelli, especially those fostered by one powerful enemy who is not named, but who is probably Innocent Gentillet.[23] Wolfe's letter to the reader, at first referring to "the malicious and

---

[22] *I Discorsi di Nicolo Machiavelli, sopra la prima deca di Tito Livio . . . in Palermo appresso gli heredi d'Antoniello degli Antonielli* (1584), bound with *Il Prencipe di Nicolo Machiavelli . . . con alcune altre operette,* "Lo stampatore al benigno lettore, " fol. 2.
[23] Gentillet's *Discours contre Machiavel* appeared in Geneva in 1576. Though shorter attacks on Machiavelli had appeared in print, Gentillet's was the first published book devoted to the condemnation of Machiavelli.

lying opinion of these slanderers," singles out one "Momus" in particular and says that if anyone read both Machiavelli's works and those
of his opponent, they would see that the one was worthy of eternal
memory and the other "fit to be a salesman of sausage and dried
fish."[24] Gentili offers his defense of Machiavelli by way of "reviewing
the book issued against him" (Laing tr., p. 156). Both Gentili and Wolfe
believe that Machiavelli dealt with the subject of tyranny in order to
oppose it, and they recognize in the text a republican tendency. This
is, of course, quite explicit in Gentili and is implied in Wolfe's contrast
between the "good many" and the "bad few." Another similarity is
that both Wolfe and Gentili associate their defense of Machiavelli more
closely with the *Discorsi* than with *Il Principe*, though most of the controversy centered upon the latter. Gentili's defense comes in the context of a recommendation that ambassadors read the *Discorsi* for its
historical and political lessons; Wolfe's defense, though it appears at
the beginning of a composite volume containing both of Machiavelli's
major works, is framed as a preface to the *Discorsi* alone. Both writers
draw the terms of their defense principally from the *Discorsi*, emphasizing Machiavelli's repudiation of tyranny and preference for government by the many – themes that receive ample treatment in that
work and do not appear in *Il Principe*. Finally, both authors stress
Machiavelli's value as a guide to the best way of drawing profit from
the reading of history.

[24] Fol. 3r. The frontispiece of the book depicts a palm tree rising above serpents that
entwine its base and a crowd of frogs beneath it, with the motto "Il vostro malignare
non giova nulla." This is in keeping with preface and refers to the eventual triumph
of Machiavelli's reputation in spite of detraction. The suggestion has been made that
this device referred to the personal triumph of Petruccio Ubaldini, who worked with
Wolfe on his Italian printing, and to his safety in exile (*Annali di Gabriel Giolito de' Ferrari*
[Rome 1890–3], II, p. 419), but Ubaldini had been a resident in England since the
reign of Henry VIII (see Giuliani Pellegrini, *Un fiorentino alla corte d'Inghilterra nel cinquecento: Petruccio Ubaldini* [Turin, 1967]), and it is difficult to see why a frontispiece
would be devoted to symbolizing his biography, for even if he did assist Wolfe in this
work, perhaps translating the preface and checking the printing of the Italian text, the
significance of such a gesture would be wholly lost, as he is nowhere mentioned in the
preface. The frontispiece, on the contrary, echoes the text of the preface and its attributions of Machiavelli's bad reputation to slander. It is a traditional device with specifically literary meaning: The palm of eternal memory rises above venom and calumny.
References to hostile critics were fairly common in Machiavelli publishing. As we have
seen, Giunta sought to defend *Il Principe* in 1532 against attackers. In 1514, Biagio
Buonacorsi expressed similar sentiments in a letter to Pandolfo Bellaci: "Acerrimo de-
fensore contro a tutti quelli, che per malignita o per invidia lo volessino secondo l'uso
de questi tempi mordere e lacerare" (see Adolph Gerber, *Niccolò Machiavelli: Die Handschriften, Ausgaben und Ubersetzungen seiner Werke im 16. und 17. Jahrhundert* [Gotha 1912–
13; repr. Turin, 1962], I, p. 84n, and Luigi Firpo, "Le origini dell'anti-machiavellismo,"
in *Machiavellismo e Antimachiavellismo nel cinquecento: Atti del Convegno di Perugia 30.IX–
1.X. 1969* [Florence, 1970], pp. 18–19, 27ff).

As mentioned previously, Wolfe had begun to print Gentili's own books in 1582, publishing six titles between 1582 and 1589. The two were literary associates with essentially similar views, and perhaps Gentili even puts in an appearance in Wolfe's preface, in the guise of the wise and profound student of politics who favored the printer with a copy of Machiavelli's book and who was ready to defend him against his bad reputation.

There are differences, however. Gentili is more markedly and aggressively republican, making no distinction between tyrants and just monarchs, specifically praising Machiavelli as a *laudator democratiae* and offering a fuller account of Machiavelli's doubleness of intention. We cannot take the Wolfe preface, as Panizza does, as evidence of any systematic republican ideology — and still less can we take the relationship between these texts as suggesting that the circle of Leicester and Walsingham and Sidney, to which Gentili and Wolfe had connections, attempted to put through a program of legislation inspired by republicanism of the Italian exiles.[25] But the connections that can be demonstrated between Gentili's reading of Machiavelli and the views of the printer of the 1584 London edition are significant in another sense, for they argue a close relation between the surreptitious printing of Machiavelli in England (indeed, according to Woodfield, the first surreptitious printing of any book in England) and an interpretation of Machiavelli that regarded the original publication of the text as itself a surreptitious act, a disguised revelation of the arcana of tyrants.

Wolfe's friend, Gabriel Harvey, also provides evidence that Wolfe not only printed but also read Machiavelli attentively. Harvey first encountered Machiavelli at Cambridge and wrote, rather boastingly, of his familiarity "with a certain parlous booke called, as I remember me, Il Principe di Niccolo Machiavelli," as well as with the *Discorsi*, the *Historia florentina*, and the *Arte della guerra*.[26] There are many other references to Machiavelli in Harvey's letters and marginalia, and Harvey appears to have regarded him with a mixture of seriousness (as the "great founder and master of policies") and undergraduate interest in the forbidden.[27] Later he was to become quite friendly with

---

[25] Diego Panizza, "Machiavelli e Alberico Gentili," in *Machiavellismo e antimachiavellici nel nel cinquencento*, pp. 148–55. This article also appeared in *Pensiero Politico*, II (1969), 476–83.
[26] Edward J. L. Scott, ed., *Letter Book of Gabriel Harvey, A.D. 1573–1580* (London, 1884), p. 79.
[27] Ibid., p. 174; see also pp. 134, 135; G. L. Moore-Smith, ed., *Gabriel Harvey's Marginalia* (London, 1913, pp. 84, 94, 96, 147, 149–50, 183, 195, 201, 209; Virginia F. Stern, "The *Bibliotheca* of Gabriel Harvey," *Renaissance Quarterly* XXV (1972), 58–9 and Stern, *Gabriel Harvey: His Life, Marginalia and Library* (Oxford, 1979), pp. 41–2, 106, 112, 121, 150, 153, 161–3, 174, 195, 226, 266, 268; T. H. Jameson, "The Machiavellianism of Gabriel Harvey," *PMLA* LVI (1941), 645–56.

Machiavelli's publisher, and in fact, according to Nashe, resided with Wolfe from September 1592 to April 1593.[28] Harvey refers to Wolfe's knowledge of Machiavelli in his *New Letter of Notable Contents* (London, 1593) addressed to "my loving friend John Wolfe, printer to the City." The reference occurs in the context of Harvey's apology for having spoken too freely in denunciation of the Turk. Fearing he has said too much, he explains:

> You know, I am not very prodigal of my discourse with everyone: but I know unto whom I write: and he that hath read, and heard so many gallant Florentine discourses, as you have done, may the better discern what is what; and he that publisheth so many books to the world, as you do, may frame unto himself a private and public use of such conference. (Sig. A4r)

It is impossible to guess what the private or public use hinted at might be, for Harvey is being deliberately obscure. It seems to do with advancing the cause of militant Protestantism in some way that uses the resources of the printing press. The particular reference here is not so important for our purposes as the fact that Harvey regards Wolfe's value to the cause as closely related to his career as a publisher and his Machiavellian political sophistication.

"Machiavellian devices": Wolfe as rebel printer

Wolfe had served an apprenticeship to John Day, and he had traveled to Italy to master the techniques of Italian printing. Nevertheless, he was not a member of the Stationers' Company and did not enjoy the exclusive privilege afforded by the patent system. Shortly after he began to print, he came into conflict with the company over the issue of infringement of patents, and his own troubles with the company intersected with something of a crisis in the industry over patents, for as early as 1577, formal complaints against the patent system had been made to the city chamberlain by thirty-five printers, and at the time when Wolfe began to print, tensions between the few rich printers who enjoyed the protection of patents and the several hundred other practitioners of the art had reached a boiling point.[29]

The practice of granting patents for the printing of particular books had begun with a grant made by Henry VIII in 1538 and was at first

---

[28] See Hoppe, "John Wolfe," p. 268.
[29] W. W. Greg, ed., *A Companion to Arber, Being a Calendar of Documents in Edward Arber's "Transcript of the Registers of the Company of Stationers of London 1554–1640" with Text and Calendar of Supplementary Documents* (Oxford, 1967), p. 18; Arber, *Transcripts* I, p. 111; Judge, pp. 18–33.

limited to two years.[30] By the 1580s, the patent system had been extended in such a way that there was a virtual class distinction between most of the several hundred persons engaged in the trade and the eight or nine rich and heavily patented printers. The number of patents had grown, and it had also become customary for the queen to grant patents for classes of books: Tottell printed law books, Seres prayer books, Barker had bibles, and so on. By this time the grants were of very long duration, some for twenty-one years, some for life, and some for the lives of father and son, so that although the number of competent printers and the demand for books were great, the patent system hindered even distribution of the work. Sometimes, in fact, as in the case of Roger Day, the patentee even lacked the means to print all the books permitted by his patents, and a valuable privilege would go unused while printers who might have done the work went idle. This situation led to protests by the poorer printers, who petitioned the Stationers' Company for fair prices, restraints upon cheap or unpaid labor, and assurances of work. The initial response of the company was conciliatory, promising redress of abuses and limited sharing of patents in cases in which the patent holder did not make full use of his privilege.[31] But these early negotiations did not settle the grievances, and John Wolfe was to play a central role in the period of greatest strife between the patentees and the poorer printers.

Almost as soon as he began to print, Wolfe began to infringe on patents. In June 1582, Wolfe was ordered not to print the *Accidences* to which Francis Flower held the patent.[32] Over the next year, a battle between the insurgent printers and the holders of patents was waged, through a series of petitions, counterpetitions, commissions of inquiry, and so on. Many aspects of the struggle and details of the chronology of the affair are still obscure, despite the labors of Greg and others. In September 1582, in response to a petition by the journeymen and workmen of the Stationers' Company, the Court of Aldermen commissioned an inquiry into the complaints of the dissident stationers.[33] By this time, Wolfe had been jailed briefly and then released at the instance of George Goring.[34] Goring attempted to influence the commission to favor the dissidents, and especially Wolfe, asking that he be given work or that his interest in the printing business be bought

[30] Judge, *Elizabethan Book Pirates*, pp. 12–13.
[31] Ibid., pp. 31–2.
[32] Ibid., p. 33, citing John Roche Dasent, ed., *Acts of the Privy Council of England*, n.s. XIII, 88.
[33] Greg, *Companion*, p. 21.
[34] Judge, *Elizabethan Book Pirates*, p. 33.

out. The city remembrancer, Norton, who was a member of the commission, replied to Goring that an agreement had been worked out that was acceptable to all of the dissidents except Wolfe and four others, and further concessions would be inconsistent with the queen's prerogative.[35]

In late 1582 or early 1583, a petition signed by Wolfe and twenty-one stationers was presented to Lord Burghley, complaining of Norton's partiality and his threats of imprisonment. A second petition went to Walsingham, suing for release from prison for several of the dissidents and complaining of illegal seizure of property.[36] The response of the Stationers' Company to these charges names Wolfe and six others as leaders of the insurgents and claims that they had been fairly dealt with, especially Wolfe.[37] According to this document, Wolfe had been offered admission to the company in the spring of 1582 and had been given work out of Christopher Barker's patent, but executed the work poorly. As his skill increased, he began to print whatever he wished, in disregard of patents. When Barker challenged Wolfe, asking why he printed books on which Barker held the patent, Wolfe replied, "Because I will live":

But much more talk having past between them, Barker replied, saying, "Wolfe, leave your Machiavellian devices, and conceit of your foreign wit, which you have gained by gadding from country to country, and tell me plainly, if you mean to deal like an honest man, what you would have."[38]

Wolfe's demands included admission to the company, a loan of twenty pounds, and the right to employ the five apprentices he already employed. This was refused, and Wolfe continued his disruptive activities. According to the Stationers, these were of a rebellious character, involving mass meetings, challenges to the queen's prerogative, and threats of violence.

What did Barker mean by "Machiavellian"? He associates the term with disorder in the printing trade, with foreign wit, and, perhaps most interestingly, with doubleness of utterance, with the refusal to state plainly what one "would have." The epithet also announces the theme of the set of notes[39] prepared by the Stationers' Company to document Wolfe's misbehavior. The picture of Wolfe that emerges from this document, however one-sided, has at least the consistency

[35] Greg, *Companion*, pp. 22–3.
[36] Ibid., p. 21.
[37] Arber, *Transcripts*, II, p. 779.
[38] Ibid., p. 780.
[39] Ibid., pp. 781–2.

of political myth: It is the portrait of a vigorous, amoral, and anarchic rebel. For Barker and the Stationers' Company, these qualities, when acquired abroad and masked by dissimulation, were the traits of a Machiavellian.

The Stationers claimed that Wolfe boasted that "he was a freeman, and had as great a privilege as any of them all, and would print all their books, if he lacked work." When he was committed to the Clink for "contempts against her majesty's grants," he gathered about him poor men from many trades "as unto one to be a mean to make them rich."[40] Upon his release, Wolfe and his confederates vowed "to withstand her majesty's grants wholly," and collected funds and held meetings in the Exchange and at the church of St. Thomas of Acres in furtherance of their cause. At one point, Wolfe and part of his group came into the Stationers' Hall itself, openly affirming that "it was lawful for all men to print all lawful books, what commandment soever her majesty gave to the contrary." In fact, according to his enemies, Wolfe denied obedience to any of the queen's commandments

further than in the written or printed law were contained, in matters specially of printing, whereof he is now somewhat reconsidered in words, nevertheless in execution continueth the same unto this hour, saying, "he will live."

Wolfe is also accused of making "disloyal" and "unreverent" speeches against the queen's government, "not once giving her highness any honorable name or title, as 'she is deceived, she shall know she is deceived,' also 'she is blindly led, she is deceived.' "

Wolfe collected money, "insensed the meaner sort of people" against all privileges and against the queen's government itself, and set a monstrous example for servants, apprentices, and journeymen, so that, for a time, the Stationers were afraid of violence in their own hall, and the apprentices even "married wives, and for a time did what they list." When Wolfe was admonished that he was only one man, and a humble one, to presume against established order, he responded:

"Tush," said he, "Luther was but one man, and reformed all the world for religion, and I am that one man that must and will reform the government in this trade."[41]

---

[40] In another entry (ibid., I, p. 144), it is said that while Wolfe was in the Clink, his associates continued to attack patents and "incensed the whole city, saying their ancient liberties were thereby infringed . . . some, when they are charitably demanded what they should gain, if all were in common, and made havock for one man to undo another, they answer, 'we should make them beggars like to ourselves.' "
[41] This quotation and those in the preceding two paragraphs are drawn from Arber, *Transcripts*, II, pp. 780–2 (see n. 38).

Barker's remarks and the complaint of the Stationers' Company against Wolfe depict an organized movement, with a small group of working printers and their associates at the center, acting as organizers and fund-raisers, and a larger following drawn from the 100 to 200 journeymen and apprentice printers, as well as the poor members of other trades throughout the city.

The account given of Wolfe's activities is a biased one but it must contain some truth, and it is remarkable that Wolfe got away with his stand against the queen's patent right. As Judge puts it, "The wonder of it is that Wolfe did not lose his head, or at least his ears, for such audacity" (*Elizabethan Book Pirates*, p. 40). For several rounds of the conflict, Wolfe had the support of Goring, and, when he was released from prison, fled to the court,[42] an unusual procedure for a rebel. It is also somewhat surprising that the Privy Council was more favorable to the rebels than were the London authorities. When the dissidents complained of the bias of the original commissioners, the council enlarged the commission, adding Bishop Aylmer, Alexander Nowell (dean of St. Paul's), and William Fleetwood, the city recorder. The instructions to this new group, unknown to scholars until Greg published them in 1967, shed some light on the context of Wolfe's challenge to the Stationers' Company, for the Privy Council, though it had received the rebuttal of the dissidents' charges against the company, instructed its commissioners to make many of the reforms requested. Abuses in pricing and quality of printing are to be redressed, and patents of violators revoked and given to the poorer printers. The issue of patent infringement is addressed in a surprising way:

We think it meet that you deal first with the patentees, who by so large construction of their grants and privileges (as it is informed) embrace more than by the said grants is intended, that they take order that the poorer sort may be set on work, by allowing unto them the printing of some part of the books granted in their patents, or at least such as they seem to challenge by their said patents, and are not directly comprised in them and to that end you shall do well to view their patents, the better to discern what they ought to have by right.[43]

What seems to be called for here is a construction of the patentees' rights so strict as to amount to the kind of sharing that the dissidents had requested. Greg comments: "The Privy Council, while endeav-

---

[42] Greg, *Companion*, p. 22.
[43] Ibid., p. 124.

ouring to maintain an impartial attitude, was evidently inclined to sympathize with 'the poorer sort' and to view with suspicion the actions of the wicked capitalists" (p. 152). In such a context, Wolfe's alleged *lèse-majesté* may appear less anarchic than his enemies wished it to appear, and his rebellion more contained. Apparently he did not transgress the limits of acceptable rebellion in the view of the Privy Council, or at least did not transgress them far enough to trouble about.

However, the commission was less favorable. In the covering letter to their final report, submitted in July 1583, they claim that the dissidents had "no great causes to complain" in the first place, and report that such abuses as there were had been corrected.[44] The final report of the commissioners recommends a series of reforms: uniform pricing, restriction of the patents for schoolbooks, a moratorium on the granting of patents for general classes of printing, a limitation on the number of apprentices and foreigners, and revocation of patents for poor work. But it also suggests measures against the rebels, recommending a reduction in the number of printers, seizure of all books printed in contempt of privileges, a ban on the printing of unlawful books, registry of presses and type specimens, a provision that printers be bound not to resist search, and severe penalties for counterfeit printing or the use of another printer's ornaments or name. In addition, nine members of the company declared themselves willing to yield part of their privilege, and specifically offered eighty-two titles to the dissidents.[45]

In July 1583, Wolfe himself joined the Stationers' Company. He "acknowledged his error," according to his former enemies, "and is relieved with work."[46] The settlement with Wolfe included a share in John Day's lucrative patent,[47] and after 1584 Wolfe became perhaps the most active printer in London, despite the fact that there was an attempt to limit his presses to two. Gerber calculates that he printed between a third and a quarter of all titles printed in London between the time of his admission to the company and his death.[48] The benefits offered may have changed his views, or it may be that, as Barker suspected, Wolfe's aim had always been to manipulate the tensions between the poorer and richer printers to his own advantage. In any

[44] Arber, *Transcripts*, II, pp. 783–4; Greg, *Companion*, p. 125.
[45] Greg, *Companion*, pp. 126–33, 136–7; Arber, *Transcripts*, II, pp. 786–9.
[46] Arber, *Transcripts*, II, pp. 688, 784.
[47] W. W. Greg and E. Boswell, eds., *Records of the Court of the Stationer's Company 1576–1602 from Register B* (London, 1930), p. lxv.
[48] Gerber, "Fictitious Italian editions," pp. 132–3.

case, after the admission of Wolfe to the company, others had to lead
the faction that still remained intransigent. In his new role, Wolfe
soon became active in the efforts of the company to suppress his former allies. On the death of the beadle in 1587, Wolfe assumed that
post, which carried with it lodging in the Stationers' Yard and a salary
of six pounds a year, later raised to ten. He held the post until 1598.[49]
The post of beadle entailed police functions. In fact, Wolfe became
the chief enforcer of the rules that constituted the settlement of the
struggle of 1582–3, serving arrest warrants on former associates, defending patent holders from encroachments, and prosecuting infring-
ers.[50]

The best-known of his acts as beadle was the raid on Thomas Waldegrave's house during the Martin Marprelate controversy. Though the
Marprelate tracts came close to religious sedition, the search for
the secret presses from which the tracts issued was apparently entrusted to Wolfe, and "Martin Marprelate" describes one of Wolfe's
searches:

You know that Waldegrave's printing press and letters were taken away: his
press being timber was sawn and hewed in pieces, the iron work battered and
made unserviceable, his letters melted, with cases and other tools defaced by
John Wolfe alias Machivill, Beadle of the Stationers and most tormenting
executioner of Waldegrave's goods.[51]

Wolfe's alias fit the "executioner" as well as it had the rebel. A Machiavellian was one who destroyed secret presses, as well as one who
used them; one who knew many excellent Florentine discourses, as
well as one who printed those discourses while pretending to be someone else. Wolfe was made printer to the City in 1594 and admitted
to livery in the Stationers' Company in 1598.[52]

Wolfe's reputation for Machiavellism predated his printing of Machiavelli and survived his abandonment of the cause of the rebel
printers. Both Barker and Martin Marprelate reprove as Machiavellian
the quality of amoral ambitiousness in Wolfe's conduct. He could lead
a rebellion or help to suppress one. In either case his ends were his
own, and he could change his behavior to suit the varying tides of
fortune. Barker's blaming of the printers' revolt on the instigations

[49] Greg and Boswell, *Records*, pp. xxxvii, lxv, 23, 24, 38.
[50] Arber, *Transcripts*, I, pp. 527; Greg and Boswell, *Records*, pp. 38–9.
[51] "Martin Marprelate," *Oh, Read over "Doctor John Bridges," For it is a Worthy Work* (n.p.,
n.d.), p. 23.
[52] Judge, *Elizabethan Book Pirates*, pp. 41–44.

of a widely traveled Machiavellian rebel is no doubt a simplification, but the protests against the patents did have an incipiently ideological, antiauthoritarian dimension. Wolfe was clearly the central figure in this protest, and he published *Il Principe* and the *Discorsi* surreptitiously within a year of the end of the rebellion, with a preface stressing Machiavelli's antityrannical and antiaristocratic teaching.

Surreptitious printing as propaganda

Wolfe pioneered the use of false imprints for foreign propaganda purposes in the period 1588–98. In this he must have worked closely with Lord Burghley, for as Woodfield has shown, the first text of this sort, the *Essempio d'una lettera mandata d'Inghilterra a don Bernardino di Mendoza,* is a translation of a letter of which there is a draft in Burghley's hand. Also, the surreptitious printing of propaganda that began with the publication of this letter in 1588 abruptly ceased at the time of Burghley's death in 1598. In the intervening decade, dozens of falsely imprinted works were issued, first by Wolfe himself and then by Richard Field, jobbing for Wolfe.[53]

The *Essempio* purports to be a letter from English Catholics to friends abroad, lamenting the failure of the Armada and expressing the belief that a pro-Catholic uprising in England was not possible. The publication of this fraudulent letter was an attempt to demonstrate that Cardinal Allen's call for rebellion in *An Admonition to the Nobility and People of England and Ireland* was based upon a gross misconstruction of the strength and loyalty of English Catholics. When this scheme proved successful, French translations of the letter followed, and then various other false letters of news in French. Wolfe's already successful attempts at surreptitious printing set the stage for this particular kind of propaganda, and Burghley may have known of them through his own well-attested efforts to secure copies of Machiavelli's works.[54] Here, as in the case of his destruction of Martin Marprelate's hidden presses, Wolfe's expertise in all aspects of clandestine printing was, after his youthful rebellious phase, enlisted in the service of established authority.

We are in a poor position to recover or assess Wolfe's political ideas:

[53] Woodfield, *Surreptitious Printing,* pp. 27–30.
[54] Ibid. p. 25 (thesis, p. 56), citing Cecil Papers CCLXXIII, fol. 3; *Calendar of State Papers, Foreign, 1547–53* (London, 1861), p. 204. See also *Calendar of the Hatfield Papers* XIV (London, 1923), p. 339, and Christopher Morris, "Machiavelli's reputation in Tudor England," in *Machiavellismo e antimachiavellici nel cinquecento,* p. 90.

We have his preface, which is richly suggestive but brief, and much of what else we have comes from his enemies. But what he thought about politics is less important than what he did. He published Machiavelli surreptitiously and achieved a reputation for Machiavellism in his own political activities. One cannot make the kind of separation Woodfield does between his "commercial" use of false imprints (including the Machiavelli editions) and the "political" use of the same technique, which Woodfield believes began at Lord Burghley's suggestion in 1588.[55] It is logical, rather, to see in Wolfe's propaganda work for the government a further indication that Wolfe had always been keenly aware of the political implications and possibilities of his craft, especially in regard to its capacity to generate texts that were other than they seemed to be. It would be close to the truth to say that for Machiavelli himself, the production of such texts was synonymous with the exercise of political power: To regard the surreptitious printing of Machiavelli by a rebel printer within a year of his reception into the printing establishment as an act with no political significance is to miss an important dimension of Renaissance political discourse. Machiavelli's influence was not solely a matter of the reception of doctrines and concepts; it is felt also in new patterns in the transmission of political texts, in a transposition from the domain of action to the domain of printing and publication, of Machiavelli's emphasis upon secrecy, dissimulation, and the effacement of the traces of power.

The shield of Ajax

The final aspect of Wolfe's career that conerns us here is his role in the publication of John Hayward's *Henry IV* in 1599. The book, a prose history of Bolingbroke's life up to the point at which he became king, was issued with a dedication to Essex that compared the earl, then in disfavor with the queen, to the usurper Bolingbroke. The Archbishop of Canterbury ordered the dedication cut out, and Wolfe and Hayward were arrested and confined to the Tower. Wolfe spent several weeks in confinement, but Hayward was imprisoned for three years, during which he was examined about his intentions concerning the book several times, the last time in January 1601, shortly before Essex's attempted revolt in early February.[56]

[55] Woodfield, *Surreptitious Printing*, pp. 6–18, 24–33.
[56] On Hayward see Norman Scarfe, "Sir John Hayward, an Elizabethan historian," *Suffolk Institute of Archaeology* XXV (1952), 79–97. Also H. R. Plomer, "An examination of some existing copies of Hayward's *Life and Raigne of King Henry IV*," *The Library*, n.s.

Essex had been linked to Bolingbroke before. Shakespeare's *Richard II* presented a Bolingbroke in whose popularity and ingratiating attitude toward the common people it was possible, though not obligatory, to find a hint at Essex's own manner. Essex himself liked the play, and on their return from the unsuccessful Azores expedition of 1597, some of Essex's followers had grumblingly compared their general with Bolingbroke, a man unfairly banished by his sovereign who not only regained his rights but became king himself. Such talk was not very serious, mere grumbling at Essex's disfavor with Elizabeth, but the association of a popular general with the king-deposing Bolingbroke was potentially dangerous, and, after all, the openly seditious tract on the succession by the Jesuit Parsons that had been issued two years before had been dedicated to Essex, though not with his permission.[57] When Shakespeare's play was printed in 1597, it appeared without the deposition scene. By 1599, then, there had been enough association between Essex and the king-deposing Bolingbroke to suggest that Hayward, in taking up Shakespeare's subject matter again, in writing strong speeches for the rebels, in dedicating *Henry IV* to Essex, and in prefacing the book with an insistence on the contemporary lessons one could learn from historical examples, was either extremely naive and unlucky or was toying injudiciously, as many people did, with half-formed notions of Essex succeeding the queen. Many others shared such notions, and the currency of such views was a factor in Essex's ultimate decision to launch his ill-fated revolt. Whatever Hayward's motive, the book was quickly perceived as dangerous and the author was jailed.

It is unclear why Wolfe was released so quickly. The author remained a prisoner in the Tower for three years and was tried twice, whereas the printer was let go, even though he admitted to a large share in the decision to dedicate the book to Essex. By Wolfe's own account, the author brought the book to him without a dedication and decided to dedicate it to Essex only after discussing the subject with Wolfe, who carried the book to Essex House himself to present it to the earl. Wolfe's reason for the choice of Essex was that Essex, like Bolingbroke, was a martial man, "and the book treating of Irish causes"

III (1902), 13–23; Evelyn May Albright, "Shakespeare's *Richard II* and the Essex conspiracy," *PMLA* XLII (1927), 686–720; Margaret Dowling, "Sir John Hayward's troubles over his life of Henry IV," *The Library*, ser. 4, XI (1930), 212–24; Ray Heffner, "Shakespeare, Hayward and Essex," *PMLA* XLV (1930), 754–80; S. L. Goldberg, "Sir John Hayward, 'politic' historian," *Review of English Studies*, n.s. VI (1955), 233–44; Anon, "Sir John Hayward," *Notes and Queries* CCII (=n.s. IV) (1957), 288–90.
[57] G. B. Harrison, *The Life and Death of Robert Devereux, Earl of Essex* (New York, 1937), pp. 214, 88–9.

was topical, for Essex was then making preparations for his Irish campaign.[58] The dedication was the reason for the book's being suspected of a disloyal intention at first. Then, in the subsequent examinations, Hayward's alleged slanting of the story toward the rebel cause, and his introduction of unhistorical material in order to make that cause more attractive, were added to the charges against him. The dedication was especially suspect for its inclusion of the words "you are great, both in present judgment, and in expectation of a future time," but the entire dedication elevated Essex inappropriately, even by the standards of the lavish Elizabethan dedication:

Aristo kai gennaiotato: to the best and noblest (as Euripides says), which title you have merited preeminently and uniquely. O illustrious earl – whose name, if it shone upon our Henry's front, he would go forth among the vulgar more fortunately and more safely – you are great, both in present judgment and in expectation of a future time, in that fortune, blind before, now seems to have regained her sight, for she goes about to load with honors one who is already notable for all the virtues. Therefore if you will deign to pick him up with favor, he will hide most safely under your name, as Homeric Teucer did under the shield of Ajax. May the best and greatest God preserve your highness *(celsitudinem)* safe for our commonwealth for a long time, for by you we may long enjoy safety and glory, as much by your faith as by the weapons of your powerful right hand by which we have so long been defended and avenged.[59]

The author humbly asks the great lord to protect his book – as was entirely traditional – but, because the book and its protagonist are, by metonymy, spoken of as if they were indistinguishable, the posture of authorial self-abasement has the effect of making Essex greater than "Henry," an English king who had deposed a reigning monarch, of making the published book the arbiter and protector of royalty. Teucer was not only defended by the shield of Ajax but shot arrows from its protection. Printing, despite, or in fact because of its blurring of the origins of utterance, did not merely reflect political power, but could contest it as well.

The dedication does not play down, but rather emphasizes, the parallels between the dedicatee and Bolingbroke, embracing Essex's own view of the unfairness of his disfavor (it was Elizabeth who was re-

[58] *Calendar of State Papers, Domestic Series, Elizabeth, 1598–1601*, ed. Mary Anne Everett [Wood] Green (London, 1869), V, pp. 450ff. It has been shown that the first edition was actually printed by Edward Allde for Wolfe. See William A. Jackson, "Counterfeit printing in Jacobean times," *The Library*, ser. 4, XV (1934), 372–3.
[59] *The First Part of the Life and Raigne of King Henrie the IIII* (London, 1599), Sig. A2r. My translation.

sponsible for the decline in Essex's fortune, who was temporarily blind to his merits, and who, with his appointment as Earl Marshal and the command of the Irish expedition, might be thought of as having recovered her judgment to load him with new honors).

According to William Camden, the main offense of the dedication was the reference to Essex's future expectations, for he was already earl marshall of England. To what else could he aspire and still remain a loyal subject?[60] At least one contemporary, John Chamberlain, who sent a transcript of the preface to Dudley Carlton in a letter of March 1, 1599, found Hayward's wording innocuous:

> For lack of better matter I send you three or four toys to pass away the time . . . the treatise of Henry the Fourth is reasonably well written. . . . Here hath been much descanting about it, why such a story should come out at this time, and many exceptions taken, especially to the epistle, which was a short thing in Latin dedicated to the Earl of Essex and objected to him in good earnest, whereupon there was commandment it should be cut out of the book. Yet I have got you a transcript of it that you may pick out the offense if you can; for my part I can find no such bugs' words, but that everything is as it is taken.[61]

Most modern scholars agree with Chamberlain, but the government did not. The questions put to Hayward show that far more than the preface was involved. The examiners were not satisfied with his defense against the charge that he had altered the record – inserting events from one reign into the history of another – in order to emphasize the parallels between his history and current events, and they clearly believed he had favored Henry the usurper over Richard in his treatment, and had put powerful and dangerous speeches in the mouths of the supporters of Bolingbroke, to the effect that "it might be lawful for the subject to depose the king" and that "subjects were bound for their obedience to the state and not to the person of the king." They also charged that he had omitted "every principal point that made against the traitor or rebels."[62] In his answers Hayward claimed, for the most part convincingly, that he was fulfilling the duties of a historian and composing, with traditional license, speeches suitable to the facts: "There can be nothing done, be it never so ill or unlawful, but must have a shadow, and every counsel must be according to the

---

[60] William Camden, *The Historie of the Life and Reigne of the Most Renowmed and Victorious Princesse Elizabeth* [Camden's "*Annals*"] (London, 1630), pp. 192–3; see Heffner, "Shakespeare, Hayward and Essex," p. 757.

[61] Norman Egbert McClure, ed., *The Letters of John Chamberlain* (Philadelphia, 1939), I, p. 70.

[62] *Calendar of State Papers, Domestic, Elizabeth* V, 40.

action."[63] It is also probably much more exciting to write good speeches for rebels than for upholders of the status quo. But Hayward's bias toward the rebels is is amply attested by the text (e.g., "the king, having a heavy hand upon his subjects . . . the people at length resolved to revolt, and rather to run into the hazard of a ruinous rebellion, than to endure safety joined with slavery"; p. 56). In addition, even when examined he did, as author, stand behind the references in his book to the principle that allegiance is owed to the state rather than to the sovereign (an idea that he claimed to have read in "Bodius," perhaps Bodin[64]) and to the necessity of limitations upon royal power, which he affirmed "to be a true opinion if rightly understood; did not intend it to be taken generally, but that princes were to be limited by the law divine and the law of nature only."[65]

These opinions were similar in certain ways to Essex's protests against Elizabeth's arbitrary treatment of him. In correspondence with Egerton, for example, Essex had been urged to submit to Elizabeth "between whom and you there can to be no proportion of duty. And God Himself requireth it as a principal bond of service to himself." Essex had replied by pointedly rejecting the absolutist implications of Egerton's advice:

Doth God require it? Is it impiety not to do it? What, cannot princes err? Cannot subjects receive wrong? Is an earthly power or authority infinite? Pardon me, pardon me, my good Lord, I can never subscribe to these principles . . . let them acknowledge an infinite absoluteness on earth that do not believe in an infinite absoluteness in heaven.[66]

Hayward's book, like Essex's response to Egerton, certainly may be taken as a spirited protest against absolute or arbitrary royal authority, and, without imagining that the author had any seriously seditious intention or that he was "set on" to write it, as his examiners asked, by someone in the Essex circle, it is reasonable to see in it a reference to the general character of Elizabeth's conduct after Essex's return from the Azores as perceived by one who resisted the more extreme implications of divine-right kingship and who associated that resistance with the Earl of Essex.

As Essex's own behavior became more rebellious, the book, which had been considered dangerous from the start, seemed ever more

[63] Ibid., 540.
[64] Ibid.
[65] Ibid.
[66] Harrison, *Robert Devereux*, pp. 197, 200–1, citing Thomas Birch, *Memoirs of the Reign of Queen Elizabeth* (London, 1754), II, pp. 385ff.

conspiratorial, until, at Essex's trial the claim was made that it was a cunning attempt to imply, by falsely attributing contemporary slanders against the government to past times, that "the same abuses being now in this realm that were in the days of Richard II, the like course might be taken for redress."[67] Even Essex's attempts to have the book suppressed were held against him, because he objected to it only after it had been released, to do its damage on his behalf. Hayward was not released from the Tower until 1602.

The protest against absolute authority embodied in Hayward's book may recall Wolfe's own protests against the queen's prerogative some years earlier. Neither in the movement of insurgent printers of which Wolfe was the leader, nor in the dissatisfactions of Essex, his supporters, and his admirers, can one find any consistent republicanism of the kind that would justify Panizza's claims for an English body of republican opinion, nourished by contact with the Italian exiles and by the *Discorsi*. But here, too, we find Wolfe in the midst of an antiauthoritarian publishing incident, and his own role in the affair was undoubtedly to make the implicit protests of Hayward's book more pointed by influencing the decision to dedicate the book to Essex.

Wolfe can be thought of as a Machiavellian in several senses. He was influenced by Gentili's notion of Machiavelli as an opponent of tyranny, and perhaps still more by the idea, implicit in Gentili's analysis, that the publication *Il Principe*, which argued for the necessity of saying one thing and meaning another, was itself an act of equivocation and doubleness of utterance, meaning one thing to the prince and another to the people. Wolfe's career, with its reversals of loyalties and tactics, does not consistently display the ideological commitment of Gentili's view of the publication of Machiavelli as a republican political act.[68] Wolfe was drawn to protests against arbitrary authority and tyranny, and the *Discorsi* preface shows that he associated such protests with Machiavelli; but he was just as much drawn to advancing his own interests under the cover of principled protest, of exploiting class tensions for his own benefit, as Barker sensed at the outset of the printers' revolt, calling him a Machiavellian in quite a different sense from Gentili's. He used his presses for books, like the Machiavelli editions and *Henry IV*, that were potentially dangerous in the political views they expressed; but he also used them to create a new and powerful kind of government propaganda. What ties his diverse activities as a

---

[67] *Calendar of State Papers, Domestic, Elizabeth* V, 567.
[68] In the reign of James, Gentili too reversed direction, and his *Regales disputationes* (London, 1605) take an extreme view of the royal prerogative, based on its precedent in Roman law.

printer together is that, among the printers of the late sixteenth century, it was Wolfe, the surreptitious printer of Machiavelli, who explored most fully the potential of the art of printing for anonymity, ambivalence, equivocation, and the creation of political mystery. His debt to Machiavelli lay not in his embracing of republican ideas, but in his adherence to Machiavelli's advice to vary one's position with the winds of fortune,[69] and more particularly in his exploitation of the special ways in which the printing press could be used in the service of that principle, creating new kinds of anonymity, new relations between an utterance and the aim or intention that lay behind it. In Wolfe's Machiavellian use of it, printing was an art uniquely suited to sustaining, as well as unmasking, the political arcana.

---

[69] "E però bisogna che egli abbia uno animo disposto a volgersi secondo ch'e venti della fortuna e le variazioni delle cose li commandano" (*Prin.* 18).

4

Machiavelli and the *arcana imperii*

This study has shown that early interpreters of and borrowers from Machiavelli often had recourse to ideas of political mystery, or mystery of state. Cardinal Pole regarded the publication of *Il Principe* as the biblically predicted revelation of the "mystery of iniquity"; Gardiner, in a treatise itself intended as a breviarium, or secret manual of counsel, compared the political wisdom he had to offer to the secrets of the hermetic tradition; and Alberico Gentili thought that Machiavelli's intention was to lay bare the arcana of tyranny. This chapter examines a closely related but rather more complex shift in political vocabulary. The authors we have dealt with so far all make some kind of equation between Machiavelli and political arcana, and thus in some ways anticipate the French seventeenth-century synthesis, in which the mystery of kingship is asserted in bolder terms than ever before in the West, even as the sacred king takes upon himself the typically Machiavellian trait of being willing to employ immoral methods in the maintenance of his image and his power.

Reason of state and the *arcana imperii* before Clapmar

What comes between the attempts to associate Machiavelli and the arcana we have already dealt with, and the French absolutist use of Machiavellian insights in the service of a paradoxically revised ideology of sacred kingship, is a complex shift in political terminology that involves not only Machiavelli and ancient notions of political arcana, but a third, mediating set of ideas – ideas closely related to those this study has repeatedly touched upon, but described in the new vocabulary of reason of state.

The relationship between Machiavelli and the doctrine of reason of state is itself a very large subject, and the primary sources on reason of state – mostly Italian and French treatises of the late sixteenth and early seventeenth centuries – constitute an immense body of literature that has been studied many times in great detail.[1] For our purposes, several features of this body of material are most important. The first is that the writers on reason of state often think of themselves as dealing in the same subject matter as Machiavelli, and often in fact look back to his work as the first, or first modern, treatment of their subject. This subject is, in the words of Giovanni Botero, the author of the first treatise to bear the title *Della ragion di stato* (Venice, 1589), and who is really the founder of the school, even though the actual term "reason of state" had been used earlier, "knowledge of the means suitable for founding, conserving and increasing a dominion."[2] Rodolfo De Mattei has shown that Botero, as well as Frachetta, Ribadeneyra, Zuccolo, Campanella, Albergati, and others, regarded Machiavelli primarily as a writer on *ragion di stato,* even though he never actually used this term.[3] But – and this is the second feature of the reason of state literature we shall need to keep in mind – though they recognize Machiavelli as a writer on the same subject, the reason of state authors almost always reject Machiavelli's amoralism and, at some point in their discourse, accept the more traditional subordination of political theory to moral or religious principles. Reason of state is a doctrine that attempts to justify, in a way alien to Machiavelli, the necessities of rule that Machiavelli had merely attempted to posit as effective. The reason of state writers take up, endlessly, questions of the use of deception, extralegal force, and the political manipulation of religion. They tend to find that some stretching of conventional moral restrictions is indeed necessary in political life, but they insist on justifying such exceptions on the basis of subordination of the good of the individual to the good of the state. When political tactics cannot be justified in such a way, they must be condemned. Thus these writers attempt to admit the necessity for some "Machiavellian" strategies while setting a limit to their use. Girolamo Frachetta in *L'Idea del libro de' governi di stato e di guerra* (Venice, 1592) speaks about these limits, in terms that were to be widely imitated, when he distinguishes between

[1] See, for example, Giuseppe Ferrari, *Corso sugli scrittori politici italiani* (Milan, 1862); Friedrich Meinecke, *Machiavellism* [Eng. trans.] (New Haven, Conn., 1957); Rodolfo De Mattei, "Il problema della 'Ragion di Stato' nel Seicento," *Rivista Internazionale di Filosofia del Diritto* XXVI (1949), 187–210; XXVII (1950), 25–38; XXVIII (1951), 333–56; 705–23; XXIX (1952), 406–24; XXX (1953), 445–61; XXXI (1954), 369–84; XXXIII (1956), 439–49; XXXIV (1957), 166–92; XXXV (1958), 680–93; XXXVI (1959), 517–43; XXXVII (1960), 553–76; XXXVIII (1961), 185–200. Much of De Mattei's earlier work reappears in his *Il problema della "ragion di stato" nell'età della controriforma* (Milan and Naples, 1979); Etienne Thuau, *Raison d'état et pensée politique à l'époque de Richelieu* (Paris, 1966); William F. Church, *Richelieu and Reason of State* (Princeton, N.J., 1972).
[2] "Notitia de' mezi, atti a fondare, conservare, & ampliare un Dominio" (p. 1).
[3] De Mattei, "Il Problema" (1949), 196ff; *Il Problema,* pp. 34ff

"buona ragione di stato," which stays within the moral limits, and "cattiva ragione di stato," which does not, and which includes the immoral recommendations of Machiavelli.[4] This division into good and bad reason of state – with the bad associated with Machiavelli – is the third feature of the literature that is important for this study, as it played a role in attempts that were made to correlate *ragion di stato* with the *arcana imperii*.

Thus, the reason of state literature was a large body of literature of wide influence that attempted to present Machiavellian subject matter in a morally correct form. Its importance here is that the good/bad reason of state scheme was taken over by a group of writers, of whom Arnold Clapmar was the first, who effected a further and decisive transformation in terminology, identifying in great detail the strategies of *ragion di stato* with the *arcana imperii* of Tacitus and the *sophismata* of Aristotle. Such a shift in vocabulary had the effect of linking reason of state, which sounded like a recent Italian coinage, with traditions of ancient political thought, and it also had the effect of emphasizing the mysterious or numinous character of the morally problematic political tactics included under the term arcana. Even if reason of state and *arcana imperii* referred to the same realities, the latter term was one that evoked a sense of religious or cultic mystery, and therefore provided a way of conceiving of the sophisticated strategies of recent Italian political thought as identical to ancient and sacral conceptions of kingship.

Clapmar himself did not regard the arcana in quite so cultic a way, and he insisted upon the distinction between the arcana (= good reason of state) and the morally indefensible, Machiavellian *flagitia* (= bad reason of state). But his rewriting of the tradition of *ragion di stato* in the vocabulary of *arcana imperii* directly influenced Naudé's conception of the *coup d'état*, in which the imagery of sacred, magical kingship and the moral principles of *II Principe* are fused (see Chapter 5, this volume).

The specific lines of influence traced here (from Bodin and Ammirato to Clapmar; from Clapmar to Naudé) constitute a case study in the literary sources of French absolutist thought and demonstrate the importance of Clapmar's innovation in terminology. The Italians had already found ways of dissociating Machiavelli's subject matter from the moral errors of *Il Principe*. Clapmar and his school showed that this same subject matter could be thought of as identical to the arcana that ancient writers had discussed, and the French developed

---

[4] Pp. 37–46 and passim. See De Mattei, "Il Problema" (1953).

this notion in the direction of a defense of Machiavellian tactics –
usually not called such – based on the notion that they were the arcana
of sacred kingship. In the works of several of the most interesting
authors – Naudé and Louis Machon especially – the indirect influence
of Machiavelli through the reason of state and *arcana imperii* schools
in combined with a fresh reading of the actual Machiavellian texts.

Jean Bodin was the first writer to associate Machiavelli with an ancient
literary tradition[5] of writing about the *arcana imperii*. In the *Methodus
ad facilem historiarum cognitionem* (Paris, 1566) he lists Machiavelli with
Tacitus, Guicciardini, and Plutarch as a revealer of "hidden counsels,"[6]
and in addition joins Machiavelli's name to those of Sleidan and several
others as a writer on the "arcana of princes" (p. 56). But the principal
passage making a connection between Machiavelli and the arcana, and
the passage that was to be most influential, comes in chapter 6 ("De
statu rerumpublicarum"), where Bodin laments the meagerness of
writings dealing with the form and modes of change of states *(rerumpublicarum statu et conversionibus)*, especially after the lapse of the ancient
tradition. Machiavelli stands out as an exception:

> After Aristotle, Polybius, Dionysius Halicarnassus, Plutarch, Dio and Tacitus
> . . . left many excellent and grave things scattered in their histories concerning
> government, as did Machiavelli, who was the first, in my opinion, to write of
> government after about 1,200 years during which barbarism buried every-
> thing. (pp. 177–8)[7]

Machiavelli himself is criticized for being insufficiently learned in ancient philosophical and historical literature, but his work nevertheless
remains almost unique in its resumption of the ancient interest in *statu
et conversionibus:*

> After him, Patricius, Thomas More, Robert of Brittany, and Garimbertus
> touched profusely and seriously upon many things concerning the institution
> of customs, the restoring of peoples, the founding of a principate, and the
> stabilizing of laws; but only sparsely have they treated of the state, not at all
> of the alterations of empire, and they did not even touch those things that

---

[5] Reginald Pole regarded Machiavelli's teaching as the *mysterium iniquitatis* that had been
at work in the world since biblical times, but that had taken literary form only in *Il
Principe*. See Chapter 1, this volume.
[6] P. 58. See G. Cardascia, "Machiavel et Jean Bodin," *Bibliothèque d'Humanisme et Renaissance* III (1943), 129–67.
[7] "Post Aristotelem Polybius, Dionysius Halicarnassus, Plutarchus, Dio, Tacitus . . . multa
de Republica praeclare et graviter in historiis dispersa relinquerunt. Multa quoque Machiavellus, primus quidem ut opinor, post annos mille circiter ac ducentos, quam bar-
baries omnia cumularat, de Republica scripsit."

Aristotle called the *sophismata* or *kruphia* and Tacitus called the *arcana imperii*. (p. 178)[8]

The equation between the Aristotelian sophismata, the Tacitean arcana and, by implication, the tricks of state of Machiavelli, about which those who came after him were silent, is something of an afterthought in the sense that Bodin had been discussing Aristotle and Tacitus more generally, as writers on the wider subject *de republica*. Machiavelli resumed this tradition: He was the first person in 1,200 years to write on republics, and though several later writers took up one or another aspect of this capacious subject, they largely abandoned the ancients' interest in the best form of government (which Machiavelli had taken up in the *Discorsi*) and in the ways in which states change from one form to another (also a characteristic Machiavellian interest). Machiavelli's successors also omitted treatment of a third aspect of the ancient tradition, not mentioned before and undoubtedly suggested by the introduction of Machiavelli into the discussion: the ruses and secrets of state. Machiavelli had been cited as an author concerned with these subjects twice before in the Methodus, as we have seen, and in the later *Six livres de la république* (1576), where Bodin takes a consistently condemnatory attitude toward Machiavelli, he is again regarded as interested in the mysterious side of politics, in the "sacrez mysteres de la philosophie politique," though in the later work as one who "profaned" those mysteries.[9]

I have been at pains to show that Bodin regarded Machiavelli as a writer on the arcana, indeed as the only modern writer on that subject, because several later writers – Johannes Clapmar and Naudé – who refer to this passage in the *Methodus* do so in a way that implies that Bodin thought *no* modern treatment of the subject existed. This was not the case, but selective quotation could make it appear to be, thus clearing the field for the claim that Arnold Clapmar's *De arcanis rerumpublicarum* or Naudé's *Coups d'état* was the first book to take up the ancient mysteries of state, while at the same time avoiding the implication that full quotation of Bodin's passage would have made inescapable, namely, that in writing of the arcana one was following in the footsteps not only of Aristotle and Tacitus, but of Machiavelli. Johannes Clapmar's preface to his brother's *De arcanis*, published

---

[8] "Hunc secuti Patricius, Th. Morus, Rob. Britannus, Garimbertus, multa graviter et copiose, de serendis moribus, de sanandis populis, de principe instituendo, de legibus stabiliendis. Leviter tamen de statu, nihil de conversionibus imperiorum, et ea quae Aristoteles principum sophísmata seu kruphía, Tacitus imperii arcana vocat, ne attigerunt quidem."

[9] Jean Bodin, *Six livres de la république* (Paris, 1576), preface, Sig. Ailiv.

posthumously in 1605, does exactly this. Clapmar tells us that his brother left many treatises in manuscript form at his early death at the age of thirty, and that of these it was decided to publish the *De arcanis* first, because of the novelty of the subject. He cites Bodin as if the latter had said that no one else had ever written on the arcana.[10] Naudé does exactly the same thing. After dismissing Clapmar's book on the arcana for the timidity of its treatment of the subject, he cites chapter 6 of Bodin's *Methodus* and, like Johannes Clapmar, changes the subject of Bodin's sentence from that list of Machiavelli's successors to the vaguer "multi," making Bodin agree with Naudé's view that no adequate treatment of political arcana had yet been written.[11] It is less clear whether Arnold Clapmar's own sense of the novelty of his project derives from Bodin: One passage in the text may echo the Bodin passage on the dearth of writing on the arcana,[12] but there is no direct quotation.

The *Sphaera civitatis* (Oxford, 1588) of John Case, the Oxford Aristotelian, also consistently uses the term arcana for those aspects of Machiavelli's teaching that most resembled the sophismata of Aristotle. As N. W. Bawcutt has shown, Case's book includes quite a sophisticated treatment of Machiavelli that draws heavily on Gentillet's *Contremachiavel* for the terms of its condemnation, but it also reveals detailed knowledge of Machiavelli's actual text, independent of Gentillet.[13] The work is a commentary on Aristotle's politics, but the attack on Machiavelli is used as a kind of framing device. The work opens with a discussion of whether there can be any "true and effective" politics without virtue, as Machiavelli, that "Florentine monster" had affirmed,[14] and ends with the image of Machiavelli as Phaethon, overreaching mortal limits of the "sphaera civitatis" and heralding, as in Pole's *Apologia,* the end of the world and the coming of Antichrist. In

---

[10] Arnoldus Clapmarius, *De arcanis rerumpublicarum libri sex* (Bremen, 1605): "Qui enim de Arcanis Rerumpublicarum ex professo scripserit scio neminem, quod ipsum Johannes Bodinus vir plurimae lectionis multi, inquit, graviter et copiose de serendis moribus . . . et ea quae Aristoteles principum seu, Tacitus Imperii arcana vocat, ne attigerunt quidem" (Sig. [a]3r).

[11] Gabriel Naudé, *Considerations politiques sur les coups d'état* ("Rome," 1639): "Et d'autant que cette matiere est si nouvelle, et relevée par dessus le commun sentiment des Politiques, qu'elle n'a presque encore esté effleurée par aucun d'eux, comme l'a remarque Bodin au sixieme de sa Methode en ces mots: multi multa graviter et copiose . . ." (pp. 28–9).

[12] "Etenim absque Aristotele et Tacito esset, nihil, vel parum, de Imperiorum arcanis posteritate constaret" (p. 50).

[13] "Some Elizabethan allusions to Machiavelli," *English Miscellany* XX (1969), 64.

[14] "Machiavellus Florentinum illud monstrum affirmat esse: Socrates, Plato, Arist. omnesque et singuli, qui vere philosophantur, negant" (p. 1).

addition, the body of the book contains numerous asides contrasting the sound doctrine of Aristotle with its perverse Machiavellian counterpart.

The term arcana is used by Case as a Latin equivalent of sophismata, a term that appears several times in Aristotle's *Politics* (e.g., 1297a35 [= IV:13] and 1308a2 [= V:8]). It refers to institutional arrangements that seem to offer political rights or power to those outside the ruling group without actually doing so, as, for example, in oligarchies where the common people are *permitted* to bear arms and to participate in assemblies but the nobles are *required* to do so. Such practices have the effect of disenfranchising the group whose participation is optional, while at the same time allowing them to feel that they have had a choice in the matter. Such methods, called "reipublicae mysteria et arcana" (p. 387),[15] are legitimate and do not constitute a defrauding of good citizens so much as "a certain concealment of the mysteries" ("occultatio quaedam mysteriorum"; p. 388), which is permissible when practiced with an eye to avoiding the downfall of the state or for the purpose of healing the wounds of the city. The sophismata are like the deft hands of the skilled physician, and the magistrate will employ such "subtle art" when needed to restore the republic to health.

But the arcana have debased forms, too, and these are associated with the "archsophist" Machiavelli, who behaved more like a black magician than a philosopher and used the arcana to delude the people and change good forms of government into bad ones. Such strategies, according to Case, ought to have a different name (though he himself continues to use the term arcana for both the good and bad varieties).[16] In the section devoted to Aristotle's discussion of tyranny in *Politics* V, Machiavelli is again the touchstone by which one may draw a distinction between a benign and a malignant treatment of the *arcana tyrannica*.[17] Aristotle is praised as a revealer of tyrants' methods (as

[15] "Res quinque (ut hic docet Philosophus) quibus in politia nobiles et opulenti viri, callide decipiunt populum, nimirum concio, magistratus, iudicium, arma et exercitatio, rei militaris; haec reipub. mysteria et arcana discuntur, in quibus vis magna rectae administrationis latet" (p. 387).

[16] "Facessat hinc longe archisophista ille Machiavellus, qui verba et sensum Aristotelis pervertit: Haec enim in monstris rerumpublicarum nutriendis sophismata non permittuntur Politici enim non sunt, ut magici, qui falsis caracteribus effascinatos animos multitudinis perstringunt, sed ut philosophi, qui mysteria suae artis cuius non referant et aperiunt. Si ergo in malis civitatis formis conservandis haec adhibeantur arcana, non stratagemata, sed consilia haberi ac nominari debent" (p. 389).

[17] "Aliud Machiavellus, aliud Aristoteles sibi proposuit, ille enim ad monarchiam, hic ad tyrannidem has causas retulit: quippe Philosophus admodum sapienter arcana tyrannorum hoc modo retexit, at Machiavellus istas vitae et administrationis labes tanquam leges in regno et rege posuit" (p. 504).

Gentili had praised Machiavelli himself!), whereas Machiavelli is condemned for recommending these techniques.

Case was heavily influenced by Gentillet in his attack on Machiavelli, and many of his themes – the poison of Machiavelli, the danger of vernacular versions of *Il Principe* becoming widely available, the *translatio* of Machiavellian ideas from Italy to France (pp. 1–4, 741–2) – are directly traceable to Gentillet or to the Latin epistle of the 1577 Latin version of the *Contremachiavel*.[18] As we have seen, the notion of Machiavellism as a kind of secret, wicked art goes back to Pole. But the specific terminology by which the sophismata of Aristotle are equated with the *arcana rerumplicarum,* and the fact that Machiavelli is thought of as a student of these (albeit in a perverse and debased form), may indicate that Case was developing Bodin's insight into the relation between Machiavelli and the ancients. At any rate, the two authors share a series of terminological equations that was to prove central to the way Machiavelli's works would be thought of in the course of the following century.

It is worthy of note that before Bodin, the normal Latin translation of the word sophismata was not arcana, but rather *machinamenta, callida consilia,* or *callida artificia* (see *Politica* [Rome, 1492], p. 117v; [Basel, 1582], p. 381). In both Case and Bodin, the sophismata are equated with the arcana, and the arcana, in turn, are associated with Machiavelli. That a single term covers Aristotelian as well as Machiavellian stratagems is significant, and the particular term chosen is crucial, for arcana, unlike its near synonyms in Latin, suggests not only secrecy but tradition. Machiavelli had surely written of the tricks, the artifices, and the plots that Aristotle referred to by the term *sophismata;* to call these techniques the arcana of politics was to suggest that they belonged to a mysterious and ancient body of knowledge.

In the year after Case's book appeared, Giovanni Botero initiated the school – or at least the fashion – of reason of state, the general relation of which to Machiavelli has been mentioned. In 1592, Frachetta's *L'Idea* systematized the notion, implicit in Botero, that there was a bad and a good reason of state, and connected Machiavelli with the bad variety (p. 45), a connection that was all but inevitable, and was widely echoed by other writers.

Another early treatise in the reason of state tradition, the *Discorsi sopra Cornelio Tacito* of Scipione Ammirato (Florence, 1594), explicitly con-

---

[18] On the importance of this preface, see Antonio D'Andrea, "Machiavelli, Satan and the Gospel," *Yearbook of Italian Studies* I (1971), 156–77, and Innocent Gentillet, *Discours contre Machiavel,* ed. Antonio D'Andrea and Pamela Stewart (Florence, 1974), p. lxiv.

nects the term reason of state with the arcana, and is especially significant because Arnold Clapmar borrowed from Ammirato a number
of his key ideas – not only this equation of terms but the concept of
reason of state as a "derogation" from other kinds of reason, justified
by the public good, and various aspects of Ammirato's discussion of
Machiavelli.[19]

Ammirato's definition of reason of state depends upon the idea
that each form of reason or law is corrected or completed by another
that seems to contravene it. Natural law is abrogated by civil law, civil
law by the "law" of war (pp. 230–1). In a similar way, reason of state
is a "contravention of ordinary reason in favor of the public benefit,
or in favor of greater or more universal reason" (p. 238). In some
ways, reason of state is like the *privilegia* of Roman law: As privilege
is an exception to civil law for the benefit of an individual, so reason
of state corrects ordinary law for the benefit of many (p. 238). Examples of such "correction" include the rape of the Sabine women,
necessary to the founding of Rome, and Moses' institution of the privilege of asylum, which was a derogation from his own code in the
interest of the public good.

But despite the wide latitude such a principle offers in the choice
of means to be used in the pursuit of the public good, reason of state
has its "termini e confini," and anyone who exceeds them must be
considered a tyrant. "Divine reason" always takes precedence over
reason of state (p. 232), and when a conflict arises between religion
and reason of state, "reason of state must be accommodated to religion,
and not religion to reason of state" (p. 237).[20] According to Ammirato,
reason of state, so conceived, was discussed by Tacitus under the term
arcanum and its abuse or excess under the term *flagitium*.[21] Reason of
state is the reverse of the doctrine that the prince should follow his
own interest: In fact, when the public good and the good of the prince
conflict, the prince ought to subordinate himself to the people, even
sacrificing his life for them, if necessary, as the Emperor Otto offered
to do (p. 241). In a passage that was to influence later ideas of reason

[19] The relationship between Ammirato and Clapmar was pointed out by De Mattei, *Il
pensiero politico di Scipione Ammirato* (Lecce, 1959), pp. 111, 135, 149–50.
[20] "Bisogna accomodar la ragion di stato alla religione, e non la religione alla ragion
di stato."
[21] "Ragione di stato, per conseguente, altro non sara che ragione di dominio, di signoria,
di regno, d'imperio, o d'altro. Onde fù poi questa per avventura da Tacito chiamato
arcano d'imperio, o arcano di signoria, cioè certe profonde, e intime, e segrete leggi o
privilegi fatti a contemplazione della sicurezza di quel'imperio over signoria: si come
volle scuoprire la cattiva ragione di stato, quando disse cuncta eius dominationis flagitia"
(p. 240).

of state as self-sacrifice,[22] Ammirato even finds precedent for his extreme emphasis upon the public good in the sacrifice of Christ.[23] Machiavelli is never mentioned by name in the *Discorsi* of Ammirato, but his works are discussed in many passages. Machiavelli is always referred to by a vague pronoun ("altri," "alcuno," etc.), even when an exact citation of his work is provided in the margin. As De Mattei has shown, circumlocutions like these were common at the time, but despite them, Ammirato's engagement with Machiavellian issues is serious and scholarly.[24]

Like Machiavelli, Ammirato accepts the necessity for deception in political life (V:1), and we have seen how the necessities of the public good may lead, in Ammirato's recasting of the doctrine of reason of state, to derogation of the moral law, as they do in Machiavelli. Most of Ammirato's specific disagreements with Machiavelli have to do with the extent to which such necessities dominate political life: We often find him arguing against Machiavelli's various demonstrations that immoral methods are effective as a general rule. For example, Ammirato holds that new cities are not safer for destroying their neighbors, that a new prince is not more secure for employing harsh methods, and that the way to rise from a low to a high fortune is not through fraud but through virtue.[25] One of Ammirato's main points of difference with Machiavelli as a historian concerns the alleged abuse of religion by the Romans, which Ammirato denies, both as a historical fact and as a model for imitation by Christians (Ammirato, *Discorsi*, pp. 51ff, 185). He denies that the Romans habitually manipulated the auspices, "as it seems that a certain person ['alcuno,' i.e., Machiavelli; cf. *Disc.* I:14] has tried to prove, showing that the Romans used them for their needs, interpreting, distorting, and accommodating them as their convenience required, and, in a certain sense, teaching us to do the same" (p. 185).[26] In the section on reason of state itself, Machiavelli is not mentioned even by circumlocution. De Mattei regards this piece

---

[22] See the discussion of Clapmar, Naudé, Mirandola, Senault, and Machon in chapters 5 and 6, this volume.
[23] "Fù consiglio della santissima Trinità, che l'innocentissimo agnello di Dio volantariamente portasse sopra la sua persona tutti i falli de peccatori per salvezza del genere humano. La qual verità se a me non sarà creduta, credasi allo Spirito santo, dal cui fiato benche per mezzo di lingua peccatrice fù pronunziata quella veracissima e nobil sentenza, che era cose utile, che uno morisse per tutto il popolo" (p. 242).
[24] See especially De Mattei, *Ammirato*, p. 55.
[25] Ibid., pp. 58–64.
[26] "Come par che voglia provar alcuno, mostrando che i Romani se ne servissero per i loro bisogni, interpretandola, tirandola, e accomodandola secondo metteva lor commodo, e in un certo modo insegnandoci che il medesimo far noi."

of negative evidence as an indication of respect.[27] This was the place
where nearly all other anti-Machiavellians made sure to execrate Machiavelli and to dissociate themselves explicitly from the bad variety
of reason of state that Machiavelli stood for. In insisting on limits to
the principle of reason of state, and especially in his belief that religion
should never be accommodated to it, this chapter of Ammirato's *Discorsi* is consistent with his major objections to Machiavelli, as explored
elsewhere in the text: His paired terms (*ragion di stato/cattiva ragion di
stato; arcano d'imperio/flagitia*) arise in a context closely related to the
project of correcting Machiavelli, both in his own book and in the
reason of state literature just preceding him (Botero and Frachetta),
and his imitator Clapmar was to use the arcanum/flagitium distinction
with specific reference to Machiavelli. But Ammirato himself does not
make this application.

Ammirato's principal reason for equating *ragion di stato* with the
arcana imperii differs somewhat from Bodin's interest in lapsed ancient
traditions or Case's deft use of arcana as a term that permits vivid
contrast between Aristotle the philosopher and Machiavelli the pres-
tidigitator or "Merlin" of political theory. Ammirato is writing a commentary on Tacitus, in whose work the term frequently appears, and
is concerned, inevitably, with the relevance of Tacitus to the contemporary debate over reason of state. Because of this focus, Ammirato
does not exploit the cultic or mystical associations of the terminology.
There may be a trace of such an association in his moving from reason
of state as contravention of law to reason of state as the self-sacrifice
of the ruler in imitation of the "consiglio" of the Trinity, whereby one
man had to die for the people, but by and large, the term arcana and
a quasireligious "mystery of kings" have no close association in the
Discorsi sopra Cornelio Tacito.

Arnold Clapmar and the *De arcanis rerumpublicarum*

Arnold Clapmar is the central figure in any study of the literature
concerned with the *arcana imperiorum,* for though Bodin, Case, and
Ammirato had produced an association of terms in which ancient notions of the arcana of state were considered in relation to Machiavelli
and/or reason of state, Clapmar was the first to write an entire treatise
developing this terminology; moreover, he was widely imitated and
may be thought of as having founded a school or tradition. Clapmar
was an extraordinary youthful prodigy. Born in Bremen in 1574, he

---

[27] De Mattei, *Ammirato*, p. 82; cf. p. 56.

studied at the universities of Helmstedt, Heidelberg, and Marburg, traveled throughout Germany, the Low Countries, and England, and by the age of twenty-six (1600) was appointed professor of politics and history at the University of Altdorf. His early death came only four years later, in 1604, and he left behind an extraordinary number of finished and unfinished works on political and legal subjects.[28] In the preface to the *De arcanis*, his brother tells us of a "Tractatus de iure sacro, commentarius de publicis iudiciis, libellus de vectigalibus, libri quattuor de iure publico, libri tres de foederibus, liber de magistratu, notae in politicam Aristotelis, commentarius in C. Cornelium Tacitum," and other works. In addition to these, Clapmar had written a treatise on education, the *Nobilis adolescentis triennium* (published in 1611), a "Miscellanea politica," and had contributed a disputation on Tacitus to the composite volume *Conclusiones de iure publico* (published in 1602).[29] This last work anticipates many of the central motifs of the *De arcanis* and appears to be a preliminary study for it. It is far briefer and is conceived more strictly as a commentary on Tacitus, but, like the later work, is centrally concerned with *arcana imperii*. The full-scale work on the arcana was selected by Johann Clapmar for publication out of all the manuscripts Arnold had left – "not so much on account of the dignity of the subject, which is yet not slight, as for the novelty of the material."[30] Johann quotes Bodin's remarks on the scarcity of writing on the arcana, changing, as has been noted, Bodin's sentence so that it seems to say that no one had touched the subject since ancient times, and ignoring Bodin's naming Machiavelli as the modern reviver of the tradition. In addition, the volume was published with a quotation from Lipsius's letters emphasizing the audacity of such an enterprise:

Who is he that is so bold or so stiffnecked as to dare to write a history that is true in all details? Who would wish to make public the *kruphia* of kings, or, as our Tacitus calls them, the *arcana imperii*?[31]

---

[28] For Clapmar's life, see S. J. Apinus, *Vitae professorum philosophiae qui a condita academia altorfina ad hunc usque diem claruerunt* (Nuremberg and Altdorf, 1728; bound with G. G. Zeltner, *Vitae theologorum altorphinorum*, 1722), pp. 100–4, and Hermann Hegels, *Arnold Clapmarius und die Publizistik über die arcana imperii im 17. Jahrhundert* (Bonn, 1918), pp. 17–23.

[29] See Hegels, *Arnold Clapmarius*, pp. 25–6, 67.

[30] "Non tam dignitate rei, quae tamen non exigua est, quam novitate materiae" (Sig. [a]3r).

[31] "Quis ille tam confidens, aut tantis cervicibus, qui audeat Historiam usquequaque veram scribere? Quis regum illa *kruphia* & ut Tacitus noster appellat Arcana Imperii prodi vult?" (title page).
    Cf. *Iusti Lipsii epistolicarum quaestionum libri V* (Antwerp, 1577), p. 205 (Lipsius to Petrus Divaeus).

The commendatory verses by Michael Piccartus and "JGHA" also present Clapmar as the heroic uncoverer of secrets hidden in shadows, "shut off, for so many years, from so many peoples."[32]

Actually, the book is a far tamer performance than all this suggests: The "secrets," such as they are, had often been treated by Machiavelli and the writers in the reason of state tradition, and the terminology employed in classifying these secrets is adapted from Aristotle and Tacitus, following hints laid down by Bodin and, especially, Ammirato. There are, furthermore, none of the special insights brought to the subject of secrets of rule by men of practical and contemporary experience, like Machiavelli or Guicciardini. Nevertheless, even before one gets to the first word of the treatise, the power of the myth of the *arcana imperii* is evident: The scholarly commentator on Aristotle and Tacitus has become a heroic quester in search of hidden wisdom. The discovery of arcana previously unknown, or the recovery of secrets known only to the ancients and later forgotten, is of course a commonly encountered motif in Renaissance literature in many fields. By recasting the central concerns of the reason of state tradition (especially the interest of that tradition in politics as false consciousness, as illusion making, and as morally problematic) in terms that evoke this Renaissance theme of secret knowledge, Clapmar brings into play a range of associations different from those of the reason of state terminology: The sacral character of political knowledge, the analogy between political men and priestly or hermetic elites, and the justification of apparent immorality in politics by analogy with the moral privilege or exemption of such elites – all these connections are suggested far more by the vocabulary of arcana than by that of reason of state. And, perhaps most importantly, when the reason of state doctrines are translated into such a vocabulary, they become more available for use by theorists of absolutism and divine right kingship. Though Clapmar himself does not use his terminological innovations to this end, he prepares the field for theorists like Naudé and Louis Machon, in whom the claims of the sacred French monarchy and the politics of Machiavelli are thoroughly fused in the concept of mystery of state.

The word *arcanum* was derived by Festus, Clapmar tells us, from *arx*, a place where sacrifices to be withheld (*arcenda*) from common view were performed; or from *arca* (also ultimately from *arcere*, to shut up or prohibit access to), meaning chest or strongbox, a word

[32] "JGHA" compares Clapmar's disclosure of the *arcana* to the discovery of medical secrets. Michael Piccartus's verses depict Clapmar as a hero, bringing the *arcana imperiorum* out of the darkness in which they had been concealed for centuries.

that had religious connotations in Christian usage on account of its use in the Vulgate for the Ark of the Covenant.[33] Clapmar reminds his readers of other sacral uses of the word as well: the "arcana sacra" of Tacitus and the arcana or mysteries of Venus and of Ceres in Horace. Thus it is in the general sense of secrets or mysteries that Clapmar introduces the word. All human sciences have some analog to the secret mysteries of religious cults: There are secrets of theology, of jurisprudence, tricks of perspective in the visual arts, military and domestic arcana, medical secrets and deceptions, mathematical fictions, and rhetorical ones (p. 4). One moves from sacred rites to tricks of the trades. Like other fields of human endeavor, politics has strategies that must be kept hidden in order to work:

I define *arcana rerumpublicarum* as the private or hidden procedures or counsels of those who would obtain power in a state, sometimes for the purpose of maintaining its tranquility, sometimes for conserving the present form of its government, for the public good. They would be those things by which, as Velleius says in his second book, "one thing is said and another is understood," or, as Servius says in *De dolo,* "one thing is done, and another thing is simulated." (p. 9)[34]

Clapmar's sense of the term arcana comprises the full range of meanings associated with the word by Festus: Arcana are both secret practices and means of protection or defense.[35] Clapmar will presently draw up a series of distinctions between the arcana proper; the *iura imperii,* or general principles, of which the arcana are the instruments; the flagitia, which are the political excesses similar to the arcana, except that they cannot be justified morally; and the *simulacra imperii,* or the creation of illusions of power. These refinements upon the terminology are not employed with complete consistency in the book, and at this point in the text the word arcanum has a broad meaning, re-

---

[33] Compare Pole's association of *arcanum imperii* and *arx:* "Et ideo arcanum illud imperii tuendi cum omni securitate, atque felicitate, ad leonis violentiam, et vulpis dolos transfert, in quorum custodia, tanquam in arce munitissima, contra omnes fortunae casus illum suum Principem relinquit" (*Apologia,* p. 140).

[34] "Arcana rerumpublicarum sic definio; esse intimas et occultas rationes, sive consilia eorum qui in Republica principatum obtinent, tum ipsorum tranquillitatis tum etiam praesentis Reipublicae status conservandi, idque boni publici causa et fere sunt talia quibus, ut ait Velleius liber 2. Aliud dicitur, aliud intelligitur, sive ut de dolo scribit Servius aliud agitur, aliud simulatur agi."

[35] "Dico esse occulta consilia, et sunt certe duseximeta, tum quod ea vulgus non facile perspicit: quod enim de sacris Poetae, odi profanum vulgus et arceo, nos non immerito de arcanis usurpemus, tu etiam quod plerumque; clanculum iis imponunt, qui praesentem in civitate statum videntur odisse. Porro finis eorum duplex est: salus et diuturnitatis praesentis Reipublicae: hoc est ne in aliam formam mutet; et eorum securitas qui imperant" (pp. 9–10).

ferring to the general issue of hidden and deceptive methods. Since arcana are practiced by a ruling group on others, Clapmar divides them into six kinds, corresponding to Aristotle's three kinds of polity: There are arcana by which kings protect themselves from aristocrats or from the populace; others by which aristocratic regimes protect themselves from the other two potential forms of government; and so on. In addition, there are the *arcana imperii* properly so called, which aim at the preservation of a particular form of government – royal, aristocratic, or democratic – and the *arcana dominationis,* which have as their aim the maintenance in power of a particular regime or administration.

The problem of the morality of such methods arises at once. Arcana are a kind of deception, yet they are, Clapmar insists, "an honest simulation, a licit simulation."[36] The Roman legal principles of private contracts, as well as the Bible itself, provide precedent for political deceptions in the public interest: Clapmar cites the instance of Saul's pretending not to hear insults in I Samuel 10 and the verse in Wisdom 11 in which God is said to "overlook men's sins that they may repent" (v. 23). When the argument from divine example is used, as here, to justify political deception or other tactics in conflict with morality, it becomes necessary, if the imputation of evil to the divine nature is to be avoided, to set limits, and to distinguish licit and illicit forms of deception, as Clapmar goes on to do:

But certainly there are limits to these arts, which may not be transgressed with impunity, as faith, honesty, virtue; and he who forgets these no longer merits the name of a prudent man or a politician, but rather that of a wicked, cunning and nefarious one.[37]

Applying such limits, however, is no simple matter, for there are cases in which the same actions would have to be condemned if performed by a private individual and approved if used in politics, actions fraudulent in themselves but "tolerated for the sake of the public good and the state of the commonwealth."

---

[36] "Ceterum simulatio quaedam sunt arcana Rerumpublicarum quae veluti glaucoma obducitur civibus, ut illud quod non habent, tamen se habere putent, qua re freti praesentem Reipublicae statum ne turbent . . . Sed est simulatio honesta, sed licita: quae si in privatis contractibus locum habet veluti Labeo dicit in d. L. I De dolo malo: posse sine dolo malo aliud agi aliud simulari. Quanto magis in publicis negotiis, quorum maius momentum est, maiorque dignitas" (pp. 10–11).

[37] "At enimvero sunt limites huius artis, quos egredi impune non licet, ut sunt fides, honestas, virtus: quorum qui obliviscitur, non amplius prudentis aut politici nomen meretur, sed vafri, astuti ac nefarii hominis" (p. 13).

If part of the justification for these acts derives from biblical example and part from the classical idea of the public good, part, too, derives from the Roman idea of majesty, which is the basis for what Clapmar calls the *iura imperii* or *iura maiestatis*. The *ius imperii* is the absolute power over all matters that pertain to the "majesty" or sovereignty of a state and includes the right to create magistracies, the power over life and death, the regulation of religious institutions, the power to conduct diplomacy, make war, coin money, levy taxes, and so on. Underlying all these activities is the principle that the ruling power in a state makes law and does not receive it, that it is, in the well-known phrase of the Digest, *legibus solutus* (pp. 23ff.). In the Civil Law, of course, this freedom from law was offset by other principles: The prince was *legibus solutus;* his will had the force of law ("quod principi placuit legem habet vigorem"). But there were countervailing texts as well. The ultimate source of law was the people, who had invested their sovereignty in the emperor, and, as the "digna vox" text asserted, though in some sense free of the laws, the good ruler would voluntarily follow them.[38] The Christian prince had, in addition, to qualify his theoretical freedom with the responsibilities he had as *imago* and vicegerent of God. So, although Clapmar cites the passages in the civil law and in Plato and Plutarch that place the ruler above the laws or make of him a "living law," he also respects the principle of obedience to God ("for he gives laws, and does not receive them *except from the highest God*"; p. 26, emphasis added),[39] and points out that true majesty lies in submission to law and is sanctioned by analogy to a God who, although superior to all law, nevertheless kept his covenants faithfully (p. 27).

Nevertheless, the *legibus solutus* principle is used here to justify the deceptive practices of the new politics, for the *legibus solutus* is the basic principle of the *iura imperii* (p. 23), and the *iura imperii* justify the use of the arcana. The relation between the *iura* and the arcana is that, in Clapmar's simile, between a citadel and its outer walls, between the rights and privileges of rulers in maintaining the state and the particular strategies employed to implement and protect these

---

[38] See *Institutes* I. ii.6: "Quod principi placuit, legis habet vigorem, cum lege regia quae de imperio eius lata est, populus ei et in eum omne suum imperium et potestatem concessit. (*Corpus Iuris Civilis*, ed. Paul Krueger and Theodor Mommsen" [Berlin, 1954–9]).

Cf. *Digest* I.iv.1 and *Code* I.xiv.4: "Digna vox maiestate regnantis legibus alligatum se principem profiteri: adeo de auctoritate iuris nostra pendet auctoritas. et re vera maius imperio est submittere legibus principatum."

[39] "Is enim leges dat non accipere, nisi a summo Deo."

rights. For example, one "law of majesty" is that no one must take up arms without the consent of the prince. The corresponding *arcanum imperii* is the devising of means whereby the plebs will be content ("contenta plebs et quasi fascinata") with this arrangement. If the right of assembly pertains to the *ius imperii,* the corresponding arcanum is the deception permitted ("licita aliqua fraude") in order to keep those outside the ruling group happy in their exclusion from assembly:

For, as the *imperium* is like an ark or citadel, so the *arcana imperii* are like walls or ramparts which protect this ark from the assaults of the factious.[40]

The *iura imperii* are invariant: They are the defining characteristics or marks of sovereignty, whereas the arcana vary with the form of government and with the particular circumstances. Clapmar defines the *arcana imperii* as "hidden counsels or contrivance for the conserving of the present state in which one thing is done, and another is simulated" (pp. 65–6).[41] Like Case, Clapmar draws his list of *arcana aristocratica* and *democratica* from Aristotle's *Politics* IV:13, equating the arcana with the sophismata, those deceptively disenfranchising privileges allowed the plebs by aristocratic governments and vice versa: The right to stay away from assembly, to refuse office, to remain unarmed – all these are perfect examples of arcana because they appear to offer freedoms to those outside the ruling class while protecting the class in power. In addition, a crucially important arcanum of aristocracy is, for Clapmar, the manipulation of religion, especially, as in the Roman examples Clapmar takes from Livy, the use of the auguries to strengthen the aristocratic constitution.

Clapmar agreed with Bodin that very little had actually been written on the arcana.[42] What enabled Clapmar to write a rather large book about them, based primarily upon the ancient sources that contained so little material on this subject, was his oscillation between a broad and a strict definition of the term. The title of the book, and the interest the author takes in all forms of political deception ("aliud agitur, aliud simulatur agi") correspond to the loose sense in which the arcana are commonly understood. But in the strict sense, *arcana imperii* or *rerumpublicarum* refer only to these apparent grantings of power or freedom, aimed at preserving the present form of government; of these the

---

[40] "Ius enim imperii est instar arcis vel palatii, arcana vero imperii sunt veluti muni ac propugnacula sive cuniculi qui hanc arcem a factiosiorum iniuriis defendunt" (p. 18).
[41] "Machinationem sive occulta consilia conservandae praesentis Reipublicae quibus aliud agitur, aliud simulatur agi."
[42] "Etenim absque Aristotele et Tacito esset, nihil, vel parum, de Imperiorum arcanis posteritate constaret" (p. 50).

ancients had spoken comparatively little, and the section of Clapmar's book devoted to them is small, despite his title. Of the *arcana imperii*, the *arcana regia* are the rarest of all. In Aristotle there is almost nothing. The sophismata and antisophismata of Book IV are aristocratic and democratic, and there is no explicit treatment of analogous devices used by kings. Something on the subject may be gleaned from the treatment of tyranny in Book V of the *Politics*, and there is a little in Ammianus Marcellinus, but, apart from Tacitus, the royal arcana remain for the most part in obscurity (pp. 49, 50, 77), so that in dealing with them Clapmar claims a special freedom of interpretation, deriving from other authors certain things at which they had merely hinted.[43] Even with this interpretative license, however, the list of *arcana regia* is short: It includes the devising of titles to occupied territories, *akkismos* or feigned unwillingness to serve as ruler (one thinks of Shakespeare's Richard III), the corruption of the plebs by offering them ease, the establishment of the succession, and so on. Closely related to the *arcana imperiorum* are the *arcana dominationis*. These are directed not at preserving the form of government but at keeping a particular administration in power, and they too have three subdivisions, corresponding to Aristotle's tripartite distinction among kinds of politics. There are *arcana dominationis regia, aristocratica*, and *democratica. Dominatio*, or the keeping in power of a particular regime, is never far removed from injustice. Clapmar associates the term with vernacular equivalents – *signoría, herrschaft, altesse* – and defines it in a way that reveals a close similarity to Machiavelli's interest in new regimes with their problematic moral foundations. It is "that greatest force of ruling, and properly pertains to those who newly, by force or right of law, or, as Pomponius terms it, by royal hand occupy or hold an *imperium*" (p. 100).[44] There is some confusion in the use of the term, for it refers to the keeping of power by any regime but also designates a particular style of rule, midway between tyranny and laxity, a *legitimum imperium sed paulo violentius*, and this style of rule is especially necessary in a newly occupied state ·or in one full of seditious or violent subjects (pp. 100–2). States of this kind were the special subject of Machiavelli's *Principe*, and in fact Clapmar cites Machiavelli several times in this section (pp. 97–151) on the use of fortifications (p. 114; cf. *Prin.* 20) and on the necessity of taking up residence in a new possession (p. 131; cf. *Prin.* 3).

[43] "Quaedam etiam ex Scriptoribus aliis excerpsero; quae latent, et vix ab ipsis autoribus exprimuntur" (p. 77).
[44] "Summa illa vis imperandi proprieque competit iis qui noviter, vi et iure belli, sive, ut Pomponius loquitur, manu regia imperium occupant vel tenent."

The most significant indications of Clapmar's relation to Machiavelli, however, are reserved for the following section on the *iura* rather than the arcana of domination.

It is not easy to separate the *arcana imperii* from the arcana of domination for the simple reason that what serves to keep a regime in power also helps maintain the form of polity that the regime represents and, to a certain extent, vice versa. Restrictions on publishing state records fall into this category, as do limitations on the building or destruction of walls, on private building at too sumptuous a level, on the use of flags and insignia, on the worship of effigies other than those of the prince, mention of possible heirs while the prince lives, and divination or the casting of horoscopes concerning matters of state or the health of the ruler. Laws forbidding the killing of any prince, even of a hostile state, are also *arcana dominationis*. These are all derived from Roman imperial practice and have aristocratic and democratic analogs. The Lex Portia forbade the killing of a Roman citizen; the tribunes were sacrosanct and had the power to arrest those who threatened popular liberty; and so on. The most powerful *arcanum dominationis* of all is the deification of the ruler. The Persian kings had themselves worshipped as gods, the Roman emperors used divine titles, and even the Christian ones called themselves "eternal, holy, divine" (p. 124); though Clapmar disapproves of this practice, and refers to Ammianus's mockery of it, it has its place among the *arcana dominationis*.

Up to this point in the treatise, Clapmar has been concerned with political methods that involve deception, manipulation, and question- able morality – that is, with the kinds of issues current in the reason of state literature. His most direct recognition of the relation of his own work to this school is found in the section on the *iura dominationis*, which must be considered here in some detail, as it is both the the- oretical core of the *De arcanis* and the place where Clapmar's debt to Ammirato's formulation of the doctrine of reason of state is most clearly revealed. Clapmar's treatment of the *iura dominationis* is closely modeled on Ammirato's chapter "Della ragion di stato" (pp. 228–42), often quoting from it but not giving explicit credit, though, as we shall see, Ammirato is explicitly cited in many other places in the *De arcanis*.

Ammirato's concept of reason of state was, as we have seen, based on the notion that various kinds of law or reason are corrected by others. Clapmar borrows this essential idea of derogation for his own explanation of the *iura dominationis*, as a comparison of the two texts shows.[45] Ammirato had equated reason of state with Tacitus's *arcana imperii;* Clapmar adapts the passage where he does so, replacing the arcana with the *iura dominationis.*[46] It would seem that although Clapmar obviously knows Ammirato's equation of the *arcana imperii* with reason of state, and sometimes borrows word for word from Ammirato's discussion of this relationship, he finally rejects Ammirato in favor of his own association of reason of state and *iura dominationis.* This is only partly true, for we must remember that the iura, flagitia, and simulacra are all, in the larger and looser sense, the sense in which Clapmar's title understands the term, arcana. Thus, one finds that the *iura dominationis* are defined here as exceptions to the laws ("quae a regulis Iuris communis recedunt, legibusque derogant"), echoing Clapmar's notion of reason of state as *deroga.* But similar language is used in the opening sentences of the *De arcanis* in reference to the subject matter of the book as a whole.[47] Clapmar also follows Ammirato closely in his formal definition of *iura dominationis,* in his comparison between this principle and the closely related idea of privilege, and in his insistence that the principle of the public good takes precedence not only over the ordinary restrictions of law but over the personal interest of the ruler.[48] Clapmar, like Ammirato, uses the Emperor

[45] "Vedesi dunque e la natural ragione dalla civile, e la civile dalla militare, e la militare dalla ragion delle gente essere in certo modo stata coretta . . . Dichiarate queste quattro ragioni, bisogna vedere che cosa e ragione di stato, e se ella, come la civile, e una cosa che distrugga verbigrazia in parte la naturale e in parte sia distrutto alla ragion di guerra" (p. 230).
   "Sicut igitur ius naturae corrigitur a iure gentium, ius gentium a iure militare, ius militari a iure legationis, ius legationis a iure civili: ita hoc ius civile iterum corrigitur, sibique veluti fraenum iniici patitur, a iure quod apello Regni sive dominationis" (p. 154).
[46] "Ragione di stato per consequente altro non sara che ragione di dominio, di signoria, di regno, d'imperio, o d'altro. Onde fù poi questa per avventura da Tacito chiamata arcano d'imperio, o arcano di signoria, cioe certe profonde, e intime, e segrete leggi o privilegi fatti a contemplazione della sicurezza di quell 'imperio over signoria" (p. 240).
   "Quod ius dominationis varie appellatur . . . Itali, Ragione di dominio di signoria, di regno d'imperio, et omnium elegantissime, ragionamente di stato" (p. 155).
[47] "Quae causa est propter quam nonnumquam quibusdam institutis opus est, quae et iuri communi derogant, et speciemquandam iniquitatis repraesentant, ad quam tamen connivendum est boni publici causa." (p. 2)
[48] "Concludiamo dunque ragione di stato essere una contravenzione di ragion ordinaria per rispetto di maggiore e più universale ragione, o veramente per esser meglio intesi diremo, ragione di stato esser una cosa opposta al privilegio; che si come il privilegio coregge la legge ordinaria in beneficio d'alcuno: onde si può dire il privilegio esser trapassamento di ragion civile in beneficio di particolari, cosi la ragion di stato coregge la legge ordinaria in beneficio di molti" (p. 238).
   "E che necessario e verissimo sia, che s'habbia sempre in essa ragione di stato a con-

Otto as an example of a prince willing to sacrifice even his life for the public good (*De arcanis*, p. 156; Ammirato, *Disc.*, p. 241) and follows Ammirato in that extraordinary final passage of the reason of state chapter, in which reason of state is located even in the counsels of the Trinity.[49] Clapmar's expansion of this motif extends the notion that there is a kind of religious mystery attached to reason of state, for the public good may require not only that the ruler transgress ordinary law but also that he die for the people, or, even worse, take on sins for them or risk damnation for them, in a curious imitation of Christ's sacrifice and his assumption of the burden of human sin. The *iura dominationis* always have about them "some kind of iniquity," and even a good man must perform morally questionable acts for the safety of the state or the prince, because "honestas" and the "salus reipublicae" are often different (p. 158). Here, and with the notion of going to hell for one's country, Clapmar formulates the moral issue of reason of state in a more pointed way than Ammirato, in a way closer to Machiavelli's concept of necessary evil. Nevertheless, Clapmar, like Ammirato, does set limits to the *iura dominationis* beyond which one

siderar il ben publico, nè mai a distaccarlo da lei: quindi manifestamente apparisce: che quando possa avvenir caso, che il principe istesso ancor che giusto e leggitimo principe venga in qualunque immaginibil modo in concorso col bene universale, dee il principe cedere al ben publico, e non il publico bene al principe" (p. 241).

"Quare sic definio, esse supremum quoddam ius, sive privilegium, bono publico introductum, contra ius commune sive ordinarium; sed tamen a lege divina non alienum, atque est ius veluti legitimae tyrannidis: sive, ut Alciat. definit, iuris communis quaedam relaxatio, sive correctio, quod privilegium dici potest: quod quamvis ibi de privatis intellegitur, tamen huc accomodari potest. Sicut enim alias privilegia in iure civili sunt correctio legis, circa unius atque alterius commodum: ita iura dominationis sunt correctio legum circa salutem et commodum multorum: hoc est ipsius principis et civium. Addo boni publici causa, cuius tam sancta tam antiqua ratio haberi debet: cui omnia iura adeoque ipse princeps cedere debet" (p. 156).

[49] "Ma che non mi sollevo io, e a un trato non mostro a principi, quanto rettamente debbano usar la misure, che hanno in mano di questo publico bene, poi che fù consiglio della santissima Trinità, che l'innocentissimo agnello di Dio volontariamente portasse sopra la sua persona tutti i falli di peccatori per salvezza del genere humano. La qual verità se a me non sarà creduta, credasi allo Spirito Santo, dal cui fiato benche per mezzo di lingua peccatrice fu pronunciata quella veracissima e nobil sentenza, che era cosa utile, che uno morisse per tutto il popolo" (p. 242).

"Sed cur ego de mortalibus solis agam? Inspice sis, summi atque immortalis Dei actiones atque consilia, an non eadem sunt? Quid? An non filium suum unicum et incocentissimum neci dedit boni publici causa, id est, propter salutem humani generis; secundum illud Caiphae Ioann. cap. 8 *Expedit hominem mori pro populo*. De quo tamen exemplo, aliisque id genus, quod *mystikotera* sunt et supra captum humanum, reverenter et sobrie sentiendum est: quemadmodum et de illos Moisis *Dele me potius ex libro vitae et populo peccatum condona*. Quam vocem hac aetate nostra, bellicosissimus atque incomparabilis Rex protulisse fertur; se pro salute populi vel ad infernos iturum. Magna vox, dii immortalis! Neque facile ex nostro ingenio metienda, neque imitanda facile" (pp. 156–7).

may no longer speak of *iura,* but rather of crimes, injustices, or *fla-gitia.*[50]

The use of the term *flagitia* for tactics that transgress divine law derives from Ammirato, who believed that it was Tacitus's term for *cattiva ragion di stato,* just as *arcanum imperii* was the Tacitean equivalent of *buona ragion di stato* (p. 240). Clapmar's fifth book is devoted to these flagitia; there he notes their equivalence to bad reason of state ("Itali la cattiva ragione di stato," p. 200) without mentioning Ammirato. Thus Clapmar was influenced by Ammirato not only in his formulation of the concept of *ius dominationis* as an equivalent of reason of state, but in the term used for tactics that were too immoral to be justified by the doctrine of the public good. Furthermore, Clapmar explicitly associates the flagitia with Machiavelli, offering *consilia Machiavellistica* as another synonym for flagitia (p. 200). That is, he follows the reason of state tradition both in distinguishing a good from a bad reason of state and in associating the latter with Machiavelli or with Machiavelli's excesses. We have noted that Ammirato's chapter on reason of state, which is Clapmar's model, abstains from explicit mention of Machiavelli, and even from the circumlocutions (such as "alcuno" or "altri") that Ammirato frequently uses elsewhere in his text when he wants to take issue with Machiavelli. Clapmar's adaptation of Ammirato, however, shows very clearly that its author understood that the distinction between *buona* and *cattiva ragion di stato* was relevant to the contemporary debate over Machiavelli.

In this connection, it is significant that in every case in which Clapmar refers openly to Ammirato in the *De arcanis,* with one exception, the reference is to Ammirato *as a commentator on Machiavelli,* either in agreement or disagreement. This connection is made in reference to the wisdom of maintaining a militia, on the right of accusation, on the use of fortifications, and, most importantly, on the Roman manipulation of the auspices. Machiavelli, whom Clapmar here calls a

---

[50] "E non è alcun dubbio, come Camillo dice: sunt et belli sicut pacis iura; che vi sieno anche i diritti della ragione di stato, e suoi termini, e confini: i quali che trapassasse, commetterebbe ingiustizia, e malvagità, e per consequente più di tiranno, e di carnefice, che di principe pietoso, e giusto meriterebbe haver nome. Come ella dunque tutte le altre ragioni da noi prodotti precede; cosi non si ha punto a vergognare, che una sola è questa è la ragion divina a lei preceda" (p. 232).

"Postremo minime contradicunt haec iura legi divinae, ceteroquin non essent iura sed flagitia. Sicut enim iura belli, iura fisci, iura Reipublicae, legationis, suos certos habent terminos, e quibus si evagantur, non amplius iura sunt, sed summa iniusticia . . . sic etiam iura dominationis suos certos habent limites, e quibus si excurrunt, et in vitiorum confinia atque possessiones involant, non amplius iura sunt, sed scelera, sed, ut Tacitus appellat, dominationis flagitia" (pp. 160–1).

politician "great in judgment and acumen, but less sound and pious of mind," had attempted to prove the irreligion of the Romans by showing how they had manipulated the oracles for political ends, "which judgment of Machiavelli Ammirato rightly disputed" (p. 207).[51] This section in Clapmar is indeed based closely upon pages 51–4 in the *Discorsi sopra Cornelio Tacito* – "Che i Romani nell'interpretare gli auspici procedevano secondo i riti, et costumi della loro religione" – and discusses the same examples of the condemnation of manipulation of religion by the Romans, the cases of Papirius and Gabinius. As De Mattei has remarked (*Ammirato*, p. 135), these citations[52] are the more noteworthy because Ammirato does not refer to Machiavelli by name, but by circumlocution, or, as in this section on the auspices, not at all: Clapmar detects Ammirato's implicit polemic against Machiavelli or, when the two Florentine authors agree, points out their agreement. If we knew Ammirato only from Clapmar's references, we would think he had written a commentary on Machiavelli, not on Tacitus.

The only passage in which Ammirato's name is not paired with Machiavelli's is also the one in which Ammirato is quoted in Italian and with credit rendered. As we have seen, Clapmar sometimes translates bits of Ammirato into Latin without credit and makes use of several Italian phrases like *ragione di dominio* that come from Ammirato, also without explicit reference. The fact that Ammirato is both cited and quoted in this passage without Machiavelli being mentioned might seem to go counter to the view that Ammirato is presented as a commentator on Machiavelli – but the subject of the quotation, like the passage on the auspices, concerns the relation of religion and reason of state.[53] The connection to Machiavelli is also indicated by the context, which is Clapmar's attempt to distinguish between the *iura dominationis* (= *ragion di stato*), which are bounded by religion, and the flagitia or *consilia Machiavellistica*, which are not.

[51] "Quam sententiam recte disputat Ammiratus contra Machiavellum."
[52] P. 60: "Adeoque in equitatu tota militiae Romanae dignitas consistebat, ut et hodie in militiae Turcica: veluti hac de re egregie disputat Scipio Admirates contra Machiavellum"; p. 74: "Aliud est enim calumniare, aliud praevaricari, aliud accusare: quod docet Cujac. in observat. lib. 4. et 10 et vide hac de re duos prudentissimos scriptores ac populares, Machiavellum et Ammiratem"; p. 114 (on fortifications): "sed de his etiam vide quae accurate disserit Florentinus ille Ammiratus, contra popularem suum Machiavellum."
[53] "Mihi hoc caput concludere libet pulcherrima atque vere Christiana sententia Scipionis Ammirati in Tacit: Et perche, inquit, la relligione e cosa maggiore, come habiam detto, della ragione di stato, e fasi conti suoi diversamente da quelli degli uomini, e non si da proportione dalle cose temporali all'eterne: conviene, in tali accidenti, ricorrer premieramente alla religione, e veder se ella ci si oppone; perche in tal caso bisogna accomodar la ragione di stato alla relligione, e non la relligione alla ragione di stato. Et quae plura hac de re disserit prudens sane ac disertus scriptor" (p. 195).

Clapmar's debt to Ammirato was thus very great: The terms arcana and flagitia as equivalents for good and bad reason of state, the concept of reason of state as derogation, and the boundary between licit and illicit forms of reason of state set by religion – all these come from Ammirato, as does Clapmar's sense, deriving from Ammirato but made more explicit than in that author, that such a scheme is necessary in order to distinguish what is useful in Machiavelli from what is wicked. In Ammirato this connection between reason of state and the debate over Machiavelli is implicit, and must be derived from the text by the reader's noticing that what distinguishes good from bad reason of state, namely, the violation or manipulation of religion, is also what Machiavelli, not directly named, is criticized for finding erroneously in Roman history and setting up as a model for contemporary imitation. In Clapmar, the connection is made explicit in the definition of flagitia as *consilia Machiavellistica* and is indicated in a number of other ways, including citation of passages in Machiavelli not used by Ammirato.

The *iura dominationis* correspond to Ammirato's reason of state, and, indeed, several of the specific tactics enumerated, like the biblical use of asylum in contravention of existing laws (*De arcanis*, p. 161; Ammirato *Disc.*, p. 231), the rape of the Sabine women (*De arcanis*, p. 165; Ammirato, *Disc.*, p. 232), and Romulus's breach of justice in the founding of Rome (*De arcanis*, p. 166; Ammirato, *Disc.*, p. 231), derive from that source. But other examples derive from Machiavelli: The importance of maintaining residence in occupied territories (p. 131) is glossed by reference to Machiavelli's example of the imprudence of the French leaving Naples; the foolishness of being overly kind to subject peoples is supported by Machiavelli's opinion on the folly of the Florentines in allowing Arezzo to rearm (p. 179); and Machiavelli's discussion of the necessity of eliminating "the sons of Brutus" is discussed in the section on the necessity for harshness to the children of proscripts (p. 190). In addition, the presence of Machiavelli can be felt in the entire section on cruel methods (pp. 178ff.) and in the section on "Preempting those who can harm you" ("Praevenire iis qui nocere potest"; pp. 171ff.), though in these cases a specific source is not indicated. Likewise, in the chapter on those who attack the use of iura, Clapmar takes up the Machiavellian motif of the boldness of spirit necessary to be effective in political life: Attacks on the iura spring from excessive piety, more appropriate to the hills and caves of hermits than for men of the world. For Clapmar, as for Machiavelli in *Principe* 15, there are no perfect republics, and he who behaves as if he lived in one is bound for ruin.[54] In this spirit, Clapmar cites Tacitus's remark that every great "exemplum" has something iniquitous about it (*Annals* 14:44) and Plutarch's principle that he who would do justice in large matters must accept injustice in small ones. Such an emphasis seems closer to Machiavelli's idea of necessary evil than to Ammirato's concept of reason of state, although Clapmar insists in several places that the iura have moral limits, and does so in a way that rejects, even more explicitly than Ammirato, the principles of *Il Principe*, especially the view, taken in chapters 15 and 18, that effective political action must conflict with virtue and faith. Dissimulation must be limited by "fides, honestas, virtus" (p. 13). The *iura dominationis* do not contradict divine law but are limited by it.[55]

The principle of majesty from which the iura derive their justification is also limited by "religio, pudor, fides" (p. 194), and these limits are reiterated in the section on flagitia (p. 201). As Machiavelli had said that it was often necessary, in maintaining one's state, to act in a manner opposed to trust, charity, humanity and religion ("contro alla fede, contro alla carità, contro alla umanità, contro alla religione" [*Prin.* 18]), we may observe here Clapmar's setting of his own limits to the iura, accepting Ammirato's requirement that they not conflict with religion, but adding other criteria as well. The enumeration of the flagitia bear this out: *Fidem frangere* is one of these *consilia Machiavellistica,* as are incest in the interest of state, the avenging of private wrongs under the guise of reason of state, fratricide in the Turkish manner (cf. Gardiner's *Machiavellian Treatise,* pp. 86–7), atheism, and a number of other breaches of rules held to be essential to the maintenance of *fides, pudor* and *religio* (pp. 206ff.). Clapmar's scheme is thus derived very directly from Ammirato but differs from it in several ways:

1. The term *iura dominationis* is substituted for *arcano d'imperio*, though the latter term is retained as the title of the whole book.
2. The distinction between the permitted and the forbidden is developed in ways that make explicit the relation of the discussion

---

[54] "Ac primum dum omnium ita comparatum est, ut rarissime, imo numquam, Politiam aliquam Platonicam repperias: quin potius pleraeque sunt turbulentae, vel saltem minus compositae, in quibus omnia exacte et ad unguem agere extremae dementiae est" (p. 160).
[55] "Quare duo sepimenta, sive terminos huic iuri statuo: Divinum numen, sive Relligionem; et fidem sive pudorem. Quae si integra maneant, nihil prohibet, nonnumquam a communi iure recedere, pacis ac quietis causa" (p. 161).

to Machiavelli, both by using examples from his works, with citation of authorship, and by associating the flagitia with his name.
3. The vague terms in which Ammirato restricts the scope of reason
   of state to those tactics not in conflict with religion is made more
   precise, as Clapmar enumerates the categories of iura and flagitia,
   and this enumeration is a further clarification of Clapmar's relation to Machiavelli: The moral difficulty of the *iura dominationis*
   is fully accepted. They always have some appearance of immorality, and one must be strong enough to accept this reality, for
   there are no Platonic republics: Cruel methods are unavoidable,
   and specific categories of necessary cruelty are set forth; at the
   same time, Machiavelli's extension of the necessary evils of political
   life to religion and the keeping of faith are rejected.

This position is not far from that of Ammirato, but it shows Clapmar
revising his source with Machiavelli in mind, stressing the irreducible
moral dilemmas faced by the good man in a wicked world more directly
than Ammirato did, and also, most basically, foregrounding the ancient
rather than the modern terminology. Clapmar notes the equivalence
of his subject matter to that of reason of state, but uses the ancient
terms arcana, iura, and flagitia as his analytic categories and explores
their implications through generous reference not only to Tacitus but
also to Livy, Plutarch, Aristotle, Servius, Labeo, and a host of other
authors of classical antiquity and Roman jurisprudence.

The final book of Clapmar's *De arcanis* is devoted to the *simulacra imperii*. This phrase refers specifically to the creation of illusions of power.
I am not sure that Clapmar succeeds in distinguishing them in a wholly
convincing way from the *arcana imperii*, but the difference he proposes
is that the arcana are "hidden but sound arts" ("occulta, sed valida
artes"), whereas the simulacra are "empty and hollow arts . . . by which
one thing is done and another simulated" (p. 243).[56] If one thinks of
the sophismata of Aristotle, those rights and privileges of exemption
from assembly, magistracy, and the bearing of arms discussed in *Politics*
4:13, which for Clapmar are models for the *arcana imperii*, one sees
that the intention is hidden, but both the right and the exemption
from exercising it are "solid" in the sense suggested here: The people
may bear arms and may choose to abstain from bearing them. Such
an arrangement is a sophisma or arcanum because in fact such arrangements have the effect of disenfranchising the exempted class
and empowering the class that is in law less "free" to ignore the re-

---

[56] "Sunt occultae artes, sed inanes, sed cassae . . . quibus aliud agitur, aliud simulatur."

sponsibilities of power. But the simulacra are wholly illusory retentions of the names and titles of power when the reality is absent. The simulacra, called by Tacitus *arcana inania* and by Pliny *libertatis umbra*, include all political strategies and institutions in which the appearance of power, or of change or retention of a former constitution, are offered instead of the reality. The simulacra were in fact Tacitus's great subject: He showed how the imperial power grew while leaving old forms and old names intact. Clapmar strongly dissents from Machiavelli (referred to here as "acutus scriptor ex Hetruria"; p. 252), who believed that when the form of government is altered, all things should be made new (p. 252; cf *Disc.* I:26). After all, it was too rapid change that brought about the fall of Caesar, whereas Augustus and Tiberius moved slowly, assuming imperial power but using the title *princeps*, or first citizen, rather than the hated *dominus*, allowing the senate nominal powers and freedom of discussion, and flattering the plebs with games and spectacles (pp. 251ff.).

Clapmar's whole treatise has been concerned with deceptions of various kinds, but the simulacra have several special associations. One is with god making, or manipulation of the appearance of the supernatural. When the simulacra are first mentioned in the book, that is the context:

The plebs is to be managed by enigmas, and, as it were, by evasions and simulacra, which, when cloaked in the image of liberty or power, present a greater outward appearance than the things themselves have. In keeping with this principle, the ancient writers described the simulacra of gods, and superhuman specters, in order to evoke terror. (pp. 2–3)[57]

Examples of this making of simulated gods for political effect are cited from Pliny, Livy, Vergil, and Juvenal. Clapmar does not offer these citations as models for contemporary imitation: Indeed, his acceptance of the rule that reason of state be accommodated to religion, and not the reverse, would seem to rule such an interpretation out.[58] Nevertheless, he recognized, as Naudé was later to do more enthusiastically, that among political illusions, the illusion of deity is among the most potent. This is also a concern of Machiavelli in Book I of the *Discorsi*, where Numa Pompilius's use of the simulacrum of converse with the

---

[57] "Etenim *en ainigmois* et veluti per ambages atque simulacra plebs tractanda est, quae ubi libertatis aut imperii imagine teguntur, majorem speciem prae se ferunt quam reipsa habent. Quo consilio antiqui Scriptores simulacra deorum et *phasmata* illa ultra modum humanum descripserunt, terriculamenti causa."

[58] Later, Clapmar explicitly condemns the deification of the Roman emperors, while noting its effect on the populace: "quod nihil animos plebis magis percellit quam relligio" (p. 124).

nymph Egeria is discussed, though Machiavelli is not referred to at this point in Clapmar's text. Another association that the use of the term simulacra suggests is with the representational or mimetic arts, particularly the art of drama. Clapmar tells us that all human sciences have their arcana (taking the term in its general sense of hidden or questionable or deceptive methods or tricks): There are tricks of color in painting, medical tricks, mathematical "fictions," rhetorical sophisms, and so on (p. 4). The simulacra are a subset of such tricks, the ones that involve illusion, and the political ones have something in common with the dramatic ones, "for public action is like comedy, in which one character is assumed and another is discarded, and, as the satyr sings, the true face returns, the dissimulated one passes away" (p. 9).[59] The simulacra are closely related to the illusions of the stage, and to the literary distortions ("tumores" or "fumi poetici" [p. 245]) authors use to portray what appears to be rather than what is. Because of this affinity between political and theatrical or literary deception, the user of the arcana must be something of an actor, practiced in showing an assumed expression and in manipulating appearances.[60] In treating the simulacra, Clapmar yields for a moment to the impulse to regard all human affairs as deception and vanity: "for what else is human life but deception and vanity? No one speaks from the heart. No one openly lies, but mixes true with false" (p. 281).[61] Machon later devoted a whole chapter of the *Apologie pour Machiavel* to a justification of political deception on the grounds that all human life is necessarily and unavoidably bound up with deception from birth to death.[62] Machon develops the motif of *vanitas* far more fully, and has behind him a more highly developed tradition of skeptical declarations of this kind, particularly in Montaigne and Charron – but Clapmar does see, though he touches on the subject so briefly, how one kind of defense of the arcana might be advanced on the grounds of the necessarily deceptive character of all human intercourse in an imperfect world. But this line of thought is not developed: Indeed, Clapmar has been at pains to limit the arcana to those that do not conflict immoderately with religion, faith, and decency, and the simulacra likewise, though they are a necessary part of political life, cannot dominate it. Illusion

---

[59] "Sunt enim actiones publicae veluti comaediae in quibus persona sumitur ac deponitur, et ut canit satyr. vera redit facies, dissimulata perit."

[60] "Sed nec omnes ad hanc rem apti sunt, verum ii demum qui sunt *praktokatoi*, versatiles, exercitatoque vultu atque ingenio, quive videri nolunt, quod sunt" (p. 289).

[61] "Quid enim aliud est haec vita hominum, quam deceptio et simulatio? Nemo ex animo loquitur; nemo palam mentitur; sed vera falsis miscet."

[62] See Chapter 6, this volume.

must yield to reality, the false face, in Petronius's description of comedy, must give place to the true, and, as Aristotle had somewhat inconsistently said of the sophismata that he had elsewhere recommended, "one should not trust oneself to those things which are feigned and shadowed to the people, for they are insubstantial in their effects" (*De arcanis,* p. 282; *Politics* V:8; cf. IV:13).[63]

Clapmar's book remains, in a very important sense, wholly within the reason of state tradition and relies, as De Mattei recognized, specifically upon Ammirato's formulation of the doctrine for its own central distinctions. Clapmar more explicitly recognizes the relevance of this scheme of Ammirato's to the debate over Machiavellism than Ammirato himself did, and in this sense is also in the main line of the reason of state authors, many of whom associate *cattiva ragion di stato* with Machiavelli, while drawing on the less morally objectionable aspects of Machiavelli's works for their own explorations of the good reason of state. Clapmar even derives his most important equations between ancient and modern terminology (*arcana,* or more properly *iura dominationis* = *ragion di stato; flagitia dominationis* = *cattiva ragion di stato*) from Ammirato. The principal difference between Clapmar and the reason of state school is his thorough commitment to the ancient terminology and his elaborate use of ancient terms – arcana, iura, flagitia, simulacra to classify the subject matter of reason of state and find ancient equivalents for the tactics so much discussed by moderns.

This shift in terminology, hair splitting and antiquarian though it sometimes seems as one reads the *De arcanis,* represented an extremely significant development in the history of European political thought, especially in the history of the reaction to Machiavelli. Not only did Clapmar have many followers and imitators in Germany – Christoph Besold, Corvino, Saggitarius, and others who largely accept his terminology – and produce their own volumes "de arcanis imperii," but the work was read in France and inspired Naudé, who thought that Clapmar had done a poor job on the arcana, to write a book provisionally entitled *De arcanis imperii.* When the book was published in 1639, however, the shift in terms from reason of state to secrets of power was succeeded by a further modification, for the *De arcanis imperii* had become the famous *Considerations politiques sur les coups d'état,* a work whose wide influence assured that Clapmar's joining of the

---

[63] "Non esse confidentum his, quae finguntur et adumbrantur ad populum; suis operibus vana sunt."

modern doctrine of reason of state with the ancient *arcana imperii* would have a lasting effect, becoming a central feature of the absolutist synthesis of Machiavellian and sacral conceptions of royal power.

The *De arcanis rerumpublicarum* was therefore, despite its lack of originality of conception, more than another treatise on reason of state. Clapmar's preference for the ancient over the modern terminology, and the thoroughness with which he applies it, have the effect of emphasizing the secret, mysterious, covert, illusory, and morally problematic side of the political philosophy loosely included in reason of state. The connections of the new doctrine with the arts of illusion and with the mysteries of religion and cult are thus foregrounded, and what had seemed to many an atheistic or antireligious doctrine emanating from Machiavelli is thus translated into terms that stress its ancient origins and make its tenets available for use in a new fusion of Machiavellian political theory with the doctrine of the sacred and mysterious character of kingship.

5

Gabriel Naudé
Magic and Machiavelli

The first edition of Gabriel Naudé's *Considerations politiques sur les coups d'état* bears the imprint Rome, 1639. The place of publication is almost certainly false, and the actual date of publication might have been somewhat later.[1] The book was reprinted many times in the late seventeenth century and was translated into several other languages. It enjoyed a wide and lasting influence on European political discourse, and its title gave currency to a locution still common, though now with a slightly different meaning. Naudé's *coups d'état* do not always involve the overthrow of a government: His usage includes the modern meaning but extends beyond it to encompass any extraordinary act by which a state, a religion, or a constitution is established. The founding of Rome, of the Hebrew nation at the time of the Exodus, and of the Muslim religion all qualify as *coups d'état*, as do the giving of laws by Romulus or Moses. In addition, a *coup* can occur whenever extraordinary or surprising means are employed to maintain an existing state, especially when these involve the use (or abuse) of religion as an instrument of state: The conversion of Henry IV of France and the St. Bartholomew's Day Massacre were just as much *coups d'état* as the sudden military usurpations and palace revolts to which modern use of the term has been limited.[2]

Naudé drew heavily on Machiavelli in defining the *coups*, and this fact, amply recognized by René Pintard in his monumental work on Naudé's circle, *Le libertinage érudit* (Paris, 1943), and by Meinecke,[3]

[1] *Considerations politiques sur les coups d'état / Par G. N. P. [= Gabriel Naudé, Parisien] / A Rome /1639*. See this chapter for a discussion of the place and date. As with other texts examined in this study, the publication history is relevant to the author's belief that his work was a kind of secret or private teaching. French editions include those of 1667, 1673, 1679, 1712, 1715, 1723, 1744, and 1752. A German translation was published at Leipzig in 1688 (*Politisches Bedencken über die Staats-streiche*), and an English translation by William King appeared at London in 1711 (*Political Considerations upon Refin'd Politicks, and the Master-strokes of State, as Practis'd by the Ancients and Moderns*).
[2] For Naudé's definition, see *Coups d'état*, pp. 65–75, and the discussion in this chapter.
[3] Pintard, *Libertinage*, pp. 545–7; Friedrich Meinecke, *Machiavellism* (English trans., New Haven, Conn., 1957), chap. 7.

who devoted a chapter of his *Machiavellism* to Naudé, will not surprise
those familiar with the modern term: If we hear that a *coup* has occurred, we are not surprised that it was a "Machiavellian" *coup*, for
both terms share a common association with intrigue, violence, and
conspiratorial amorality. Naudé was influenced, centrally and per-
vasively, by *Il Principe* and the *Discorsi*, and one purpose of this chapter
is to demonstrate and assess that influence in greater detail than Pintard and Meinecke thought necessary. This look at Naudé's Machiavellism is called for partly because the old view has been challenged
– Anna Maria Battista has argued, in *Alle origini del pensiero libertino:
Montaigne e Charron* (Milan, 1966), that Naudé and the other "libertines" belong to a distinctively French, skeptical tradition deriving from
Montaigne and Charron – and partly because the way in which Naudé
uses Machiavelli is an important instance of the translation of Machiavellian terminology into the language of sacred kingship. Distinctively Machiavellian ideas and themes appear in the *Coups d'état*
as "mysteries of state," or "secrets of state," or *arcana imperii*. In fact,
coup d'état is actually a synonym, in Naudé's usage, for *arcana imperii*,
and the original title planned for the book that eventually appeared
as the *Coups d'état* was *De arcanis imperiorum*.[4] Indeed, throughout the
book, the *coups* are presented as the fruits of an ancient and secret
political tradition Naudé claims to be reviving, a tradition with strong
links to sacral kingship as well as to magic, hermetism, and the "ancient
wisdom" of Renaissance occultism.

The hermetic tradition as political charlatanism: Naudé's *Apologie*

Naudé himself did not believe in the magic of kings; in fact, he was
well known as a great debunker of the magic fad and of superstition
generally. What he believed in was an ancient tradition of apparent
magic, mostly fake, but of immense political importance, and it is this
tradition to which he regards Machiavelli as belonging and in which
he places his own political writings. In fact, the *Coups* bears a close
and thus far insufficiently recognized relation to Naudé's early book
on magic, the *Apologie pour tous les grands hommes qui ont esté faussement
soupçonnez de Magie* of 1625. In that book he developed a skeptical,
Machiavellian interpretation of the occult sciences and of the myth of

---

[4] Pintard, *Libertinage*, p. 615, citing Gabriel Naudé, *Bibliographia politica* (Venice, 1633),
p. 47; *Syntagma de studio militari* (Rome, 1637), p. 2; and L. Allacci, *Apes urbanae, sive
de viris illustribus, qui ab anno MDCXXX per totum MDCXXXII Romae adfuerunt, ac typis
aliquid evulgarunt* (Rome, 1633), p. 116.

the *prisca theologia,* or hermetic tradition. In doing so, he laid the foundation for the central ideas of the *Coups d'état,* including the idea that the doctrines of Machiavelli constituted a kind of mystery of state. Because the two treatises are so closely related, with the latter sometimes quoting verbatim from the former, we shall need to discuss the *Apologie* first, and at some length.

The *Apologie* was not Naudé's first book, though it was published in 1625, when he was only twenty-five years old. Naudé had been a brilliant student at an early age, and at the College de Navarre came under the influence of Claude Belurgey, the well-known skeptic.[5] In 1620 he became the librarian of Henri de Mesmes and at the same time began to study medicine. His first published works were the *Marfore,* a defense of the Duke of Luynes, (1620), the *Instruction à la France sur la verité de l'histoire des Frères de la Roze-Croix* (1623), and the *Apologie* (1625). A major preoccupation in the pamphlet on the Rosicrucians, as in the book on magic, is the folly and superstition of the masses, and the necessity for the wise man to free himself from their errors, to become *déniaisé,* or undeceived. Just how far *déniaisement* is supposed to extend, and whether the attack on superstition is at the same time a guarded assault upon Christianity itself, is a debated matter, but this interest in demystification, as well as a complex web of personal and literary relationships, made Naudé a member of the circle, including Gassendi, La Mothe Le Vayer, and the brothers Du Puy, whom Pintard named the "erudite libertines."

In 1626 Naudé traveled to Padua to continue his medical studies, and there came into contact with wider currents of skeptical and heterodox Aristotelian thought. In 1631 he moved to Rome and for the next twelve years was in the service of Cardinal De Bagni, for whom, if what he tells us in the preface is true, he prepared the *Coups d'état* as a private manual of advice. On De Bagni's death, Naudé briefly entered the service of Cardinal Antonio Barberini. He then also briefly became Cardinal Richelieu's librarian and later held the same position under Mazarin, whose collection became, under Naudé's direction, one of the greatest in Europe, the first great public library in Europe. After the seizure of the collection in 1651, Naudé spent several years at the court of Queen Christina of Sweden and died at Abbeville in Picardy in 1653.

The *Apologie pour tous les grands personnages qui ont esté faussement soupçonnez de Magie* was Naudé's youthful tour de force, lavishly ded-

---

[5] The biographical details presented here follow Pintard, *Libertinage,* pp. 156–73, 207, 245–70, 304–11, 390, 415.

icated to his patron, Henri de Mesmes, president of the Parliament of Paris, and accompanied by commendatory verses by Patin, Colletet, Gaffarel, and others.[6] The *Apologie* is an exercise in historical criticism of sources, and its aim is to show that most of the magic imputed to famous figures of the past never happened. In this spirit of "censure et critique des autheurs" Naudé offers the outline, later to be expanded in the *Syntagma de studio*, of a method of historical criticism whose principles include distrust of all books written in the last 800 years, the systematic attempt to establish an author's bias, and the search for the first extant source of any questionable opinion.

Naudé's recurring image for the clearing away of accumulated error is that of illumination, as, for example, in the preface, when he compares the accusations of magic made against the great men of the past to the croaking of frogs:

The only way to remedy the croaking of frogs is to bring a light into the place where they are: I assume you [i.e., the dedicatee] will expect no less effect from this *Apologie*. (Sig. Aivv)

He expects his book to be a lighthouse in the darkness of "opinions communes," "a torch that can illuminate [*esclairer*] for us the palpable darkness of lies." He uses the word *éclaircissement* and its related forms for the activities of the critical intellect, and in this, as in the opposition of this term to the "darkness" of popular error, anticipates what would later become the well-known image of philosophical "enlightenment." At the outset, the project of enlightenment is presented as an enterprise whose audience is a small, endangered intellectual elite in perpetual conflict with the mass of "crédules." Truth is hidden and masked, and the ordinary person never sees through the mask. Those who do are often lonely and persecuted, for unless they are extremely circumspect, their knowledge inevitably brings them into conflict with the rest of humanity.

Naudé's view of the history of thought is based upon this opposition between intellect and error. Wise men have often had to teach secretly and make a mystery of their learning so as to avoid persecution by an uncomprehending multitude, and even though the renaissance of learning after the fall of Constantinople (1453) created new opportunities and moderated the persecution of the learned, caution was still necessary and always likely to be. The Renaissance itself is thus a flowering of ancient and secret intellectual traditions, which now can be made partly, though not completely, public.

[6] Gaffarel wrote his commendatory verses in Hebrew, a foretaste of the showy erudition of the book itself.

For Naudé, in contrast to other writers on the secrets of the ancients, the reasons for the secrecy of the tradition were prudential rather than mystical. Pythagoras, Galen, Apuleius, and others were "magi" only in a metaphoric[7] sense, demigods only insofar as their knowledge, acquired in natural and not supernatural ways, elevated them above others. They made themselves mysterious by necessity, teaching

by cabal and tradition, secretly and to disciples, not daring to divulge their doctrine to the people who were, in all eras, convinced that only rash and impious men would investigate the reasons for all the extraordinary effects that depended upon the immediate will of their gods, whose liberty they judged incompatible with the assured order of causes the Philosophers wished to demonstrate in Nature: that is why they punished them severely. (p. 62)

Protagoras was exiled, Anaxagoras imprisoned, and Socrates executed because they were thought to possess illicit supernatural or magic powers and because their teaching seemed to challenge the common beliefs in the gods. And if antiquity was a time of ignorance and intolerance, the Middle Ages were even worse, for then (in an image contrasted with the "enlightenment" of the sages and, like that image, having a long history of subsequent use) darkness reigned supreme. As we might call a man a wizard who could produce a summer flower in the middle of winter, so

all those spirited men who appeared, like brilliant stars in the midst of that sombre and dark night, and who produced admirable effects by their learning in that most cold and icy season for letters have passed, up until our own time, under the like title. (p. 116)

The fall of Constantinople marks the new era. Pico was still considered a magician because in his time "good letters had only just begun to bud upon the thorns of barbarism," but after 1453

all the world began to change face, the heavens to roll according to new hypotheses, the air to be better known in its meteors, the sea to make itself more easy and open, the earth to reveal to us another hemisphere, men to communicate among themselves by navigation, the arts to produce their marvels of cannon and printing, and the sciences to take up their former luster. (p. 113)

These changes produced a climate more favorable to critical inquiry:

Before the humanities and good letters had been rendered common and available to everyone by the felicity of our last century, all those who delighted in cultivating and polishing them were reputed grammarians and heretics;

[7] Naudé is fond of St. Jerome's definition of the magus: "magi sunt qui de singulis philosophantur" (p. 60).

those who penetrated further into the understanding of natural causes passed for Adiaphorists and irreligious; whoever had better knowledge of the Hebrew language was taken for a Jew or Marrano, and those who researched mathematics and the less common sciences were taken for enchanters and magicians, although this was a pure calumny, founded on the ignorance of the vulgar or the envy it always bears toward great people. (pp. 22–3)

Naudé thought his own age had attained a degree of maturity in intellectual culture. Claims of demonic possession and other superstitions found less credence in his own time, when the world had become "more adult and *déniaisé* than ever before" (p. 440) than in times when the world was in its cradle (p. 436). The praise of the learning of his own age was developed further in *Addition à l'histoire de Louis XI* (1630), in which he devotes one chapter to the advancement of learning (pp. 132–224) and another to the history of printing and its role in that advancement (pp. 224–320). He saw his own period as an intellectual renaissance and himself as a leader in the restoration of ancient learning, a bringer of light into darkness.[8]

Yet his project in these early works is not the simple one of educating as many people as possible, for the ancient need for secrecy in intellectual matters persists into the age of renaissance. The opposition between the *déniaisés* and the *crédules* remains perilous, and in nearly every one of these early works there is a troubling ambivalence about the act of publication. In the *Instruction à la France* he speaks of doubts about publishing because of the massive quantity of literature already written and the hostility of the common people. Yet he did publish his work:

I recognized that the saying of Pythagoras, "don't kindle a blaze upon the public way," was destructive and prejudicial to good letters, and capable of casting a man into an inextricable labyrinth from which he could never carry forth any glory except to have served as victim to a Minotaur, while his fellow citizens enjoyed an agreeable tranquillity. (p. 10)

Publication has its dangers, but in isolation intellectual labors face one with a monstrous, malevolent, and insoluble maze. The desire to communicate what one has learned, though it entails risk, is the thread of Ariadne that connects the scholar to others, justifies his search for the truth, and augurs its success.

The image of the monstrous secret or puzzle is one that recurs in Naudé's work, often, as here, in reference to the question of whether to publish. In the *Apologie* the image is used in a related but somewhat

---

[8] See also the prefatory letter to Gabriel de Guenegault in the *Instruction à la France*, where Naudé proclaims his intention "d'opposer auz tenebres palpables du mensonge le soleil de la verité."

different way: The ignorant masses are pictured as a Sphinx, ready to destroy those who will not answer its foolish riddles, and the secrecy of the sages is seen as a necessary precaution against this intolerant demand for intellectual conformity (pp. 21–2). Naudé does publish, but he makes a gesture toward restricting access to his teaching by leaving his Latin and Greek citations, of which there are a great many, in the original languages "because there is no need that they be understood by the populace" (preface, Sig. Aviir). Of course, he might have written the whole book in Latin, so that his ambivalence about the extent of his intended audience is merely underscored by this use of untranslated citations in a French text. The two-sidedness of his attitude can perhaps best be seen in his remarks on the invention of the printing press: It is the glory of the age and makes possible the work of demystification in ways never before possible (p. 9), but it is also the nurse and nourisher of rampant fantasies (loc. cit.). With the rise of inexpensive pamphlet printing, rumors of magic or miracle could spread rapidly through a city, and a whole industry had come into being that catered to the ignorant masses' taste for frivolous and superstitious reading matter.

Because the printing press is such a double-edged instrument, serving ignorance as well as wisdom, the ancient conflict between the ignorant and threatening masses and the searchers after truth persists even in an age of renaissance. Naudé's *déniaisés,* the libertines of his own circle, are the spiritual heirs of the ancient magi. Like the magi, they are subject to suspicion of heresy or necromancy, and must communicate what they know in guarded ways, disseminating knowledge within their own circle but leaving the illusions and fictions under which the majority live intact and even, in certain cases, helping to create them.

In discussing the great men of the ancient world who were reputed to be magicians, Naudé secularizes the myth of the *prisca theologia,* accepting the notion of a secret wisdom passed on in disciplic succession, but holding that such wisdom consisted of knowledge of natural, rather than supernatural, causes. The source of the ancient tradition, for Naudé, is Hebraic. After the Flood, the sciences that had been lost in the deluge were reestablished in schools founded by Shem and Heber. From these schools, the learning passed to Zoroaster, who, in Naudé's account, was the son of Ham. Zoroaster brought the sciences to Chaldea, Abraham himself brought them into Egypt, and from Egypt they were carried into Greece by Orpheus (pp. 168ff.).[9] But

---

[9] In many other versions of this myth, the *prisca theologia* begins with Hermes Trismegistus. In placing the Hebrew patriarchs at the source, Naudé follows Agostino Steuco, *De perenni philosophia* (Leyden, 1540). Steuco also provided many of the details of the passing down of the tradition from Hebrews to Greeks.

though all the names of the ancient magi are here (even Trismegistus finds a place later in the sequence) and the list is sanctified by locating its origins among the patriarchs, it is not a magic or mystical tradition in the usual sense, for the "magic" of Orpheus, Zoroaster, and a host of others is explained on natural grounds or revealed to be politically motivated stagecraft, and even the patriarchs are denied their tutelary angels (pp. 55–6). In addition, though Naudé presents his sequence as the most probable one, he pokes it so full of holes, pointing out impossibilities of chronology and other problems, that his commitment to its historical truth comes to seem doubtful. At one point he expresses doubt that Zoroaster ever existed, and asserts that the whole notion of an ancient tradition must be regarded with suspicion, like other legends of antiquity (pp. 141ff.). But if such a tradition did exist, it was a tradition of apparent and not actual magic, a product of the popular tendency to regard everything hard to understand as supernatural and the habit of wise men exploiting appearances of the supernatural for political ends.

The idea of political magic that Naudé explored in defending the ancients is especially important for this study because it influenced the *Coups d'état* and enabled Naudé to associate the magi with Machiavelli. Magic as political fiction is taken up first in chapter 3, "That many of the great persons who were considered magicians were merely politicians":

Livy seems to offer some opening for the discovery of the primary reason so many great persons have been suspected of magic without any of them ever having practiced it when he tells us in his history that "this privilege is given to antiquity, that by mixing human things and divine, it may make the first beginnings of cities more august." From this we may conjecture that all the most subtle and tricky lawgivers, not unacquainted with the fact that the most satisfactory way of acquiring authority over their people and maintaining themselves in it was to persuade them that they were only the organ of some supreme deity that wished to favor them with his assistance and take them under his protection, have made appropriate use of these feigned deities, these supposed colloquies, these lying apparitions and in a word this Magic of the ancients the better to serve as a platform for their ambition, and establish more securely the first design of their empires, as, in fact, one sees that Trismegistus in ancient times said he had received his laws from Mercury, Zamolxis from Vesta, Charondas from Saturn, Minos from Jupiter, Lycurgus from Apollo, Draco and Solon from Minerva, Numa from the nymph Egeria, and Mohammed from the angel Gabriel, who came from time to time to whisper in his ear in the form of a pigeon, as well instructed in this stratagem as the eagle of Pythagoras or the hind of Sertorius. (p. 49)

Many of the leading ideas of the *Apologie* appear here: skepticism concerning any claims of actual magic, the association of the magi with the ancient "legislators," or lawgivers, and the equation of magic with the construction of politically useful fictions of the supernatural.

These ideas are also central to Naudé's conception of the *coup d'état*, as we shall see. Therefore, it is of special interest that there is a directly Machiavellian influence even on this early approach to the question of political magic. The relationship between this passage and *Discorsi* I:11, where Machiavelli discusses fictive converse with gods, is complex. Naudé explicitly refers to Livy, Machiavelli's own source for *Discorsi* I:11. Yet he quotes what follows neither from Livy nor from Machiavelli, but from Pasquier's *Catechisme des Jesuites* (Villefranche, 1602). Pasquier's legislators are Machiavellians before the fact:

Do you not recall that Minos, king of Crete, wishing to give new laws to his subjects, made them believe that he had held communication with Jupiter; Lycurgus in Sparta with Apollo; Numa Pompilius in Rome with Egeria the nymph; and Sertorius, to have greater authority over his soldiers, made out that he was familiar with a hind, implying that one of their imaginary gods had transformed himself into her? These were the Machiavellisms that the ancient ages produced for us before Machiavelli was in the world, and an infinity of persons Machiavellize among us today who have never read his books. (*Catechisme*, fol. 101r)

In borrowing this passage from Pasquier, Naudé has omitted the reference to Machiavelli, along with the negative judgment on the legislators that Pasquier intends.[10]

That Naudé used Pasquier and not Machiavelli as his immediate source may be established by comparing the preceding passages with *Discorsi* I:11, where Machiavelli discusses Livy's account of the "simulated domesticity" of Numa with the nymph Egeria:

Nor in fact was there ever a legislator who, in introducing extraordinary laws to a people, did not have recourse to God, for otherwise they would have been accepted, since many benefits of which a prudent man is aware, are not so evident to reason that he can convince others of them. Hence wise men, in order to escape this difficulty, have recourse to God: so Lycurgus did; so did Solon, and so have many others done who have had the same end in view.

Naudé's inclusion of Minos and Sertorius, and his listing of the deities to whom the legislators had "recourse," derive from Pasquier. Yet

---

[10] Naudé shares the tendency to regard Machiavellism as the creation of illusions of the supernatural with several writers in the anti-Machiavellian camp: Not only Pasquier but also Lessius, Garasse, Mersenne, and others make this association. See J. R. Charbonnel, *La pensée italienne au XVIe siècle et le courant libertin* (Paris, 1919), pp. 33, 37, 42.

Naudé was aware of the Machiavellian original also, for after giving several contemporary examples of the political use of the supernatural, he quotes from *Discorsi* I:11 directly:

We have this testimony of the politic Italian in his *Discourse on Titus Livy:* "the people of Florence were not stupid, yet nevertheless brother Girolamo Savanarola made them believe that he spoke with God." (p. 52)

Naudé thus acknowledges that Machiavelli wrote about such matters, yet conceals the extent of his debt to *Discorsi* I:11 and the fact that the crucial insight into the political origins of magic comes not from Livy directly, but from Livy as interpreted by Machiavelli. Like Pasquier, yet without referring to Pasquier, Naudé understands feigned converse with gods as a central Machiavellian doctrine. His own contribution, in weaving his way among these texts, is to grasp, in Machiavelli's demystified account of the recourse to God of the legislators, a key to the history of magic. For him, the heremetic tradition is a sequence of politically motivated fictions of the supernatural.

G. Spini has argued (*Ricerca dei libertini* [Rome, 1950]) that the Renaissance idea of the legislator had roots in Arabic commentaries on Aristotle of the Late Middle Ages, where the activity of the lawgiver was already associated with imposture, and that it was this skeptical tradition that Machiavelli drew on in the *Discorsi*. The idea of the hermetic tradition also had a long history by the time Naudé wrote. Naudé thoroughly conflates these two lines of thought, identifying the magus and the legislator, so that a skeptical, fictive version of the tradition of ancient wisdom is created. Zoroaster was not merely a magus, but a politician who tried to convince people that he had received his laws from Ahura Mazda; Pythagoras pretended, for political reasons, to have conversed with a river deity; and Mohammed used a hidden accomplice, who cried out from under the ground that Mohammed was the prophet of God, in founding his new religion (p. 232).

In the case of certain legislators, notably Orpheus, Naudé finds it difficult to distinguish between magic as metaphor and magic as political ruse. The fabled music of Orpheus, by which he was said to have charmed wild beasts, may have merely been a poetic figure for his activity as founder, by which he "civilized, by his laws, fierce and barbaric peoples" (p.189); and, insofar as the Orphic cult and the Orphic hymns did invoke the supernatural, the motive was likewise political, "to tame and refine the spirit of a rustic and gross people" (p. 193). Zoroastrianism, Orphism, and Mohammedanism were all started by shrewd politicians. In fact, the very diversity of pagan worship is evidence of the political origin of religion, for this variety "could only come from the ruse and subtlety of the legislators and first theologians who thus diversified their sacrifices in ways they judged appropriate to make them suitable to their people" (p. 194).

Numa, the Roman lawgiver, is a central example for Naudé as for Machiavelli. He had many legends attached to his name, including the claim that he received his laws from the nymph Egeria, with whom he had intercourse ("il quale simulò di avere domestichezza con una Ninfa," in Machiavelli's quaint phrase), that he practiced hydromancy, that he held magical banquets, and that he drew wine and honey from a fountain. Citing Lactantius, Dionysus of Halicarnassus, Livy, and Plutarch, Naudé argues that Numa feigned these things in order to civilize the Romans, transforming them from a rude, harsh, and war-like people into a gentler and more tractable nation (p. 254). He, like the other legislators, "wisely feigned communication with the gods, knowing that this fiction would be useful and salutary" (pp. 257–8). The Roman religion too, therefore, had its origins in political "foundation."

It is not clear to what extent this line of argument is meant to promote skepticism concerning the Christian religion. It is clear that Naudé is making use of the *Discorsi* and that he shares with Machiavelli the view that the founders all "had recourse to God" and knew how to use false miracles to increase their authority, institute new law, and civilize warlike populations. In addition, Naudé, like Machiavelli, includes Savanarola as a would-be legislator, and his inclusion suggests that Christian belief is not exempt from the political analysis of religion.

Machiavelli's founders of new modes and orders, like Naudé's magi, are not really in contact with the supernatural, but are "conoscitòri delle cause naturali" (Disc. I:12) – that is to say, they are natural magicians or scientists. This phrase, "knowers of natural causes," is placed rather oddly in Machiavelli's text, and he does not elaborate upon it, but the context seems to include knowledge of human nature and insight into the predictable credulousness of the people the founder wants to control, as well as an understanding of the "natural causes" by which the appearance of a miracle can be manipulated.[11] It is this

---

[11] Debbono adunque, i principi d'una republica o d'uno regno, i fondamenti della religione che loro tengono, mantenergli; e fatto questo, sarà loro facil cosa mantenere la loro republica religiosa, e, per conseguente, buona e unita. E debbono tutte le cose che nascano in favore di quella, come che le giudicassono false, favorirle e accrescerle; e tanto più lo debbono fare quanto più prudenti sono, e quanto più conoscitori delle cose naturali. E perchè questo modo è stato osservato dagli uomini savi, ne è nato l'opinione dei miracoli che si celebrano nelle religioni eziando false; perchè i prudenti augmentano, da qualunque principio e' si nascano; e l'autorità loro dà poi a quelli fede appresso a qualunque" (*Disc.* I:12).

latter meaning that is developed at length by Naudé. Indeed, in his skeptical version of the hermetic tradition, scientific knowledge, knowledge of natural causes, replaces the *gnosis* of hermetism as the quality of mind that distinguishes the magi from the masses. In most recent scholarly work on Renaissance hermetism, magic, alchemy, and occult sciences, attention has been paid to the doctrine of the spiritually transforming effects of knowledge, which stand in contrast to later conceptions of scientific knowledge, in which the acquisition of knowledge is usually held to be relatively independent of the spiritual state of the investigator.[12] The alchemist or white magician had to practice spiritual purification in order to perform his work; no set of mere procedures could suffice without a spiritual analog, and the perfection of the alchemical work, in turn, contributed to the process of spiritual transformation. It is this magical belief, drastically revised, that lies at the heart of Naudé's conception, worked out in the *Coups d'état*, of the *esprit fort* (see the section "arcana imperii" in this chapter) which is the spiritual prerequisite for effective political action. In the *Apologie*, the process of revising the meaning of hermetic gnosis has already begun: Just as Naudé substitutes natural magic for supernatural, so he substitutes *knowledge* of natural causes for the spiritual elevation of the hermetic tradition. It is the contemplation of natural causes that

lifts one right up to the azure vault of the purest part of our soul, to that terrestrial paradise of the contemplation of causes, finally to reach that supreme degree of felicity that alone permits man to dwell in those regions so boasted of by Lucretius, the serene temples erected by the teaching of wise men. This indeed is the true effect of this kind of magic, which the Persians used to call Wisdom, the Greeks Philosophy, the Jews Cabbala, the Pythagoreans science of formal numbers, and the Platonists sovereign remedy. (p. 43)

Elsewhere Naudé says that the knowledge of natural causes lifts man to the level of divinity that Homer attributed to the sun (p. 61). He does not reject but rather revises the doctrine of the spiritually elevating effects of "magical " knowledge; and, since magic and politics are so closely related, it is not surprising that later, when he returns to the same questions in the *Coups d'état* and discusses them in terms of the vocabulary of reason of state and the *arcana imperii*, he draws an analogy between the contemplative heavens of the philosophers and the spiritual qualities needed to make full use of Machiavellian tactics.

The spiritually elevating side of ancient magic also becomes a key

---

[12] Frances Yates made this point repeatedly in *Giordano Bruno and the Heremetic Tradition* (London, 1964), and it is by now a commonplace in discussions of the subject.

to the interpretation of stories concerning demonic and divine assistance in the working of wonders, for Naudé sees these as metaphoric ways of referring to the strength of mind and spirit needed to rise above the masses. The usual writers on magic always spoke of several hierarchically graded varieties: theurgic magic, in which God helped the operator; angelic; demonic; and, finally, natural magic, which for most writers on magic, including Naudé, shaded into what we would call technology, including, as in Della Porta's compendium, *Magia naturalis*,[13] all sorts of naturally achieved wonders, like the building of bridges and manufacture of dyes and cosmetics. Naudé reduces almost all magic to this last nonmagical category. He refers to the other kinds but (see esp. pp. 26–30) finds almost no instances of them outside the Bible, and even the ones in the Bible are made somewhat dubious by their formal similarity to the others. The demonic or angelic kind of magic may be explained as political trickery, as we have seen, or, alternatively, demons and angels may be regarded metaphorically, as figural representations of the powers of the human soul. Since our souls guide and protect us, and mediate between us and God, as supernatural spirits are said to do,

sometimes people have taken occasion from the resemblance between these actions and those that souls exercise over their bodies to give the name of demons to souls, and especially to such souls as are successful, in some measure, in emancipating themselves from the slavery and tyranny of matter, where they are, as it were, entombed, so that they make themselves absolute masters of all their faculties, and thenceforward produce only miracles and actions wholly similar to those of the demons. This is the real meaning of Apuleius' remark that the human soul, even as presently situated in a body, is called a demon, and Heraclitus' remark that the spirit of man serves him as a Genius (*os ethos anthropo daimon*). (pp. 306–7)

The "just desire and good operation" of the human soul has a right to be called not only a demon or a genius, but even a god ("peut estre pareillement qualifiée du nom du dieu"; p. 307) – and, if this is so, then even theurgic magic may be a way of speaking metaphorically about the divine capacities of the unassisted human intelligence. The hermetic tradition, then, secularized and demystified as it is by Naudé, yet retains analogs of the *gnosis* of the ancient theology, and of the ascent of the magus toward and even into the realm of divinity posited by the more mystical variants on the tradition Naudé was recasting. As Marlowe's Faustus had said, "A strong magician is a mighty god."

[13] Giovanni Battista della Porta, *Magia naturalis, sive de miraculis rerum naturalium libri iiii* (Naples, 1558).

Naudé appears to agree, but he understands "magic" as the ability to create wonders by natural means and regards the "deification" of the magus as a metaphor for his knowledge and power.

Machiavelli and the *Coups d'état*

We have seen that Machiavelli influenced the central conception of the *Apologie:* The key passage on the legislators as magi draws on *Discorsi* I:11 and 12, and even when Naudé refers to Livy, Machiavelli's source, or uses Pasquier, Machiavelli's opponent, he does so with the text of the *Discorsi* as a guide. When one turns to the *Coups d'état,* its debt to Machiavelli stands out more clearly when one realizes the extent to which Naudé had already come to regard the ancient magical lawgivers as Machiavellians before the fact.

It is true, as Anna Maria Battista has claimed, that Naudé quotes more extensively from Charron than from Machiavelli, and true also that the French skeptical tradition had an important influence on his work.[14] But analysis of the places where Naudé cites Machiavelli or refashions Machiavellian texts for his own purposes reveals a profound, though partly dissimulated, debt and suggests that Naudé regarded Machiavelli as the founder (or modern restorer) of the tradition in which he himself was writing. That tradition, which Naudé calls by different names – secrets of state, mysteries of state, *arcana imperii, administratio extraordinaria,* or *raison d'état extraordinaire* – has close links with the traditions of magic, occult science, and religious imposture we have examined as they appear in the *Apologie.* It is to this tradition of ancient, mysterious, but finally natural political magic that he professes allegiance and in which he places the works of Machiavelli and his own *Coups d'état.* Naudé's title, *Coups d'état* is a synonym, in his usage, for *arcana imperii.* Indeed, he insists on identifying the two terms throughout the book, as in this passage where the two locutions are first introduced:

Now, among the headings of politics, I cannot see that there is any less discussed, less worked over, and likewise more worthy of being discussed than that of secrets of state or, to put it better, master strokes of state [*coups d'état*]. What Clapmarius has said of it in his treatise *De arcanis imperiorum* does not constitute a valid exception, for, not having understood the meaning of the title of his book, he only spoke of what other writers have said and repeated a thousand times before touching the general rules of the administration of

[14] Battista, *Alle origini,* pp. 206–7, 250–1, 259–65, 279.

states and empires; and did so despite the fact that this subject matter is so new and so elevated above the common opinion of politicians that it has been unfolded by almost none of them, as Bodin remarked in the sixth chapter of his *Methodus* in these words: "many writers [multi] have touched profusely and seriously upon the institution of customs, the restoring of peoples, the founding of a principate, the stabilizing of laws; but only sparsely have they treated of the state, not at all of the alterations of empire, and they did not even touch those things which Aristotle called the *sophismata* or *kruphia* of princes and Tacitus called the *arcana imperii*." (pp. 28–9)

This makes it clear that for Naudé, arcana, secrets, and *coups d'état* are interchangeable terms. This is confirmed by the evidence, reviewed by Pintard (*Libertinage*, p. 615), that the original title of the book was *Arcana imperiorum*, also the title Naudé incorrectly ascribes to Clapmar's book, actually titled *De arcanis rerumpublicarum*. The phrase never appears in the *Apologie*, even though it turns out, as we shall see, that some of the most important arcana discussed in the *Coups d'état* are those feigned apparitions and fictional gods the *Apologie* discusses. It appears that although Naudé rejects Clapmar, perhaps for good reason, as too timid and ordinary a writer, unworthy of his mysterious and recondite title, nevertheless Clapmar's book, a systematic attempt to give content to that provocative phrase of Tacitus, *arcana imperii*, provided Naudé with a vocabulary with which to further press his view that the magic of the ancients and the political theories of Machiavelli were part of the same tradition.

Naudé's attitude toward Machiavelli as a writer on the arcana is complex and not altogether explicit: One finds in the *Coups d'état* some of the distancing from Machiavelli and concealing of his influence noted in the *Apologie*. Notice that in borrowing from Bodin, Naudé implies that no one had written about the arcana since ancient times. Actually Bodin makes it clear that Machiavelli resumed the Aristotelian and Tacitean tradition:

After Aristotle, Polybius, Dionysius Halicarnassus, Plutarch, Dio, and Tacitus (I omit those whose writings have disappeared) left many excellent and grave things scattered in their histories concerning government, as did Machiavelli who was the first, in my opinion, to write of government after about 1,200 years during which barbarism buried everything. . . . After him, Patricius, Thomas More, Robert of Brittainy, and Garimbertus touched profusely and seriously upon many things.[15]

[15] Jean Bodin, *Methodus ad facilem historiarum cognitiarum* (Paris, 1566), pp. 77–8. Naudé may have taken his quotation from Johannes Clapmar's preface to Arnold Clapmar's *De arcanis* rather than from Bodin himself. Both Johannes Clapmar and Naudé substitute the word *multi* for Bodin's list of political authors here; see Chapter 4, n. 7 and n. 8, this volume.

and here follows the passage Naudé quotes. It is these lesser writers that Bodin accuses of having said nothing about the arcana. As Naudé therefore must have known, Bodin regarded Machiavelli as the reviver of the tradition.[16] What Naudé does here is to edit the passage he borrows from the *Methodus* in such a way as to make it appear that Naudé himself, rather than Machiavelli, is the modern reviver of the arcana tradition.

The relation of Naudé's subject matter to Machiavelli's is somewhat more explicitly recognized in the *Bibliographia politica* of 1633 – published after Naudé had completed the early version of the *Coups d'état* with the title *Arcana imperiorum,* but six years before the publication of the *Coups d'état* itself. There Naudé speaks of the scarcity of works on what he calls "administratio extraordinaria" and finds Clapmar inadequate,

for although Clapmar was willing to take upon himself this burden in his book *De arcanis imperiorum,* he delivered far less than what he had promised, and offers rather the ordinary laws of administration. (p. 45)

However, a certain "politicus florentinus" had disseminated "almost all the axioms of this kind of administration in his works" (p. 45), and Naudé tells us that he himself had written a short work on the subject, which he "trusts the learned will one day find not unwelcome" (p. 47). This is very likely the early *De arcanis,* and this work shares with the works of Machiavelli credit for adequate treatment of the subject matter Clapmar had botched so badly. This passage also provides further insight into Naudé's reasons for slighting Machiavelli. His own desire to carve out a niche for himself in literary history is obviously important; the role of the first modern restorer of ancient secrets is one he clearly relished. But Machiavelli was also a banned author, and some distancing was required, so praise and criticism mingle:

However, because he imitated the more subtle philosophers, who in disputation affirm more than they actually prove, he has earned the reputation of being astute and rash rather than prudent, and has sharpened the pens of many against his doctrine, whose point will nevertheless perhaps not be left unblunted by Gaspar Scioppius, who in recent years attempted this in his most cultivated and learned little book brought out in Rome, the *Paedia politica,* which has more good thought and judgment in it than the rest of his books, as, indeed, the most fairminded judges of books have thought, and not undeservedly. (pp. 45–6)

[16] Even in the *Republique,* where Bodin's attitude toward Machiavelli is more harsh, he continues to refer to Machiavelli as a writer on the secrets of princes. See Chapter 4, n. 9, this volume.

Machiavelli is criticized for a fault irrelevant to the main issue – his failure to offer proofs of his positions – and his defender, Scioppius, unreservedly praised.

This praise is quite significant because it explicitly recognizes that the *Paedia politica* was intended as a defense of Machiavelli. Machiavelli is not mentioned in it, but Naudé is correct in seeing the book as an attempt to defend Machiavelli. Scioppius had been at work for years on a work he called the *Machiavellica,* which is still in manuscript to-day.[17] He believed that the church should lift the ban on the reading of Machiavelli and developed, at great length, the notion of a distinct political *paedia,* or subject matter, independent of theology. Scioppius had some influence with Urban VIII and with the censor, Riccardi, and believed he had a chance to convince both of them that Machiavelli should be restored, not only because the independence of political thought required it, but also because Machiavelli had already been thrown in the face of the Catholic world despite the prohibition, since a pope had licensed the original publication of his works. It was there-fore desirable, Scioppius reasoned, to face the intellectual issues squarely and attempt to defend the original papal license. The story of the relations between the censor, the pope, and Scioppius, and of the complex process by which the *Machiavellica* became the *Paedia,* pub-lished in 1623 with most of the arguments concerning the independence of politics intact, but without the specific reference to Machiavelli, is admirably told in Mario D'Addio's monograph on Scioppius.

For our purposes, it is significant that Naudé knew the *Paedia,* and knew it to be a defense of Machiavelli, for as we move from the *Bib-liographia* to the *Coups,* the connection between Machiavelli and Sciop-pius is suppressed. In the *Coups d'état* the term *paedia* occurs in the course of Naudé's apology for his own subject matter: To leave out the topic of *coups d'état* in a treatise on politics would be to display ignorance of *paedeia.* Aristotle and the author of the *De regimine prin-cipum* are cited in support of the notion that each branch of knowledge has its own appropriate subject matter, and the idea that even a dis-cussion of the means by which a tyranny might be maintained could have a legitimate place in political theory. The citations, as well as the argument itself, are borrowed from Scioppius.[18]

[17] See Mario D'Addio, *Il pensiero politico di Gaspare Scioppio e il machiavellismo del seicento* (Milan, 1962), pp. 416ff. D'Addio lists a number of manuscripts of this work and uses for his own references Cod. Vat. Lat. 13669: "Gasparis Scioppii, Comitis a Claravelle, [Machiavellica], Hoc est enumeratio utilitatum, quas examen doctrinae Machiavelli et causarum quae Ecclesiam ad vetandos eius libros impulerunt Reipublicae Christianae in primisque Societati Iesuiticae pollicetur."
[18] *Coups d'état,* pp. 11–13; *Paedia politices,* pp. 222, 281, and 286 in Hermann Conring's

The passage in the *De regimine principum* in which precepts for maintaining tyranny are given was particularly helpful to Scioppius (p. 286) because the treatise was thought to have been written by Thomas Aquinas (an attribution no longer accepted). The author of the *De regimine* had given these rules not because he favored tyranny, but because knowledge of its modes of operation could be useful in avoiding tyranny or making it more tolerable. Scioppius's *Paedia* was, as we have noted, a defense of Machiavelli from which the name of Machiavelli had been excised, but Naudé, in using it, was well aware of the connection; in his own references to "Aquinas's" discussion of the need to simulate virtue, he notes that "these are precepts surely very strange in the mouth of a saint, and that differ in nothing from those of Machiavelli and Cardan!" (p. 14). But, though the connection between Aristotle, Saint Thomas, and Machiavelli is made, Naudé's tone differs in a significant way from that of Scioppius. What, in the *Machiavellica* had originally been a serious argument for the rehabilitation of Machiavelli has become, in its altered appearance in the *Coups d'état,* merely an irony. Scioppius's project of rehabilitating Machiavelli had failed; his discussion of the principle of *paedeia,* a principle that offered a powerful justification for Machiavelli's bold political speculations, was allowed to be published, but the plan for a serious reconsideration of the prohibition of Machiavelli's works was rejected by the ecclesiastical authorities.[19] In the *Paedia* of 1623, and in the portions of the *Bibliographia Politica* (1633) and the *Coups d'état* (composed in 1632–9, published in 1639) that rely on the *Paedia,* the real subject under discussion remains Machiavelli, but there is no open or unambiguous defense of his works.

Another passage in the *Bibliographia* in which Machiavelli is referred to concerns the unveiling of the mysteries of politics. He says that it is necessary for the political man to be well versed in those books that deal in the secrets of princes and the hidden frauds of ministers, and "all those things in the political administration of kingdoms that ought to be covered in the darkness of night, like the Eleusinian mysteries" (p. 108), but that are offered to the public view in such books, like Diana unclothed. Machiavelli is on the list of such authors, as are Procopius, Matthew Paris, and "all similar pamphlets that just pour out to the common people what the king whispered to the queen, what

edition, *Gabrielis Naudaei Bibliographia politica et Casparis Scioppii Paedia politices, nova editio* (Frankfurt, 1673). Scioppius had used the same arguments and cited the same passages earlier in his "Responsio ad P. Riccardi censuram de paedia et apaedeusia," Laurentian Library, Florence, MS S 217, cited by D'Addio, p. 509n.
[19] See D'Addio, *Il Pensiero,* pp. 159ff.

Juno gossiped about with Jove" (p. 109). The passage must be read in conjunction with similar passages in the *Coups d'état*, where what Naudé appears to condemn in these authors appears as a description of his own intentions.

> Dare I get mixed up in these sacrifices more hidden than those of the Eleusinian goddess, without being initiated into them? With what assurance can I enter into the depth of these affairs, penetrate the cabinets of the great, pass to the sanctuary where these hardy designs are formed? (pp. 6–7)

> Our own century seems to favor this design, since one can have quite complete knowledge of and discover all the great secrets of monarchies, the intrigues of courts, the cabals of the factions, the pretexts and particular motives, and, in a word, "what the king whispered to the queen, what Juno gossiped about with Jove," by means of so many relations, memoirs, discourses, instructions, pamphlets, manifestos, pasquinades and similar secret pieces that come to light every day, and are in fact capable of better and more easily forming, demystifying and freeing the spirit from folly than all the actions that are practiced ordinarily at courts of princes. (pp. 25–6)

The metaphor here may be drawn from Bodin, who speaks of Machiavelli as one of those writers who "profanent les sacrez mysteres de la philosophie politique" (*République*, preface). In any case, Naudé's own project is precisely the kind of divulging of the arcana that he associates with Machiavelli. The metaphor of profanation of the mysteries is continued as Naudé speaks of the

> ruses, tricks and stratagems that many have used and still use every day to succeed in their projects. Charron, in his book *De la Sagesse*, Cardan in his works entitled *Proxeneta: On Taking Advantage of Adversity*, and *On Wisdom*, Machiavelli in his *Discourses on Livy* and in his *Prince* have amply given the precepts. It will be enough for me to report several examples, noting that although Lipsius spoke of the latter as offering . . . an honest and praiseworthy cleverness, and Scioppius wrote a little book in his defense, one can nevertheless be impatient with him for the fact that he let "the south wind blow upon the flowers, and loosed the wild boar into the liquid fountains," having first freed the pace, broken the ice, and profaned in his writings, if one may say so, what the judicious have reserved as their most hidden and powerful techniques for making their enterprises succeed. (pp. 44–5)

So, despite Naudé's gestures of criticism and dissociation, Machiavelli is presented in a number of places as a decisive figure in the arcana tradition, as the modern reviver of an ancient genre in which Naudé himself is writing: Indeed, the *coups d'état* are the arcana that Machiavelli injudiciously or rashly revealed. Machiavelli was the first modern writer on the subject, and Naudé is his successor, improver, and corrector. What Naudé most often criticizes Machiavelli for is not writing about the arcana, but profaning them, that is, publishing them. Either to publish his own book openly or to express its debt to Machiavelli openly and fully would be to repeat Machiavelli's error. The dissemination of the arcana requires special, even paradoxical, modes of publication, for the central insight of the tradition Machiavelli had revived was that power had to be concealed. Naudé's subject matter is identical to Machiavelli's, but the *Coups d'état,* unlike *Il Principe,* was not intended to be made public – or, at least, that is what Naudé would like us to believe.

The *Coups d'état* as a mock apocryphon

A major theme of the present study has been the way in which Machiavelli's major works were often regarded as a secret teaching that was only inadvertently, or imprudently, made public and that ought to be reserved for a select company, perhaps communicated only to a prince. Naudé's criticisms of previous writers on the arcana emphasize their inattention to the secrecy required for mysteries of state: Machiavelli profaned the sacred precincts; Clapmar failed to limit his treatment of the arcana to techniques that ought not to be divulged, and gave his readers a "science that is common, understood and practiced by everyone" (*Coups d'état,* pp. 37–8). For Naudé the sources of political power, like the source of the Nile and the secrets of other natural marvels, must remain undiscovered in order to inspire wonder and awe:

One can draw a good parallel between this river Nile and the secrets of state, for, just as the people who live near its power draw from it a thousand commodities without having any knowledge of its origin, so it is needful that the people admire the happy effects of these master strokes, without, however, understanding anything of their causes and divers origins. (p. 40)

Mystery is thus essential: Augustus communicated his *arcana imperii* only to two confidants, and Julius Caesar likewise limited the communication of his "mysteries" to two trusted allies (p. 41).

The evidence concerning Naudé's own intentions in regard to divulging the arcana must now be examined. The preface of the *Coups d'état* itself presents the work as an entirely private treatise:

It was not to make this work public that it was sent to the press, which rolled only by command, for the satisfaction of that great prelate [Cardinal De Bagni] who reads with pleasure only with the aid of printed books, and who, for this reason, wished to have a dozen copies produced in lieu of manuscript copies that would otherwise have been made. I know well that this number is too small to allow this book to be seen by as many people as the *Prince* of Balzac and the *Minister* of Silhon. But as the causes of which it treats are much more important, it is appropriate that they not be so common, and, in a word, the author had no other end than the satisfaction of his Eminence in the writing, as well as in the publication of this work. (Sig aii)

This story is not entirely consistent, even internally: A press run of twelve copies would not be needed for one cardinal, and the extra ones would increase the chances that the book would reach a wider audience. Other problems arise: The book is dated Rome, 1639, and is prefaced by a commendatory sonnet by Bouchard, dated "le premier de l'an 1639," which means that if the 1639 date is correct, the book appeared between March 16, 1639, and March 15, 1640, when the old-style year ended. At this time the dedicatee was terminally ill and would surely never reenter public life, and the preparation of a printed text on the political arcana for him would have far less point than in earlier years.[20] In fact, Naudé had written most of the book in 1632–3, as we have noted, at a time when the cardinal could still have made use of political theory. Was the book withheld from him then, and only prepared for his weak eyes seven years later, when trouble was taken to print it? Also, the place of publication given on the title page is almost certainly spurious, for the printer's mark (a twin compass with the motto "labore et constantia") was the device of the Antwerp printer Christopher Plantin and his heirs.[21] The particular form of this device, of which Plantin had many varieties, is that found in books printed at the Leyden branch of the Plantin press.[22] Plantin himself printed in Leyden in 1583–5 and left the press to his son-in-law François Raphelengien upon his return to Antwerp. The Raphelengien heirs were still printing in Leyden in the 1630s.[23] It is almost certain that the place of publication was not Rome, but Antwerp or Leyden, with Leyden the more probable location. Further doubt is cast upon the circumstances of publication by the fact that, though the preface tells us that only twelve copies were printed, this account is contradicted both by early evidence of a larger edition and by certain later remarks of Naudé himself. In the late seventeenth century there is testimony by Louis Jacob that over a hundred copies of this edition existed,[24]

[20] Pintard, *Libertinago,* pp. 267ff.
[21] See G. van Havre, *Marques typographiques des imprimeurs et libraires anversois* (Antwerp and Ghent, 1883), II, pp. 87ff.
[22] Ibid., II, p. 115 and fig. 43.
[23] Ibid., pp. 89, 133–58.
[24] See Jacques-Charles Brunet, *Manuel du libraire* (Paris, 1863), IV, p. 20.

yet Naudé told Mazarin in 1642 that he had shown the work only to Bouchard and De Bagni, and retained the manuscript himself. The context of this statement is a memoir addressed to Mazarin in which Naudé discusses his qualifications as a writer on political subjects. Naudé asserts that he was asked to write on a political topic by De Bagni shortly after his arrival in Rome. *Le Prince* by Guy de Balzac and *Le Ministre* by Silhon had recently appeared, and it was Naudé's intention to outdo them by writing about "plus haultes et relevées actions":

And after a labor of six whole months, I finished a book on this subject, which printed would be larger than *The Prince* or *Minister* named above. And having then presented it to my lord Cardinal when he was vacationing at Castle Gandolfo, he took the trouble to read the main chapters of it at diverse times, which did not displease him. But since he was surprised at the boldness, however well organized and firmly supported by reasons, with which I had treated the subject, I have not wished since that time to circulate this piece, except to the late M. Bouchard, a man quite exact in his judgments, who, on account of the special friendship he had toward me, took pains to read it all, and to give me his advice, which I have kept with the said manuscript, to place them one day in the hands of your Eminence.[25]

This distinctly implies that no printed version existed, not even an edition of twelve copies. The book *would* be longer than those of Balzac and Silhon if printed. Naudé retained *the* manuscript, makes no reference to other copies, and contradicts the story of De Bagni's unwillingness to read manuscripts, for he read the main parts of the *Coups d'état* in manuscript and criticized them. However, Naudé leaves the matter somewhat more unresolved than first appears. He seems to say that the manuscript was shown only to De Bagni and Bouchard, but what he really says is that he intended to show it only to them, and he leaves at least a little room for the possibility of unintentional circulation. In fact, it is difficult to see why he would need to go into such detail about his efforts to limit circulation unless he were reacting to stories at variance with his own account that Mazarin might have heard. If a printed edition did surface after Naudé's intended gift of the sole manuscript to Mazarin, he could then point to Bouchard, now deceased,[26] as the source of the unauthorized publication. But if his intention here was to disown the edition, it is not entirely convincing; the preface to the printed text would then have to be spurious (perhaps an invention of the printer), for in it the author acknowledges

---

[25] *Mémoire confidentiel adressé à Mazarin par Gabriel Naudé après la mort de Richelieu publié d'après le manuscrit autographe et inédit par Alfred Franklin* (Paris, 1870), pp. 8–12.
[26] Bouchard died in 1641. See Pintard, *Libertinage*, p. 233.

the limited edition, and it is difficult to believe that it was spurious, for it tallies too closely in certain respects with the *Mémoire*. To Mazarin, Naudé speaks of his desire to compete with Balzac and Silhon, and the same statement is made in the preface of the *Coups d'état* in the context of explaining the small press run.[27] It is most unlikely that the printer would choose to compare the book to those of Balzac and Silhon in 1640, when those books were no longer current news, whereas their importance for Naudé is made clear in the *Mémoire*: Balzac and Silhon constituted Naudé's competition at the time the book was written. We know that Naudé did work on the *Coups d'état* in 1632, and it seems likely that both the preface to the 1639 edition and the *Mémoire* are authentic recollections of the circumstances of composition.

The known facts are inconsistent. If the book fell into the hands of the printer inadvertently, it would not need its preface, explaining that it was really still a private treatise because only twelve copies were made. De Bagni, for whom the copies were made, would already know that. Yet the preface, echoing Naudé's later association of the work with Balzac and Silhon, and the dedicatory poem, confirming Naudé's claim that he showed the work to Bouchard, suggest that the printer cannot have devised the preface himself. These facts can be reconciled on the hypothesis that Naudé himself devised a story that would make it appear that the work was never intended to be published and yet would account for the existence of printed copies. The motives for this would have been primarily literary, rather than prudential. The memoir to Mazarin makes it clear that the book was withheld from the public out of deference to De Bagni; after his death in 1641, and that of Bouchard in the same year, there was no one to object to its publication or to contradict Naudé's account of the reasons for its being printed. The final piece of evidence to consider here is from the *Bibliographia*, where Naudé discusses those authors who dealt with the *vera rerumpublicarum arcana*, among whom he includes himself: "We too prepared a collection on this subject last year, which I trust the learned in political theory will at some time find not unwelcome or unpleasant."[28] Here circulation of the work is not rejected, but deferred.

The hypothesis I am advancing is that the memoir to Mazarin is almost completely true: Naudé showed the book to very few people before De Bagni's death, and then arranged to have it printed in such

---

[27] "Je scay bien que ce nombre est trop petit pour permettre que ce livre soit veu d'autant de personnes que *Le Prince* de Balsac et *Le Ministre* de Sillion."
[28] "De quibus et nos contractionem illam anno superiore accuravimus, quam aliquando Politicae doctrinae studiosis haud ingratam fore injucundamve confido" (p. 50).

a way that it would seem not only that he never intended publication, but that the copy the reader acquired was an inadvertent glimpse into the arcana themselves, that the *Coups d'état* was, like the papers of advice of William Thomas or the *Ragionamento* of Bishop Gardiner, a private manual of statecraft that had accidentally come to the notice of outsiders.

If this hypothesis is correct, Naudé had found a way, or thought he had found a way, of making the arcana secret and public at the same time. In the age of the printing press, the transmission of the mysteries of state had to take on a new and paradoxical form. Naudé's magicians maintained their arcana through secret oral teachings, to which only the initiate had access. The fraudulent title page and misleading preface of the *Coups d'état* create, for Naudé's reader, an analog to the ancient initiate's experience of illicit and unauthorized access to knowledge. Political knowledge is knowledge one is not supposed to have, an overhearing of secrets; in reading the *Coups d'état,* one reads what was written for Cardinal De Bagni and not meant for oneself. The arcana can be published only if their publication somehow replicates the act of concealment or erasure from which political power arises.

Thus it seems likely that Naudé was responsible for the form in which his book reached the press; but whether this is so or not, the book in its present form implies a double audience – the statesman for whom it was written and the reader into whose hands it has come, despite the author's intentions and the limitation of the press run. It is, like those pamphlets that tell us what Juno wispered to Jove, an unauthorized glimpse into the *arcana imperii,* and its content, in which the doubleness of political knowledge is stressed, conforms to this mode of presentation.

The claim that the treatise was intended only for De Bagni is also illuminated by the relationship we have explored between Naudé, Machiavelli, and Scioppius, taken in the context of the efforts to rehabilitate Machiavelli; the *Coups d'état* may be seen as Naudé's attempt to succeed where Scioppius had failed. His solution was not to try to defend Machiavelli but to use him, and to use Scioppius's defense of him, in his own work so that, as in the *Paedia,* the principles of *Il Principe* and the *Discorsi* might be developed, even if their relation to their originator was not made entirely clear; and to stress, from the outset, the private character of the undertaking. If Naudé did not intend to publish, then one major concern of the censor – the effect such ideas might have on the common people – was eliminated from the start.

The *Coups d'état*, whose subject matter is secrets of state, has the form of a secret treatise, but it is unlikely that it was ever intended to be quite so secret as the memoir to Mazarin implies: Its own preface admits to twelve copies; Father Jacob knew of more than a hundred. Yet even this number may be consistent with Naudé's view that the arcana should not be too widely disseminated. A hundred copies are many times fewer than the thousands of copies of Machiavelli's works that had been printed by 1640. The *Coups d'état* was not written only for De Bagni, but it was not written for the mass of *crédules* and *bigots* either. Like Machiavelli, Naudé imagines an audience not only of princes but of those who have the ability to rule, though they lack the power.[29] As in the treatise on magic, the printing press is an ambivalent instrument. Its use risks revealing the arcana, but at the same time it "favors his design" (p. 25) by making it possible, for the first time in history, for one who is not a ruler himself to have access to the inner workings of courts and the private meditations of rulers. The printed book also provides a means, if proper care is taken either to limit circulation or to write in such a way that only the intelligent will understand, to make possible the formation of a new kind of intellectual elite, self-recruited on the basis of merit, intelligence, and freedom from moral and religious scruples (pp. 193–8). The fiction or device of presenting the *Coups d'état* as a secret treatise for De Bagni actually addresses such an audience, allowing them to believe that the very mysteries of state have fallen into their hands inadvertently. At the same time, the imagery of secrecy, mystery, and cultic sacrifice underscores the initiatory function of the work, for the *Coups d'état* is not intended to reveal the arcana to everyone, but rather to initiate a select circle of readers into them.

Arcana imperii

Naudé's definition of *arcana imperii* or *coups d'état* appears in bits and pieces throughout the book. In his various statements on the subject there are several recurrent motifs: The arcana are secret in several ways; either their true causes or the details of their preparation are not revealed to the people. They are also extraordinary or unusual events; the common, everyday ruses and deceptions of princes do not qualify. For these reasons, Clapmar's arcana are regarded as unworthy of the name, for they are both well known and ordinary. The arcana

---

[29] See pp. 193–8, where Naudé discusses the question of audience, and the last section of this chapter ("Strong spirits").

also violate or transgress moral or religious law and often involve precisely those manipulations of supernatural appearances that were catalogued in the *Apologie:* A *coup d'état* is often something like an artificial or fictive miracle, secret, sudden, extraordinary, apparently supernatural. There is also an element of the dramatic or theatrical, for *coups d'état* are conceived in terms of aesthetic as well as political effect, achieving their political purposes amid awe and wonder, as public spectacles of power and majesty.

Naudé's first effort to define the arcana comes in his discussion of prudence, a moral and political virtue of which there are two varieties, "the first ordinary and easy, which marches after the common train without exceeding the laws and customs of the country, the second extraordinary, more rigorous, severe and difficult" (p. 33). This second form of prudence employs methods that are rightly termed arcana. Disguise, dissimulation, espionage, and many other of the morally dubious tactics common in political life do not, surprisingly, qualify. These are ordinary and do not merit the appellation of

secrets de gouvernement, coups d'état, and *arcana imperiorum,* as do those that are comprised under this second, extraordinary kind of prudence, and that give the impetus to more difficult and problematic affairs. These merit, particularly and exclusively, the title *arcana imperiorum,* the only title not only I, but all good writers who preceded me, have given them. (p. 36)

The adjectives applied to the arcana – *extraordinaire, difficile, rigoureux, sévère, fascheuse* – refer especially to moral difficulty. This is an important point, because Naudé wants to resist attempts to make politically necessary acts that violate moral law respectable; wants to resist, that is, the moral alchemy of the reason of state school. Naudé therefore assigns even several of the bolder speculations of his predecessors on the use of morally questionable methods to the category of ordinary prudence and denies them the name arcana. Thus the "double prudence" of Justus Lipsius, which Naudé's doctrine superficially resembles, is rejected; so is the double morality of Charron, according to which the ruler, because of his greater responsibilities, must "dodge and feint, mix prudence with justice, and, as the saying is, play the fox with the fox" (pp. 33–4). If, as these authors held, the prince is justified in using deception and other such methods, then his use of them does not fall into the range of extraordinary actions, or *coups d'état.* Clapmar, too, in equating his arcana with the good reason of state, and rejecting the bad by equating it with *consilia machiavellistica,* was too timid for Naudé and failed to treat adequately the true arcana, despite his title. In rejecting this tradition, even in its bolder manifestations, Naudé is attempting to restore to political discourse some of the more troubling aspects of Machiavellian thought, especially the notion of irreducible moral difficulty. For Machiavelli, the prince must accept necessary evils and "entrare nel male." Naudé rejects all attempts to turn that *male* into *buono*.

Naudé frequently employs images of a formless and unmanageable horror to convey this sense of moral risk. In his preface to his patron (pp. 4–7), he speaks of his fear that he will trouble De Bagni's conscience; his own spirit recoils from his subject, as did Aeneas at the sack of Troy; he remembers Nero's wish (uttered when the emperor was asked to sign a death warrant for the execution of a poor man) that he had never learned to write; he understands the position of those who might think him too rash for entering a "labyrinth of ruses and subtleties" without having in hand the thread of such knowledge as could lead him safely out again. The danger is the greater because one cannot safely speculate about the arcana from a distance:

Rather this political prudence is like Proteus, of whom it is impossible to have any certain knowledge except after having descended *in secreta senis* and having contemplated with a fixed and assured eye all his divers movements, figures and metamorphoses, by means of which he "suddenly becomes a horrid boar, a sable tiger, a scaly dragon with tawny cloak about his neck." (p. 7)

Because of the nature of the subject matter, Naudé finds it necessary to limit his imaginative identification with the arcana. He speaks of Cardan and Campanella, who recommend that when writing on a certain subject, one should try to transmute one's whole spirit and imagination into the subject. Thus Dubartas is said to have run about the room on all fours when he had to write of horses, and Agrippa imagined himself a dog when writing his *De Vanitate* [because it made vanity impossible?] and a dragon when he wrote of fireworks:

For me, when I treat or write of some wholly good and profitable subject, I am often willing to make use of such imaginations, but in this matter, which tends so to injustice, I will never imagine myself to be some Nero or Busiris, the better to find means to destroy or exterminate humankind. (p. 30)

The quest for the secret amid horrors has, of course, its heroic side, and something of value may be brought back from an encounter with the moral ambiguities and other dangers inherent in investigating the *coups d'état*. But Naudé doesn't want his reader to lose the sense of penetrating forbidden ground and doesn't allow the arcana to lose their troubling ambivalence:

These *coups d'état* are like a sword that one can use or abuse, like the lance of Telephus that can wound and heal, like that Diana of Ephesus that had two faces, the one sorrowful and the other joyous, in brief like those medallions devised by heretics that carry the face of a Pope and a Devil under the same contours and lineaments, or like those tableaux that represent life or death depending upon from what side one looks at them. (pp. 75–6)

There are rules that one may give to help ensure that the *coups* will be used for good rather than evil: One should proceed slowly, in the common interest, use the minimum amount of force necessary to achieve one's ends, and so on (pp. 76–83). But the *coups d'état* remain Protean and ambivalent, resistant both to systematization and to moral rationalization. Political evil is not wholly negated by the necessity of its performance, but remains to trouble the conscience.

Other nuances of Naudé's sense of the extraordinary in political life emerge in further definitions of the *coups*. Naudé divides political thought into three branches. First, there are the general and universal rules upon which political life rests and about which philosophers have written (p. 58). Under this head come the principles that the common good is preferable to the private, that there is a god, and so on. Next come the "maximes d'état" (pp. 59–65), comprising all the effective but morally questionable means that other writers had included under reason of state, mixed prudence, *arcana imperii* in Clapmar's sense: breach of ordinary law in the common interest like the Roman emperors' incest, the Salic law, the Chinese law that outsiders were to be put to death, the practice of killing prisoners of war when there are too many of them, and the practices of the Spanish Inquisition and other methods "that have for foundation no other right than that of the state" (p. 65). The *coups d'état* are like these in transgressing morality and law, but there are other criteria as well. They are

bold and extraordinary actions princes are constrained to employ in difficult or desperate circumstances, in violation of common law, without even taking account of the forms or procedures of justice, hazarding particular interests for the common good. (pp. 65–6)

In the case of the maxims of state, the action to be taken is rationalized and legitimized in advance. With the *coups*, on the contrary,

one sees the thunderbolt before one hears it groaning in the clouds, it strikes before the flame shines forth, here Matins are said before the bells have rung, the execution precedes the sentence, everything is done à la Judaique – one is taken in the French manner, suddenly and without dreaming of it – he receives the stroke who thought to give it, he dies who thought himself quite safe, one suffers what one never expected, all is done at night, in obscurity, in fog and darkness, the Goddess Laverna presides. (p. 66)

The baroque, chiaroscuro imagery of the passage continues several of the motifs we have noticed already – secret preparation, the sense of the unusual and extraordinary, moral daring in obscure and ambivalent circumstances (Laverna is the patron goddess of thieves, not politicians). But the controlling image here is that of the thunderbolt of the gods: the *coups d'état* stand in the same relation to ordinary politics as miracles and other direct interventions of the gods do to the regular processes of nature:

All that is marvelous and extraordinary does not show itself every day – comets appear only in successive centuries, monsters, floods, irruptions of Vesuvius, earthquakes happen only rarely, and this rarity gives luster and color to many things that would lose it if one used them too frequently. (pp. 78–9)

The *coups* – performed "à la Judaique" – are compared to the shaking of the earth, the floods and fire that characterize the modes of divine action in the Old Testament. They are human miracles, and the political operator must not only have the moral boldness to violate human laws, placing himself, as a god would be, above the restrictions that are binding upon ordinary mortals, but must make himself an imitator of god in other ways as well, mimicking divine interruption of the regularities of natural law in actions that are unpredictable and unfathomable manifestations of power and majesty.

Indeed, the motif of the artificial miracle is central to the entire book. It appears, for example, in Naudé's definition of the *esprit fort*, the bold spirit one needs in order to be able to perform *coups d'état*. To develop the *esprit fort*, one should "think often of that saying of Seneca's – what a wretched thing is man, unless he will elevate himself above the human" (p. 20). But this elevation above the human turns out to be far more manipulative and theatrical than the Stoic meditation Seneca had in mind. The would-be *esprit fort* should imagine himself

at the top of a very high tower, representing to himself all the world as a theater, rather badly ordered and full of much confusion, where some play comedies, others tragedies, and where he is allowed to interfere like some *deus ex machina*, whenever he wishes to or when various opportunities may persuade him to do so. (p. 20)

To elevate oneself above the human is always connected in Naudé's mind with the effect, particularly the political effect, that seeming to be superhuman will have on others. The godlike detachment imagined here is not contemplative *apatheia;* it is a precondition for effecting political action, for an intervention in human affairs so potent as to seem miraculous. Through image, metaphor, and simile, Naudé suggests throughout that the *coups* are a kind of political miracle and that those who employ them play the role of gods, astonishing mere mortals with their thunder like petty Joves or Jehovahs, and there are places in the treatise where this metaphor of political deification surfaces as literal advice:

Now, among the secrets of *monastique*[30] there are none more exalted in their aims than those practiced by certain persons who, to distinguish themselves from the rest of humanity, tried to instill among them some opinion of their divinity. (p. 45)

Such fictions of deification were central to Naudé's defense of the magi in the *Apologie*. Here the vocabulary of magic is replaced by a more explicitly political set of terms (*coups, secrets de la monastique*, arcana), but the subject matter is the same, and, as in the treatise on magic, Naudé connects fictions of the divine with Machiavelli.

Naudé divides the arcana into three categories, loosely Aristotelian, according to whether they are employed in the management of an individual, a family, or a state. Oddly, Machiavelli's contribution to the arcana appears at first to be limited to the first two categories:

In *monastique* or the government of an individual, and *oeconomique* or the administration of a family, which are the two pivots of politics, there are certain ruses, tricks and stratagems that many have used and still use every day to succeed in their projects. Charron, in his book *De la Sagesse*, Cardan in his works entitled *Proxeneta: On Taking Advantage of Adversity* and *On Wisdom*, Machiavelli in his *Discourses on Livy* and in his *Prince* have amply given the precepts. It will be enough for me to report several examples. (p. 44)

Naudé's modesty concerning the secrets of individual and family life is disingenuous. His own main subject is the *secrets de la politique*, and he manages to intimate his own preeminence by suggesting that Charron, Cardan, and Machiavelli were more interested in domestic and private applications. This is another of those distancing devices frequent in Naudé's treatment of Machiavelli, and it is one of the more transparent ones, for of course *Il Principe* and the *Discorsi* deal primarily with the political sphere, rather than with the stratagems of private and family life. The relegation of Machiavelli to the domestic level is not intended to put us seriously off the track, however, for it is quickly contradicted by the examples of *secrets de la monastique* that Naudé actually gives: Those who engineered belief in their own divinity did

---

[30] In this passage, *monastique*, in Naudé's special usage, means "government over one," or management of one's own image or reputation, in contrast to *oeconomique*, or government of a family, and *politique*, the management of a state.

so, Naudé shows here, as in the *Apologie*, not only for personal aggrandizement, but as founders of states and sects.

That Naudé regards fictions of the supernatural as Machiavellian is clear here. In fact, this is the place where Machiavelli is criticized for "profaning" the arcana (see the earlier discussion). That these fictions are political in nature, and therefore central to the conception of *coups d'état*, is confirmed in the section that details the circumstances under which *coups* may be employed. The chief of these is, not unexpectedly, in the establishment or alteration of states:

If we consider what have been the beginnings of all monarchies, we shall always find that they have been started by some of those inventions and deceptions, making religion and miracles march at the head of a long sequence of barbarisms and cruelties. (pp. 84–5)

Then follows the citation of Livy and the list of impostures used at the founding of states that Naudé had used in discussing the same subject in the *Apologie*. Semiramis, Cyrus, Alexander, Romulus, Numa, Mohammed, Zoroaster, and Zamolxis all feigned divine birth or communication with divine beings. Even Moses,

who was the wisest of all, describes to us in Exodus how he received his [laws] directly from God. On account of which, although the kingdom of the Jews was completely destroyed, this Mosaic religion has survived, nevertheless, superstitiously in the Hebrews and Mohammedans, and with most excellent reformation in the Christians, as Campanella says. It is this, I think, that gave Cardan the idea of counseling princes, who, because of defects of birth, lack of money, partisans, military forces and soldiery, could not govern their realms with enough splendor and authority, to have recourse to religion, as was formerly and most successfully done by David, Numa and Vespasian. (pp. 118–19)

All this is a reprise of the *Apologie*. The ancient legislators, the founders of religions, and the magi all belong to the same tradition of supernatural fakery and imaginary deification. The *Coups d'état* redescribes this view of the ancient legislators in a vocabulary drawn from the reason of state tradition, and especially from Clapmar's particular terminology of mystery of state and *arcana imperii;* further, it argues for the continuing relevance of these ancient, fictional imitations of God to contemporary political needs. The emphasis of the book is not on what the wise men of the past did, but on what one needs to know to be an effective political operator in the present. The ersatz magic of the *Apologie*, understood as identical to the "recourse to god" of the founders as analyzed by Machiavelli in *Discorsi* I:11–12, becomes the basis for Naudé's analysis of the *arcana imperii* or *coups d'état* in the later book.

With this shift in terminology comes a greater emphasis on contemporary political applications of the ancient magic, a greater concern with how the magnificent impostures of the founders and legislators can be emulated by modern men, concerned more with maintaining existing states, or with taking power in existing states, than with founding new ones. Such an emphasis is closer to the twentieth-century meaning of *coups d'état,* so that Naudé's use of the term in reference to the conversion of Henri IV, or the Bartholomew massacre, or the execution of the Mareschal D'Ancre may seem less strange to us than the use of the same phrase to describe the lawgiving of Moses or the religious fakery of Numa. But in Naudé as in Machiavelli, foundation, preservation, and decisive alteration of political entities are essentially similar events, and the ancient arcana, like the latest *coups,* depend upon the ability and willingness to arrogate to oneself the mystery and sudden power of the gods. Like miracles and other acts of God, they are apparently causeless, unpredictable, violent, and morally unfettered interventions in the regular course of ordinary politics.

The motif of *imitatio dei* had a long history in the West, with roots in biblical and Hellenistic conceptions of kingship. It was often used to justify what was harsh and violent in political life, for the ruler had to imitate not only God's love but also his justice or severity. But this principle, powerful as it was as a rationale for what was morally problematic in politics, had strict limits in its pre-Machiavellian formulations. Mercy was to be preferred to severity, and the prince was not licensed to mirror all the attributes of the divine, especially not when divine action apparently transcended or contraverted the moral laws binding upon human beings. Naudé's recommendation that the wise politician will make use of the "fear of the gods and their thunder" was an ancient idea, but one of the things that makes the *Coups d'état* such a heterodox working out of the implications of *imitatio dei* is that Naudé insists upon the political imitation of the most problematic aspects of the divine: It is specifically the violence, obscurity, and ineffable quality of the gods that must be imitated. Here again we find a connection between a Machiavellian sense of the necessity for evil methods in politics and the notion of a quasireligious mystery of state. If the ruler is a mirror of the divine nature, and if Machiavelli was right about how the ruler must conduct himself, what becomes of the prince/God analogy? That earthly politics must reflect divine led early critics, especially Pole, to see Machiavelli not merely as ignoring religion but as promoting some blasphemous, parodic, satanic form of it, as propounding a *mysterium iniquitatis*. But it was also possible to use Machiavelli's political realism, taken together with the principle of *imitatio*, to ask whether there wasn't something like a mystery of state in heaven, a mysterious interweaving of good and evil, prefigured even in Scripture, that resembled the complexities by which good emerged from evil in political life.

Naudé implicitly raises such a question when he cites the Gospel of John in his discussion of the right of the prince to exceed the law by executing dangerous persons without a trial:

[Princes] are masters of the laws to lengthen them or shorten them, not following their own whim, but according as reason or public utility permit: the honor of the prince, the love of country, and the safety of the people easily outweigh a few small faults and unjust acts, and we shall apply the saying of the prophet (if we can do so with no blasphemy) – "It is needful that one man die for the people, lest all the people perish."[31] (p. 78)

The "prophet" referred to is Caiaphas, the high priest, and the "one man" is Jesus. One may question whether it is plausible to use this particular passage of Scripture to sanction politically necessary executions, for then perpetrators of the Crucifixion would become models for imitation. It is possible that, by giving Caiaphas the title of prophet, and by treating the passage as if it set a standard of political conduct for emulation, Naudé was rejecting the example of Christ in favor of that of his persecutors.[32] But it is also possible that Naudé read Caiaphas's remark in a way less hostile to Christianity, as evidence of a biblically sanctioned mystery of state. The common good was advanced, in a sense not intended by Caiaphas, by the death of the "one man," Christ.

In this, as in other ways, the motif of *imitatio* is given an unexpected and potentially blasphemous twist by Naudé. In the traditional use of the principle, in the ordinary applications of the prince/God analogy, limits were understood to be necessary. If God's will was unfettered, the king's was understood to be bound, even if the binding was voluntary, by law and custom. If God was merciful and severe, the king was urged to prefer mercy. If God stood above human conceptions

[31] John 11:50 had been noticed as an example of biblical reason of state before Naudé – by Topius, Ramirez, Mirandola, and others. See Rodolfo de Mattei, "Il problema della 'Ragion di Stato' nel seicento," *Rivista Internazionale di Filosofia del Diritto* XXVII (1951), p. 720. But for these authors, the reason of state of the high priest was of the bad, Machiavellian, not-to-be-imitated variety.

[32] As other "libertines" were said to have done: One of the charges against Christopher Marlowe in the "Baines note" was that he had held the opinion that the Jews made a good choice in preferring Barabbas to Jesus.

of good and evil, bringing his designs to completion in mysterious ways apparently at variance with the moral laws that bound human beings, the king was not encouraged to imitate God in that respect, and, of course, if God's power and majesty were beyond human comprehension, those of the king could only dimly reflect the transcendent attributes of the divine. Yet *dei* are precisely what all these problematic aspects of the principle of *imitatio* Naudé emphasizes: The *coups d'état* are princely imitations of all those attributes of divinity that were thought to be either beyond human power (like miracles) or beyond the laws and moral prescriptions that bound men but not God. If the notion of royal *imitatio dei* had always contained within it the potential for an overly literal, God-challenging interpretation, that potential is not suppressed or explained away, but actually exploited by the theory of the *coups d'état*. Naudé does not shrink from the idea that *imitatio dei* makes the prince a partaker, with deity, in the paradoxes and complexities of the relation between good and evil; rather, his use of the imagery of mystery and cultic secrecy reinforces it. The Naudean prince is a sacred ruler, and his use of the arcana and of Machiavellian methods are part of the mystery of his state.

But this Machiavellian revival of *imitatio dei* has another side, for the mysteries of state Naudé deals in are so often fictions, recommendations to imitate the gods in the aesthetic, or representational, sense. Moreover, there are hints in the *Coups* that such imitations, in the sense of fictions, may be all there is to the supernatural world. Not only is the politician encouraged to make use of feigned appearances of the supernatural, to "feindre des miracles," but the continuity between such fakery and the Bible is suggested in various places, just as it is in Machiavelli, who tells us in *Principe* 6 that he will not speak of Moses as a political founder of states and then proceeds to do so, and who compares the Christian religion unfavorably with paganism in *Discorsi* I:12. Naudé's treatment of the Bible is very similar: He always stops short of denying its truth, but always makes us see similarities between it and the impostures of nonbiblical legislators, politicians, and magi. Thus, for example, after discussing the impostures of Salmonee, who tried to make an artificial thunderbolt to rival Jupiter; Psaphon, who trained parrots to proclaim his divinity; Empedocles, who threw himself into Mount Aetna so that it would be thought that he was taken up to heaven; and Romulus, who drowned himself in order to promote belief in his divinity, he tells of the "atheists" who held that the mystery surrounding Moses' place of burial should be understood in the same way (p. 47). Naudé claims not to believe such stories, and perhaps he did not. Nevertheless he directs

our attention to ways in which the Bible may be read as part of the
fictive *arcana politica,* consistently including biblical examples among
the various kinds of political ruses without adequately facing the question of the Bible's truth or falsehood.

It is possible to read such passages in Naudé, as in Machiavelli, as
a covert attack on Christianity, but in both cases, whatever degree of
religious skepticism or atheism may animate such comparisons, their
main purpose is political. Perhaps Moses was a true prophet, whereas
Empedocles was an impostor. Even so, reading the story of Moses,
with his miracles, divinely sanctioned laws, and mysterious death *as
if it were* a fiction provides an example of how such a founder *might*
have proceeded by entirely natural means, and it is that example that
can be emulated by modern politicians or *esprit forts,* none of whom
are or will be prophets. As with Machiavelli, the point is to make the
boldness of the ancients, particularly in regard to their willingness to
manipulate religion, available to contemporaries.

One of the ways in which the *Coups d'état* recommends imitation of
God is particularly interesting in this connection. The biblical God
frequently used weak and apparently inadequate instruments to
achieve his ends, and "it is the same in politics: a small neglected flicker
often starts a great blaze" (p. 147). By beginning with small things,
the politician "imitates his Creator, whose custom it is to draw the
greatness of his actions from the smallness of their beginnings." But
in this section, Naudé assimilates divine fiat to natural processes of
growth:

The world, according to the doctrine of Moses, was made of nothing, and
according to Epicurus it was composed merely of a concourse of atoms, and
those great rivers that flow with impetuosity almost from one end of the earth
to the other are usually so small at their source that a child can easily cross
over them. (pp. 146–7)

Nature grows great elephants and whales out of a tiny "atom" of se-
men, and great political changes may be wrought from trivial occasions.
The biblical account of creation *ex nihilo* is desacralized by calling it
the "doctrine de Moyse" (it was, in fact, still the doctrine of the Catholic
church when Naudé wrote); by offering the doctrine of Epicurus as
an alternative example; and by the analogies drawn from geology and
mammalian sexual reproduction. After creating the world from nothing, the biblical God continued to use improbable and inadequate instruments: David, Judith, and Moses, who was slow of speech, were
all unlikely choices for their great exploits, and in the Exodus, God
even made use of vermin – flies, locusts, frogs – to bring his wonders

to pass. Yet, like Machiavelli in *Principe* 6, Naudé holds that biblical examples cannot be drawn upon directly, but only insofar as they are replicated in secular contexts:

But since these actions were miracles, and we cannot, therefore, draw upon them,[33] let us make some little reflection, rather, upon the greatness of the empire of the Turk, on the marvelous progress made every day by the Lutherans and Calvinists, and I am sure that one will be forced to admire how the spite of two monks who had no other arms than the tongue and the pen have been able to cause such great and extraordinary changes and revolutions in government and religion. (p. 149)

Mohammed, Luther, and Calvin are more directly useful examples than Moses precisely because their access to the supernatural was not genuine, yet the Bible has an essential place in Naudé's treatise, for its prophets, indeed, even its God, are the ultimate models for princely imitation. The Bible may be the locus of the authentically supernatural, but it becomes available for political emulation only when it is read, as a Christian would read the Koran, as a work of human authorship whose miracles are either natural or fictional.

Such religious skepticism as there may be in the *Coups d'état* works, therefore, not to dispel but to sustain belief in the mysterious or divine sanction of political order, while making the *esprit fort* a participator in its creation. In this skeptical reworking of the doctrines of sacred kingship, *imitatio dei* has become indistinguishable from fictional representation of the supernatural.

Strong spirits

In the *Apologie*, Gabriel Naudé had tried to recast the hermetic *gnosis*, substituting for the spiritual purification and mystical elevation that was the psychological analog of the magician's wonder working an undeceived and scientific kind of contemplation. Knowledge of natural causes became, for him, what mystical experience had been for the hermetists: the crown of earthly bliss, the special mark of the magi, and the necessary condition for the working of marvels. It is significant that Naudé retains, though in a demythologized form, the idea that

---

[33] Cf. *Prin.* 6: "Ma per venire a quelli che, per propria virtù e non per fortuna, sono diventati principi, dico che li più eccellenti sono Moisè, Ciro, Romolo, Teseo e simili. E benchè di Moisè non si debba ragionare, sendo suto uno mero esecutore delle cose che li erano ordinate da Dio, tamen debbe essere ammirato solum per quella grazia che lo faceva degno di parlare con Dio. Ma consideriamo Ciro e li altri che hanno acquistato o fondato regni; li troverette tutti mirabili. E se si consideranno le azioni e ordini loro particulari, paranno non discrepanti da quelli di Moisé, che ebbe si gran precettore."

a special spiritual capacity is required for the working of wonders. That the soul of man participates in and partakes, to one degree or another, of the nature of what it knows is a central feature not only of Aristotelian epistemology, but of nearly all ancient and premodern Christian theories of knowledge, one that finds exaggerated but not radically altered expression in magical *gnosis:* The work transforms the man, and the man must be engaged in the process of spiritual transformation in order to accomplish the work. For the most part, modern science rejects such a connection. Scientific knowledge tends to be thought of as a body of objectively verifiable hypotheses, whose validity is independent of the spiritual or psychological condition of those who know or learn it. Consequently, modern science provides relatively little support for the notion of a *spiritual* elite with secret traditions and rituals of initiation. This is not to say that modern science does not shroud itself in its own kinds of mysteries, but only to indicate that modern theories of knowledge provide little support for them and make it more difficult to think of the acquisition of knowledge as a form of spiritual ascent.

Naudé, on the other hand, accepts the most elitist premise of the hermetists, the notion that knowledge is spiritually elevating and justifies its possessors' manipulation and domination of other human beings. The *Coups d'état* draws its justification for its political version of hermetic wonder working not directly from the divine right of kings, but rather from a notion of the psychological superiority of those clever and bold enough to make use of its techniques; its doctrine of the *esprit fort* is analogous to and developed from his treatment of the spiritual elevation of the great men of the ancient world whom he defended against the charge of magic in the *Apologie*. The term *esprit fort* occurs early in the treatise, in Naudé's discussion of the propriety of his subject matter. He fears that his book will "wound the ears" of his patron and trouble his conscience (p. 4). Yet he is confident, too, that De Bagni, having lived his life at court, cannot be ignorant of the "Machiavellisms" that are so frequent in political life (p. 15). An *esprit fort* (p. 16) is required in politics, and those who lack it will come to grief: One must "avoid great responsibilities, or administer them with a force and generosity of spirit so elevated above the common that it is capable of making fortune willing to favor and second it in all its enterprises" (p. 19); the man who has it can be the "worker and creator of his own fortune," like Alexander, Caesar, Romulus, Tamburlaine, or Mohammed.

The *esprit fort* is the psychological concomitant of knowledge of the arcana: One needs a strong spirit to be able to use them, and knowledge of them, in turn, helps to demystify and strengthen the spirit. Indeed, part of the reason for the secrecy of the arcana is that it takes time to evolve a spirit strong enough to use them well.

Naudé deals most explicitly with the *esprit fort* in the final chapters, which concern the opinions one needs to hold in order to effect coups and the virtues required in a minister or courtier chosen by the prince to share in the arcana. The virtues required are the classical ones of force, justice and prudence.[34] These virtues, however, do not indicate a retreat to conventional, moralized politics or a reversion to the "mirror of princes" assumption that goodness is politically effective, for Naudé intends "to explain them in a manner less trivial than that of the schools" (p. 200). Force, for example, is the ability "to see all things, hear all things, do all things without troubling oneself, losing oneself, amazing oneself" (loc. cit.), and may be thought of as self-possession in the face of moral complexity. It is acquired by contemplating the mutability of all things, including religions. A man who has it lives in the world as if he were outside it, under the heavens as if he were above them, and can contemplate even the ruin of the entire world with equanimity (p. 202). The opposite of force is not weakness, for Naudé, but *credulité:* The effective counselor or minister must not be too devout or superstitious. As usual in Naudé, it is not possible to distinguish the excessively superstitious man from the ordinary Christian very easily, or to draw a line between excessive devotion and minimal conformity; he may mean that religious belief is harmful in whatever measure it is found. In any case, credulity makes a man "incapable of seeing anything, doing anything, of judging or examining anything to the purpose, capable only of causing the loss or total ruin of whoever employs him" (p. 208). The virtue of fortitude entails a weakening of the hold of religion over the spirit and a concomitant elevation of the spirit to those regions of undismayed knowledge of the world, and effective power to act upon it, that the Christian religion as well as the pagan held to be the domain of deity.

The virtue of justice likewise appears at first to be an ancient and traditional quality for the minister to have. It is the virtue of following the laws of God and nature with integrity. Yet the practical needs of political life necessitate modification of this definition:

This natural, universal, noble and philosophical justice is sometimes out of use and inconvenient in the practical sphere. "Of true law and its cousin justice we have no distinct and solid effigy; we must employ shades and shadows of

---

[34] Temperance, the fourth cardinal virtue, doesn't seem to be required, though Naudé himself was famous for practicing it.

them." It will often be necessary to employ the artificial, particular, and political kind, constructed and adjusted to the needs and necessities of policies and statecraft, since it is soft and supple enough to accommodate itself, like the Lesbian rule, to popular, human weakness, and to diverse times, people, affairs and accidents. All these considerations oblige us quite often to do things that natural justice would reject and condemn absolutely. (pp. 210–11)[35]

This "justice" is the ability to do things that would ordinarily be considered unjust and to construct one's own ethical standards. As the image of the Lesbian rule suggests, justice in this sense also entails the ability to change oneself, to imitate the Protean nature of the arcana:

It is then a maxim that, as among lances the best are the supplest, so among ministers, one should prize most highly those who are most pliable, and can accommodate themselves to diverse occurrences to succeed in their designs, imitating thus the god Vertumnus, who says in Propertius "my nature is opportune for all figures; wherever you wish, I am capable of turning." (p. 211)

In Machiavellian terms, one must have a spirit that can turn according to the winds of fortune (*Prin.* 18). To dominate fortune, one must not only be bold, unexcessive in piety, and willing to *entrare nel male*, but must, above all, relinquish that stability of moral character that makes one's responses to fortune automatic, predictable, and thus ineffective, in favor of the ability to transform one's own nature as kaleidoscopically as the shifts of fortune require.

The third virtue, prudence, is defined chiefly in terms of what the Italian writers of this period called *segrettezza*, the ability to keep important matters (here, the arcana) secret.[36]

The chapter on what opinions it is necessary to hold in order to perform master strokes of state is likewise concerned with amplifying the psychological portrait of the politician, with preparing his spirit. The first opinion required is that of the mutability of all things, or, in the phrase of Boethius, whom Naudé cites here, "in mundo constare quantum esse nihil." The heavens themselves are subject to corruption, and religions also alter and change form, and "one should not fall into the error of those weak spirits who imagine that Rome will always be the seat of the Holy Fathers, and Paris that of the kings of France" (p. 141). In Boethius, universal mutability placed secular events under the sway of fortune, but from another perspective, the rule of fortune,

---

[35] Battista, *Alle origini*, p. 207, has pointed out Naudé's borrowings from Charron in this passage.
[36] See, for example, Scipione Ammirato, *Della segrettezza* (Venice, 1598).

in the *De Consolatione,* is only apparent: From the point of view of the all-knowing and benign Creator, a point of view outside of time (the *nunc stans,* as Boethius calls it), Providence directs events, even when they seem unfair or inscrutable to mortals. When this other side of Boethius's concept of fortune is abandoned,[37] as it is in Machiavelli and Naudé, fortune becomes the symbol of a delegitimated political universe, and virtue loses its moral and contemplative dimension and becomes the personal force (*esprit fort*) by which an individual counters fortune by recognizing the principle of change and adapting to it. The Machiavellian direction of Naudé's belief in mutability is clear in his extension of the principle to the church. (By insisting that the popes may not always live in Rome, he may have in mind some temporary absence, like the residence at Avignon, or he may mean that the Christian religion, like the pagan, will one day disappear. In either case, like Machiavelli – who includes Christianity in his discussion of the founding, maintaining, and restoration to first principles of religions – he draws attention to those ways in which the church, an institution supposedly beyond time, exists within time and is subject to the rule of mutability applicable to all human and natural things.) It is also clear in his use of the principle of mutability to demystify the process of founding and maintaining political (including religious) institutions. For the conclusion he draws from mutability is that

a good spirit will never despair of being able to surmount the difficulties that will get in the way of others in order to undertake and accomplish affairs of importance. As, for example, if a minister, be it for the service of God or that of his master, thinks of means to ruin some republic or empire, this general maxim will make him think at the start that such an endeavor is not impossible, since there isn't one that enjoys the privilege of eternal duration and existence. (pp. 141–2)

As in ruining states, so in founding them and in altering their form, Augustus made an empire of the greatest republic of all time, and one may make a republic of the greatest empire. The principle of inevitable, periodic alteration that Naudé insists upon here is very similar to the Polybian concept of anacyclosis as used by Machiavelli:[38] What is specifically Machiavellian is not variation, which is Boethian, or anacyclosis itself, but the way in which these principles of universal change make the political achievements of the past accessible to the

---

[37] The Boethian tradition and its alteration by Machiavelli are treated in detail by J. G. A. Pocock, *The Machiavellian Moment* (Princeton, N.J., 1975), pp. 36–48, 156–7ff.
[38] Ibid., pp. 189ff.

imagination and make them available as models for imitation and action:

Let no one despair, then, of being able to effect that which has been effected by others; for ... men are born and live and die in an order which remains ever the same. (*Disc.* I:11)

That order is the order of fortune, the order of constant variation and cyclical alteration of political constitutions, presenting opportunities for "virtue."

Like Naudé, Machiavelli invokes this principle in the context of the anacyclosis of religions. It is important to include religions under fortune's dominion, because it is precisely their claim to exist outside of time and to partake of a nonhistorical reality that beclouds and mystifies the entire process of the founding and altering of institutions. If we cannot see the religions that sanctify political institutions as themselves the product of time, then we cannot imitate the founders, because they all claim to have been inspired by God. It is for this reason that Machiavelli mentions Moses' divine call in *Il Principe*, only to ignore it, placing the Exodus in the context of pagan and purely human achievements; that he tells us that ecclesiastical principalities are subject to higher laws, only to analyze them according to lower ones; and why here, when he enunciates the principle of uniformity in human affairs, he does so in the context of heartening those who might wish to imitate the actions of a Numa or a Savanarola. Numa made use of religion and fictional converse with deity in founding Rome and, though he was assisted in his aims by the relative rudeness and unsophistication of the Romans at the time, the task is not an impossible one even for contemporaries:

Though it is easier to persuade rude men to adopt a new institution or a new standpoint, it does not follow that it is impossible to persuade civilized men to do so. ... It did not seem to the people of Florence that they were either ignorant or rude, yet they were persuaded by Friar Girolamo Savanarola that he had converse with God. I do not propose to decide whether it was so or not, because of so great a man one ought to speak with reverence; but I do say that vast numbers believed it was so without having seen him do anything out of the common whereby to make them believe it; for his life, his teaching and the topic on which he preached, were sufficient to make them trust him. Let no one despair, then, of being able to effect that which has been effected by others; for ... men are born and live and die in an order which remains ever the same.

Again, we find that these chapters of the *Discorsi* are central ones for Naudé. As with Machiavelli, the anacyclosis of political institutions, including religions, leads not to a belief in providence but to the view that the achievements of the founders and legislators, involving, as they did, religious deception, are imitable by modern politicians. Later in the chapter, Naudé again quotes Machiavelli on Savanarola.[39]

The second opinion one needs to hold is that it is not necessary to move the world in order to achieve great changes in states. As with the lever of Archimedes, great changes can come from small means and slight beginnings – The world was made of nothing, or of atoms; tiny seeds become great trees; God used a tongue-tied man and tiny, insignificant animals to humble Egypt (pp. 146–9) – and, as with the principle of mutability, the emphasis falls upon the imitability of such ancient examples. If anyone should suppose that such miracles are irrelevant to modern concerns, let him consider the wondrous changes wrought by Luther and Calvin, by "the spite of two monks whose only weapons were the tongue and the pen" (p. 149). As in Machiavelli, again, the miraculous character of the Exodus is not denied, but the emphasis falls upon the possibility of its contemporary imitation, a possibility that is diminished to the extent that one does accept it as a miracle. This section tells us not only that small means can effect large changes, but that contemporary equivalents of biblical miracles can be effected by purely human means.

One of the reasons they can be effected is made plain in Naudé's discussion of the third and final opinion, which concerns the populace and its credulity, particularly its easy acceptance of supposed miracles. The people believed David George to be the son of God; they credited Dooms' prophecies of the advent of Antichrist and the impostures of the Rosicrucians (pp. 154–7). Naudé's examples of the credulity of the Parisians recall biblical miracles: If one told the Parisians that a Flood was imminent, they would build arks; if one told them that the seas would dry up, they would prepare for the trip to Jerusalem. Naudé even draws an example of credulity from the New Testament, recalling the superstition of the people of Lycaonia, who thought that Paul and Barnabas were gods. Thus all three opinions centrally involve the continued possibility of creating the illusion of the supernatural for political effect. In regard to this last one, the conclusion drawn from the credulity of the people is that people can still be fooled, as they were by Serotius, Sulla, Jean de Vincence, and Savanarola, into believing in conversations with the gods, and that therefore

princes or their ministers should study how to manipulate and persuade them by fine words, seduce and fool them by appearances, win them over and turn

[39] This quotation had played an important role in the *Apologie* as well; see the section "The hermetic tradition" in this chapter.

them to one's designs by preachers and miracles under pretext of sanctity, or by making for them clandestine books, manifestos, apologies, and declarations, artistically composed, to lead them by the nose. (p. 158)

Thus, just as, in the transition from the *Apologie* to the *Coups d'état*, the vocabulary of magic is replaced by terms like *mystère d'état, secrets d'état*, and *arcana imperii*, so, in regard to the psychological or spiritual dimension of Naudé's subject, the vocabulary of hermetic contemplation and spiritual elevation is replaced by the doctrine of the *esprit fort*, with very little change in essentials. Like the magus, the *esprit fort* is set apart from the common people, knows how supernatural manifestations may be simulated by natural means, uses his knowledge to gain political control over others, and has the boldness and moral courage to use it despite the taboos, moral hesitancies, and superstitions that keep others from using it.

The term *esprit fort* itself had been used by others on both sides of the "libertine" question. It is G. C. Vanini's regular term for the man of undeceived, scientific understanding. Vanini's book *De admirandis naturae arcanis*[40] argues that by knowing the secrets of nature and by understanding the rational causes for what appears to the ignorant as mystery, one learns to manipulate those causes and becomes a natural magician. The personality trait one needs for this is precisely the *spiritus fortis*, the ability to see beyond received myths, particularly moral ones. The French term *esprit fort* appears in Garasse and Mersenne, where it is associated with the "libertine" tradition of Charron, Vanini, Cardan, and Machiavelli.[41] Like much else in Naudé's outlook, the doctrine may go back to Paduan, Averroistic sources that operated upon Machiavelli as well. The motif of the legislator who gives order to successive eras in the history of states and religions, and whose virtue or personal quality of forcefulness enables him to succeed, is common to Paduan Averroism and Machiavelli, as Spini has pointed out.[42] But whether the ultimate sources lie elsewhere or not, there is no doubt that Naudé associates the *esprit fort* with Machiavelli, who first "broke the ice" in writing about the arcana and whose texts surface at the crucial junctures we have noted in Naudé's *Coups d'état*. Machiavelli's founder of new modes and orders, too, is a natural magician or "conoscitore delle cause naturali" (*Disc.* I:12) and creates fictions

---

[40] Giulio Cesare Vanini, *De admirandis naturae . . . arcanis* (Paris, 1616).
[41] Marin Mersenne, *L'impieté des déistes, athées et libertins de ce temps* (Paris, 1624), pp. 174–5, 197–8, 210, 228; F. Garasse, *La doctrine curieuse des beaux esprits de ce temps, ou pretendus tels* (Paris, 1623), pp. 1–3.
[42] Spini, *Libertini*, pp. 17ff.

of the supernatural. Machiavelli's ordinary term for the quality needed to found states is *virtù*, but he sometimes uses terminology closer to *esprit fort*.[43]

But as this quotation suggests, the essential connection between Machiavelli and the doctrine of the *esprit fort* is not the term, but the idea that there is a necessary psychological strength that must accompany effective political action. Machiavelli is sometimes read as if he were the originator of a technology of politics, or a positive science, in which effective procedures for achieving political ends are explored without reference to the kind of person one would need to be to use them. But Machiavelli's interest in the moral or psychological aspect of his subject is signaled in many ways: by his use of a rigidly moral vocabulary that draws attention to the human and moral cost of employing the strategies he recommends; by his recognition that although extreme methods are effective, moderate ones are more humane; and by his constant posing of alternative courses of action. When one begins to see that Machiavelli sometimes writes of self-tansformation, of the preparation of the spirit for difficult choices, one soon realizes that he always writes this way, and in fact never discusses technique in isolation from moral and psychological questions.

Naudé's doctrine of the *esprit fort* differs from Machiavelli's idea of the spiritual preparation necessary in politics in many ways. The idea of an arcane, quasimystical initiation into political wisdom is absent in Machiavelli, as is Naudé's belief that the people are contemptible and are potential persecutors of the intellectual elite. Machiavelli, of course, teaches how to deceive the masses and recognizes popular credulity as a source of power. But this recognition is balanced by a respect for ordinary people that Naudé never shows. An uncorrupted populace, such as that of republican Rome, is the firmest foundation for a state; Machiavelli can even endorse, at least in a limited sense, the adage that the voice of the people is the voice of God (*Disc.* I:58), and he holds that the military defense, even of principalities, must be entrusted to them (*Prin.* 13). Naudé has no concept of citizenship – certainly no republican sense of the citizen – and his *esprit fort* draws his psychological strength, as well as his justification for manipulating the credulous masses, from his infinite intellectual and moral superiority to them.

Nevertheless, when one has pointed out the ways in which Naudé's doctrine of the *esprit fort* is not Machiavellian, much remains, partic-

---

[43] E.g., *Disc.* III:22: "l'animo suo forte gli fa comandare cose forti. . . . a comandare le cose forti, conviene essere forte."

ularly the moral tension of the original, the balancing of moral claims against political realities, the repeated confrontation of the reader with the inescapable dilemma of seeking good ends through bad means, and the sense that this confrontation with the moral issues is a necessary form of spiritual preparation for political life. Naudé set out, both in his framing of the concept of the *coup d'état* and in his portrait of the *esprit fort*, to restore this dimension of moral complexity to the political tradition Machiavelli had revived. The Naudean insistence upon the extraordinary is part of this effort. It is a quality we expect to find in aesthetics – especially baroque aesthetics – rather than in politics. Yet it was a necessary counter to the aridity of a literature of reason of state that sought to correct, rationalize, and schematize Machiavelli's sense of the need for morally flawed methods. In Botero, in Clapmar, and in many of the other writers in this tradition, the moral problems are solved, rules are established for the use of reason of state, and limits are set to it. But such clarity actually has the effect of diminishing the moral difficulty and the human complexity of the challenge to traditional political ethics that Machiavelli had raised. In fact, the reason of state school represents a return to exactly the kind of euphemizing that Machiavelli deplored. Almost none of Machiavelli's followers retain the delicate balance between moral judgment and its necessary overriding by considerations of state exemplified in the famous line "entrare nel male, necessitato," in which euphemism is refused and moral judgment passed even upon the necessitated act. It is this difficulty and complexity that Naudé aims at in the *Coups d'état*. Naudé's restoration of the Machiavellian tradition is effected through an emphasis upon mystery and upon those unformulable aspects of political action that give it grandeur and effect; and his doctrine of the *esprit fort* is his attempt to give a name to the combination of undeceived intellectual clarity and moral courage possessed by Machiavelli's founder of new modes and orders as he existed in past history and, potentially, among the readers of *Il Principe, I Discorsi,* and the *Considerations politiques sur les coups d'état.*

6

Biblical Machiavellism
Louis Machon's *Apologie pour Machiavel*

Louis Machon was born about 1600 in the Lorraine, where his father was councillor and secretary of the archdiocese of Toul.[1] We know little of his early life and education. He spent the years, 1625–6 at the College de Boncourt in Paris, and by the early 1630s was himself episcopal canon and chaplain of Toul. In 1633 the bishop of Toul resigned, and a complex and lengthy controversy arose involving the episcopal canons, the pope, and the government of Cardinal Richelieu concerning the proper way to replace him. The details need not concern us here, except insofar as negotiations between the archdiocese and Paris brought Machon into contact with Richelieu and propelled him into the midst of the complexities surrounding the question of the union of France with the Lorraine that were to occupy him for more than a decade. At first, Machon had taken the view that the king ought to recognize that the archdiocese was "entirely at the disposition of the Holy See" and had composed a "remonstrance" to the king on the question in 1633. But shortly afterward, we find him taking the opposite view and preparing memoranda for Richelieu supporting the government's position. Richelieu asked Machon to prepare a complete study of the question of the relation between papal and royal power in France; the massive work was completed only after Richelieu's death in 1642. The *Traité politique des différends ecclesiastique* ran to 1,700 pages in manuscript, but because Mazarin's administration took a less aggressive stance on the issue, Machon was unable, despite repeated attempts, to secure a license for its publication. Under Richelieu, Machon had been appointed archdeacon of Port and enjoyed various other benefices, which he held for several years after the Cardinal's death. At this time, while in the employ of the Chancellor Séguier,

---

[1] On Machon's biography see Raymond Céleste, "Louis Machon, apologiste de Machiavel et de la politique du cardinal de Richelieu: Recherches sur sa vie et ses oeuvres," *Annales de la faculté des lettres de Bordeaux* III (1881), 446–72; V (1883), 67–132; and K. T. Butler, "Louis Machon's 'Apologie pour Machiavelle – 1643 and 1688," *Journal of the Warburg and Courtauld Institutes*, III (1939–40), 208–27.

he became implicated in a case involving the unauthorized use of the chancellor's seal. The "affair of the false seals" is a difficult one to assess, as charges and countercharges were exchanged for years afterward, Machon claiming that the accusations against him were a cover for the chancellor's own misprison. At any rate, in 1648 Machon was put in prison, where he attempted suicide by cutting a vein. Upon release, he was deprived of his benefices, and remained in Paris during the period of the Fronde, composing, if Celeste is correct in his attributions, a number of "Mazarinades" attacking the chief minister. With the end of the Fronde, Machon fled to Rouen, then to Tourne, a small commune on the banks of the Garonne, where he enjoyed the protection of the bishop of Bordeaux and was appointed curate of Saint-Estienne de Tourne in 1654. In 1662 he prepared a catalog of the library of Arnauld de Pontac, first president of the Parliament of Bordeaux. He was succeeded in his curacy in 1672, and it is not known whether he returned to Paris at that time or when he died.

The *Apologie pour Machiavel* occupied Machon in one way or another for over a quarter-century. The project of defending Machiavelli was suggested by Richelieu in 1641:

Cardinal Richelieu, who may be considered a miracle of our times and a wonder for the ages to come, did me the honor (in his library, of which he himself was the finest piece) to say that he could not sufficiently wonder at the fact that all who wrote politics attended to this rare spirit [i.e., Machiavelli] without one of them ever having had the courage or the heart to defend the indispensable and reasonable maxims of this solid and truthful writer. This, the request of this peerless minister whom one could refuse nothing, made me begin the apology. (MS Bordeaux 535, preface, p. 26)

There are two distinct versions of the work that resulted from this suggestion: one completed in 1643 and dedicated to Séguier (BN 19046–7), of which there is a second, incomplete manuscript of a somewhat later date (BN fonds Séguier 642); and one finished in 1668 and dedicated to Armand de Pontac (Bibliothèque Municipale de Bordeaux MS 535). In this discussion, the complete 1643 text will be referred to, except for material added in 1668. The work has never been published in its entirety, though extracts have appeared at various times and J. A. C. Buchon printed the incomplete 1643 text in his edition of Machiavelli's works in 1836.[2] As with the *Traité*, Machon had expended an immense amount of labor on a work that was not to be printed, and owed its inspiration to Richelieu, who, as Machon

---

[2] See Giuliano Procacci, *Studi sulla fortuna del Machiavelli* (Rome, 1965), p. 195. I have not seen a copy of Buchon's edition.

poignantly puts it, "died too soon for me." In the dedication to Armand de Pontac, Machon seems to place his hope for literary survival on the *Apologie:* His own life, in exile from Paris, had been that of a "martyr of the state," but his work on Machiavelli is his "glorious child, which is most certain to be discovered after the death of its afflicted father."

In form, Machon's treatise is a defense of thirteen passages from the *Discorsi,* and ten from *Il Principe,* selected from among those most attacked by Machiavelli's critics, especially Gentillet and the Jesuit opponents of Machiavelli: Ribadeneyra, Possevino, and their successors. Machon defends Machiavelli on many grounds, some of which are familiar to us – that Machiavelli didn't actually say what his enemies claimed he said: or didn't mean it in the ways imputed to him; that he wrote to unmask the secrets of tyrants than to recommend them; and so on. But the heart of the defense, reiterated throughout the work, is that "the most approved historians and the most sacred of books are guarantors of the doctrine he puts forth," that is, that Machiavelli's doctrines are consistent with the classical political tradition, with the political writings of the church fathers, and even with the Bible itself. In his preface, Machon defends this singular undertaking by claiming that the Bible is the ultimate source of the ancient wisdom regarding secrets of state:

One may cease to be surprised that I draw parallels between Holy Scripture and the works of Machiavelli, and that I propose that his strongest and most formidable maxims were drawn from the book of books, which is the work of the Holy Spirit, if one considers that this sacred volume, which should be the study and meditation of all true Christians, teaches princes as well as subjects. . . . There is no secret of state in Plato, in Aristotle, or in Tacitus that cannot be found in Wisdom and Ecclesiasticus, and I maintain that these two books can teach great princes a politics finer and more subtle than exists among men. (1668, preface, pp. 1–2)

But this project was even more ambitious than one showing that Machiavelli had biblical precedent and sanction for his ideas. Machon read Machiavelli as an author who had actually made a contribution to Christian piety:

There is nothing religious in morals, nothing holy in politics, nothing sacred and worthy of reverence among men that he does not preach and counsel with fervor, justice and piety. (1668 preface, p. 9)

For Louis Machon, Machiavelli far from being the atheist his enemies took him to be, was a misunderstood Christian moralist, who in his appreciation for the difficult ethical questions of political life "spoke like a saint" (1643, p. 203).

Machiavellism had been found in the Bible before, but usually on the wrong side. For Cardinal Pole, Machiavelli's doctrine was the *mysterium iniquitatis* of Antichrist. The Latin translator of Innocent Gentillet's *Coutremachiavel,* in his influential preface, took an essentially similar view, as Antonio D'Andrea has shown, placing Machiavelli's doctrines in an apocalyptic framework.[3] For these authors, as for John Carpenter, Machiavellism appeared in the Bible because it was satanic:

Such a one was that Macchiavile, who persuaded men to govern in this world partly by fraud, partly by force, and partly by fortune; and not by the divine providence, whereat he jested; imitating therein not only Julian . . . but also (and that effectually) that cankered serpent, which, hearing that God had forbidden Adam and Hevah the Tree of Knowledge of good and evil, scoffed at God's word and said: Tush, it is nothing so: ye shall not die, but ye shall be as Gods.[4]

After Giovanni Botero's *Della ragione di stato* was published in 1589, a large body of political literature came into being whose purpose was to find in Scripture models for political conduct, and especially to find in the Bible a guide to a ˆgood reason of state, in order to counter the bad reason of state of Machiavelli.[5] Joan Marquez's *El governador cristiano* (1604), for example, takes the form of a joint biography of Moses and Joshua, and attempts to base its advice to Christian rulers on their practice. In France, the work of Claude Vaure (*Les politiques chrestiennes* [Paris, 1621]), Etienne Molinier (*L'estat chrestien, ou maximes politiques, tirées de l'Escriture contre les fausses raisons d'estat des libertins politiques* [Paris, 1626]), and many others testifies to the widespread belief that a recast, more specifically scriptural version of the ideologies of Christian kingship was required in an age in which reason of state was triumphant. The question was not whether reason of state was a valid category of political analysis, but whether the excesses of bad, or Machiavellian, reason of state could be moderated by Christian principles and biblical precedent.[6]

Some authors in this tradition found both the good and the bad varieties of reason of state in the Bible. Scipio Chiaramonti (*Della ra-*

---

[3] See also Chapter 1, this volume, for a discussion of "satanic" Machiavellism.
[4] *A Preparative to Contentation* (London, 1597), pp. 233–4.
[5] See William F. Church, *Richelieu and Reason of State* (Princeton, N.J., 1972), pp. 62–72; Rodolfo de Mattei, "Il problema della 'Ragion di Stato' nel Seicento," *Rivista Internazionale di Filosofia del Diritto* XXVI (1949), 187–210; XXVII (1950), 25–38; XXVIII (1951), 333–56; and De Mattei, *Il problema della 'ragion di stato' nell'età della controriforma* (Milan and Naples, 1979).
[6] See Church, *Richelieu*, pp. 42–4.

gione di stato [Florence, 1635]) devotes a chapter to the question of
"whether reason of state was known to the ancients," and discovers
evidence for the antiquity of the notion in Hesiod, in Plato, and above
all in the Bible, which provided examples of both kinds, the good
being exemplified by the political prudence of Joseph, who ensured
the safety of Israel by his government of Egypt, and the bad represented by the Pharaohs, whose "bad and tyrannical reason of state"
almost destroyed the Jews (pp. 487–91). Secondo Lancelotti's *Hoggidi*
(Venice, 1623) attributes to bad reason of state the making of the
golden calf by Aaron, Jeroboam's schism, Achitophel's temptation of
Absalom, and, above all, the role of the Jews in the condemnation of
Christ (pp. 84–6).[7] The "maladetta ragione di stato" that led to the
death of Christ was the same as that favored by modern politicians,
who daily consult, if not Machiavelli himself, then at least the "Bodins
and Tacituses" who teach a similar doctrine (p. 86). And with this
trust in human prudence – found even in the Bible, but as bad example
– Lancelotti contrasts "the true and holy reason of state," which can
be derived from Scripture, particularly from Ecclesiasticus, Proverbs,
and the books of Kings (p. 86).

Antonio Mirandola's book *Ragion di stato del presidente della Giudea
nella Passione di Cristo* (Bologna, 1630) turns upon the elaboration of
the contrast between the worldly reason of state of Pilate and the Jews
and the divine reason of state of Christ:

Since reason of state may be taken in a good and a bad sense, so that if a
prince employs true prudence and just artifice in procuring the public and
private good of his subjects in acquiring and maintaining his state it will be
good, and if he wishes to use wicked and malicious arts for his own interests
or for those of the public it will be bad and worthy of reprehension, I, wishing
that the one be avoided and the other embraced, show the mostly bad kind
used by Pilate and the Hebrews, and the good and wise kind exercised by
Christ and God in regard to the spiritual kingdom. (Preface)

Mirandola explicitly associates the "bad reason of state" not only with
the Devil, who is the ultimate inspiration for the actions of Pilate and
the Sanhedrin, but also with Machiavelli (p. 39). Yet, unlike Chiar-
monte and the other authors of the reason of state tradition, Mirandola's purpose is not to contribute to political theory but to use it
for a meditative purpose. A canon regular and abbot of San Salvatore,
Mirandola explains that his treatise is essentially devotional: "Retired

[7] This last point was also made by Clapmar (see Chapter 4, this volume); by F. Topius,
Tractatus de potestate principis secularis (Florence, 1607), pp. 67–8; and by P. C. Ramirez,
Analyticus tractatus de lege regia (Saragossa, 1616), p. 82. See De Mattei, *Il Problema*, p.
125.

in the removed cloisters of the religious, I wept for a time for the harsh circumstance of the Passion of Christ, and finally my tears have issued from my pen" (prefatory letter to Antonio Barberino). The reader Mirandola imagines is not a prince, but one who seeks to be a spiritual prince, emulating Christ's "government" over the soul to attain the kingdom of heaven. Mirandola's project may seem a strange one, but there was precedent for it in the Ignatian tradition of the meditation upon the "two standards."[8] In this meditative technique, Ignatius invites the worshipper to imagine, as fully as possible, the struggle between God and Satan as a battle, with its leaders, armies, and strategies. Mirandola extends the comparison, endowing each side with a political ideology, but his aims are likewise meditative. The book is nearly 600 pages long, and each verse of the biblical Passion narrative is discussed at length on the assumption that every detail reveals an element of the complex strategies by which both Satan and Christ attempted to establish and maintain their kingdoms through reason of state. The work is especially interesting because even the good or divine reason of state has its harsh or difficult side, entailing not only deception and "just artifice," but also the sacrifice of the innocent. Here it is not only Caiaphas who considers it necessary for one man to die for the people, but God as well:

Thus Christ was crucified for the common salvation, as was preordained by God, in order to procure true felicity for us. And the prince not only ought to have as his sole aim the safety and happiness of his subjects, as King Ferdinand the Younger of Naples said to Neapolitans according to Guicciardini . . . but he is obligated as well to give up his own life and those of his children in their defense, as did Marius (albeit unwisely), who, to benefit the Roman people whose consul he was, sacrificed his daughter to the demons, wishing to gain victory over the Cimbri. (pp. 335–6)

Like Mirandola, Louis Machon locates, in the more daring portions of his book, a complex and morally difficult reason of state in the divine counsels themselves. Unlike Mirandola, indeed, more than any other author of the period, he insists on connecting divine reason of state with Machiavelli.

In form, the *Apologie* is a defense of twenty-three controversial passages, thirteen from the *Discorsi* and ten from *Il Principe*. Each of these "maxims" is quoted in Italian and French, and defended by parallels drawn from Greek, Roman, and patristic authors, and from the Bible.

[8] For the "two standards" see *The Spiritual Exercises of Saint Ignatius of Loyola*, 4th ed., tr. W. H. Longridge (London and Oxford, 1950), pp. 100ff.

From the *Discorsi*, Machon selects the following principles for discussion:

1. It is permissible to conquer states by force. (*Disc.* I:1)
2. The prince may foment dissension for the good of the state. (1:4)
3. Popular uprisings must be put down by force. (I:34)
4. Cruelty in a good cause is blameless. (I:9)
5. Reason of state requires the use of religion, even if false. (I:12)
6. One must accommodate religion to the needs of the state. (I:14)
7. The Roman Catholic church brought confusion to its territories. (I:14)
8. One must establish colonies in newly acquired territories. (I:26)
9. The Christian religion makes men weak. (II:2)
10. Deception for the good of the state is permitted. (II:13)
11. Recent benefits do not cancel old injuries. (III:4)
12. A prince ought to keep his subjects poor. (III:25)
13. One may break faith for the good of the state. (III:42)

And from *Il Principe*:

1. One must exterminate rivals in newly conquered possessions. (Ch. 3)
2. A prince should accommodate the virtues and vices to the needs of state. (Ch. 15)
3. A prince should be parsimonious. (Ch. 16)
4. It is better to be feared than loved. (Ch. 17)
5. A prince should imitate the lion and the fox. (Ch. 18)
6. One must dissimulate to rule well. (Ch. 18)
7. It suffices for a prince to be virtuous in appearance and not in fact. (Ch. 18)
8. A prince should tolerate enemies in order to assess their power. (Ch. 20)
9. A prince should prefer his own counsel to that of all others. (Ch. 23)
10. War is justified by its usefulness. (Ch. 26)

Several of these maxims do not reveal the actual issues that made the long passages of which they are summaries controversial. For example, in the case of maxim 8 from the *Discorsi*, the passage in question is the famous one concerning the tyrannical colonial policies of Philip of Macedon, and it is the cruelty of these methods, rather than the general question of the establishment of colonies, that provoked criticism. Others more adequately indicate the shape of the debate as it had developed by the time Machon wrote, and many of these maxims will by now be quite familiar to the reader, as they have figured in our discussion of Pole, Gardiner, and Gabriel Naudé. All of them were passages that had been reproved by one or another, and usually several, of the authors who had written in opposition to Machiavelli – Gentillet, Ribadeneyra, and many others. In some cases, Machon claims that Machiavelli did not say, or did not intend in the way attributed to him, what his critics found objectionable. In other cases, the defense offered is simply that Machiavelli's critics are excessively scrupulous, rejecting what not only Machiavelli but universal custom and practice have condoned. But in the course of defending a large number of these maxims, Machon offers a more subtle and original argument based on a recasting of the ideology of sacred kingship and holding that, if both are rightly understood, Machiavelli and the doctrine of the sacredness of kings drawn from the Bible have common themes and sanction identical practices. In the following discussion, not all of Machon's maxims can be treated in detail; those in which the principles of his biblical defense of Machiavelli stand out most clearly will be emphasized.

Cruelty and reason of state

The fourth maxim from the *Discorsi* – that cruelty for reasons of state is permitted – is drawn from Machiavelli's discussion of the murder of Remus by Romulus (*Disc.* I:9). For Machiavelli, Romulus's action is a somewhat sardonic illustration of the principle that one must assume sole authority in founding a state. Machiavelli mentions Moses and Lycurgus as examples of the same principle. Machon begins his defense with this reference to Moses and argues, like Machiavelli, that founders of states fall into a special moral class. Moses founded "the commonwealth of the Jews," and Romulus "followed him and imitated him to establish that of Rome"(p. 43). It is interesting that the particular act of Moses upon which Machon bases the comparison is not, as in Machiavelli, the assumption of sole authority over the state, but the murder of the Egyptian overseer (Exodus 2:12). In the biblical narrative, this act is not presented as a political necessity at all; in fact it puts Moses, and therefore his mission, in danger. Moses' anger against the overseer does, however, testify to his unconscious intimation of his kinship with the Hebrew slaves and of his destiny as their leader. Machon's point is that in this act, as in Romulus's murder of Remus, the founder, responding to divine command, is released from the moral law. There is no such idea in Machiavelli, for whom Rome and

Israel are similar because there are general laws that govern political life, and the justification for the acts of founders comes from the success of the states they found. Machon and Machiavelli agree that the founding of great states often, perhaps always, entails what would in other circumstances be considered great crimes. But for Machon this pattern has a religious significance, and pagan examples conform to biblical analogs that sanction them.

The cruelty of Romulus and of Moses also testifies, in Machon's view, to the principle that no great human work can be accomplished without moral shortfall. Romulus' achievement would have been superhuman if there had not been

some stain, some counterweight to balance a masterwork. . . . Since a man had to be the agent, and a pagan one, there had to be some fault, something to criticize. If destiny had wanted otherwise a god would have been needed. (p. 44)

There were a number of familiar classical maxims that asserted this principle – among them Seneca's "A great necessity is the inheritance of human weakness, and breaks every law," and Cicero's "Whatever is useful becomes honest" – and Machon, like many other political theorists of the period, cites them (pp. 45–6); but the main support for this principle comes from the Bible, where it shades into the doctrine of original sin:

Men can do nothing without mixing something of humanity into it, as it is not their power to do anything without some fault, and something to criticize, especially when they try something that seems to exceed their force and the scope of their powers: Tacitus knew this well when he said "every great example has something wicked about it, because the public good is in conflict with individuals"; it is this that Holy Scripture often expresses in these terms: "all our justice is like a menstrous cloth," and the common and trivial maxim holds that the "greater the right, the greater the injury." (pp. 47–8)

The biblical citation from Isaiah 64:6 implies that, like women in menstruation, human attempts at justice cannot be ritually clean, cannot, that is, claim the same kind of holiness and sanctity as the justice of God. Machon indicates his precise understanding of the image by referring in the margins to Ezekiel 16:4 and Matthew 9:10. The passage from Ezekiel uses the blood of birth to symbolize the tainted Canaanite origin of the city of Jerusalem. Matthew 9:10 refers to the commencement of Jesus' ministry among the tax collectors and sinners. The work of salvation itself requires commerce, even intimacy, with the sinful side of human nature. Machon futher illustrates the principle with the biblical examples of necessary violence: Phineas's summary execution of an Israelite who had married a Gentile wife, for which zeal Phineas was made high priest; Peter's cutting an ear off a Roman soldier; and so on (1668, p. 50). In each case, the point is that violence is a necessary qualification for founders and leaders not only of states but of God's chosen people, the children of Israel and their successors in the church.

A third defense of Romulus holds that in cases when an innocent man, like Remus, must die in furtherance of a great cause like the founding of Rome, such a death may be considered a sacrifice, and, as such, may have biblical precedent. This argument was added to the 1668 text and is borrowed, largely verbatim, from Jean Francois Senault's *Le Monarque* (Paris, 1662):

there are circumstances in which a prince can abandon a just man for the public good, according to the maxim which the high priest of the Jews understood so well, and applied so badly: "it is expedient for one man to die for the people." (*Apologie*, 1668, p. 62; *Le Monarque*, p. 299)

This biblical citation had been noticed by Clapmar and by Naudé (see Chapters 4 and 5, this volume). Naudé had used it, as here, to justify the practice of summary execution. The conception of kinship implied is an extreme, almost cultic, one, with the sovereign playing the role of a priest preparing a human sacrifice. Machon's use of this idea differs from that of Senault, however. His point is not merely that the Bible sanctions such a practice, but that the Bible and Machiavelli teach the same doctrine. Throughout the book, Machon attempts to show that Machiavelli's influence, though widespread, is insufficiently acknowledged. By insisting on the Machiavellian as well as the biblical lineage of this motif of royal sacrifice, Machon attempts to erase the comforting distinction between good and bad reason of state, locating even the harshest moral positions of the new politics in Scripture. This is not to say that Machon held that either Scripture or Machiavelli recommended such methods lightly. Exactly as Bishop Gardiner had done in discussing necessary cruelty, Machon reads the harsher passages of Machiavelli in relation to the chapters in the *Discorsi* (III:19; III:20) in which the kindness of Camillus is praised and in which Fabius is preferred to Scipio. These chapters show, for Machon, that "our author prefers kindness to rigor, clemency to cruelty" (p. 69). But when kindness is ineffective, methods harsh to the point of sinfulness must be adopted.

In this discussion of the use of cruelty in founding and maintaining a state, one may distinguish two kinds of argument, closely related but not identical. One of these holds that human political life is necessarily distant from divine perfection and that a flexible moral standard must therefore be applied to it. The argument from original sin may be thought of as falling into this category, and its effect, roughly, is to affirm the secular direction of Machiavelli's thought. The other argument holds that Machiavellian tactics are justified by the special status of the sacred king. "The people have no knowledge of the secret motives that God suggests to princes" (1668, p. 165). Their conduct may be divinely inspired, and even in the tragic necessity of sacrificing an innocent for the good of the state, they participate in mysteries that have a religious and sacral dimension as well as a political one.

Simulation and dissimulation: Machiavellian illusion in the Bible

The issue of deception or illusion is taken up in many places in the *Apologie*, perhaps most directly in relation to maxim 10 from the *Discorsi* ("deception for the good of the state is permitted"), based on Machiavelli's discussion of the usefulness of fraud in rising from a low to a great position (II:13), and maxim 6 from *Il Principe*, which deals with the famous passage in *Principe* 18 where the need to be a great "simulator and dissimulator" is proclaimed. Machon begins his defense of *Discorsi* II:13 by claiming, as he often does, that Machiavelli was simply stating a fact, not recommending a course of action, when he pointed out that fraud is useful in political life. In Machiavelli's context, which is a discussion of the growth of the state of Rome, it is historically true that fraud was used and that the principle of its use in affairs of state was widely recognized by Roman writers (pp. 306–12). But even if Machiavelli had not meant to justify fraud, as his enemies had claimed, it can be justified, for deceptions of all sorts, "tromperies," are unavoidable in human life: "It would be a failure to know oneself not to know that deception and simulation are born with men, grow with them, and only die when they themselves quit this life" (p. 316). Tromperie begins in infancy, and in fact

the life of men is but a traffic in deception . . . we are so nurtured in this humor that that if we lack someone to fool us, we fool ourselves. (pp. 316–17)

The Machiavellian parent of this passage is *Principe* 18: "men are so simple and so ready to follow the needs of the moment that the deceiver will always find some one to deceive." But soon Machon moves beyond Machiavelli's hard-nosed witness to human knavery under pressure of ambition or neccessity to a vision of vanity and instability influenced by traditions of Renaissance skepticism:

We are fooled by the shadows of things, and, while we fool others, we take opinion for truth. An ugly face covered with plaster charms and teases us by deceiving: that is why we can say with Petrarch that blindness possesses the entry of our life, travail accompanies its progress, sorrow its result and its finish, and error and falsehood the whole. Our own senses fool us, teaching us this business: our sight makes us see oars in water as bent and broken, though one knows they are straight and whole, it makes us think that a square tower is round at a distance, and a path, although of equal width everywhere, seems narrower at the far end than where we are. (pp. 317–18)

The catalog of visual, aural, tactile, and olfactory illusions continues, to conclude with a sweeping tribute to the power of illusion: "Thus the body fools the spirit, the spirit fools the body, and 'tromperie' is our matter and our form, our end and our beginning, the stuff and substance of all our actions" (p. 318). Montaigne obviously influenced Machon here, and the debt is acknowledged in a marginal note to *Essais* III:1 ("je ne peux pas priver la tromperie de son rang"; *Apologie*, p. 320, margin).

The Bible provides a wealth of examples of trickery, many of them for good causes and some apparently sanctioned by God (pp. 320–33): Moses' deception of Pharaoh; the Israelites' plunder of the Egyptians' jewels; military trickery in the campaign for Canaan; Abraham's pretense that Sarah was his sister, not his wife; Joseph's pretending not to know his brothers; Jacob's deception of both Laban and Esau; Judith's lies; David's feigned insanity; and Jehu's misleading of the priests of Baal. In the New Testament, examples of deception are no less frequent: Jesus instructs his disciples to be as subtle as serpents, and in accepting this command they "used a thousand innocent artifices to conquer the world" (1668, p. 428). Machon collects an impressive number of testimonies from various authors (Saint Ambrose, Marcus Marulus Spalatensis, Lessius, Robert Parsons, Senault, and others: pp. 326–8; 1668, pp. 427–8) to support his opinion that the Gospels portray Jesus himself as engaged in deception. There are contradictions in Jesus' account of his powers of judgment, in his statements concerning the timing of the Second Coming, the relation of the Jewish people to the kingdom of God, and other matters. For Machon, these are to be explained as "equivocations and falsehoods he used against the Jews, to further the success of his plan to destroy their religion and their state" (pp. 327–8).

The most striking of Machon's examples of Jesus' use of deception concerns the Incarnation itself. In language that comes close to the ancient Docetist heresy, which held that Jesus' human body was illusory, Machon claims that Christ "assumed the appearance of sinning flesh," though he was without sin (p. 331). In support of this view, Machon adduces an extraordinary passage in Jerome's commentary on Galatians, in which Jesus' human body is referred to as a "simulatio," and his assumption of it is compared to the righteous deceptions of Jehu and David.[9] And, to this idea of Jerome's, Machon adds Saint Ambrose's theory that Jesus' body was a disguise, adopted to "trick the Devil" into attacking him.[10] With these speculations, grounded rather surprisingly upon patristic texts, Machon's discussion of deception approaches the paradoxical notion that the saving action of redemption entails an entering into evil, or into the appearance of evil, in order to transform it. As God tricks the Devil for our benefit, and appears to us in ways that do not fully represent his nature, so the king, sacred as his office is, must employ the deceptions recommended by Machiavelli.

The Machiavellian arts of illusion had often been condemned on the grounds that they were analogous to magic or were a kind of magic. In the 1668 text, Machon addresses this issues in terms borrowed from Gabriel Naudé's *Apologie,* denying the imputation of actual magic but firmly associating Machiavelli with the ancient arcana:

In fact, the sage politician does not at all imitate the magicians who, by impious tricks and fascinations, fill the senses with illusions and the spirit with vain images: he follows the example rather of the true philosophers, who use the mysteries of their science only to maintain them in dignity and make them objects of astonishment to those who can only wonder at what they cannot understand. It is in this same thing that the utility of those counsels which among the ancients carried the name of secrets of empire or of domination consisted, and they never spoke of them but as a species of political religion that veiled its mysteries to make them more venerable. Tacitus called them

[9] Machon quotes in Latin the following extract from Jerome's commentary on Galatians: "Utilem vero simulationem, et assumendam in tempore, Jehu regis Israel nos doceat exemplum, et David: nec mirum quamvis iustos homines, tamen aliqua simulare pro tempore, ob suam et aliorum salutem; cum et ipse Dominus noster non habens peccatum, nec carnem peccati, simulationem peccatris carnis assumpserit, ut condemnans in carne peccatum, nos in se faceret iustitiam Dei."
For the full text see Migne, *Patrologia latina* XXVI, Cols. 339–40, sects. 407–8.
[10] "Jesus Christ s'en est servy [i.e., deception] contre le Demon, qui cachant sa divinité sous sa chair, luy donna la hardiesse de l'attacquer, affin que dans le combat il nous delivrait de sa tirannie, et qu'il vanquist par la ruse ce superbe esprit qui avoit seduit la premiere femme par son artifice: fefellit Diaboloum Christus, ut vinceret" (1668, pp. 427–8, citing Ambrose's *Commentary on Luke,* II; full text in Migne, *Patrologia latina* XV. cols. 1553–4, sect. 1283). The same passage is also used by Senault, *Le Monarque,* pp. 416–17.

arcana imperii or *simulacra imperii,* Pliny shadows of liberty, and Justin blandishments of empire. (1668, pp. 444–5)

Though Machon follows Naudé's analysis of political magic here, he also has Arnold Clapmar in mind: the association of the Tacitean arcana with the *libertatis umbra* of Pliny and the *blandimenta* of Justin appears in the *De arcanis rerumpublicarum* in the section devoted to *simulacra imperii* (Book VI, p. 243). In the previous chapter, we saw how it was precisely this combination of the analysis of magic in Naudé's *Apologie* with the terminology of Clapmar, both regarded as relevant to Machiavelli's project of revealing the ancient secrets of rule, that provided the germ of the *Coups d'état.* But Machon appears to be making this association for himself: It is apparent from citations elsewhere in his text that he knew Naudé's work on magic, but the later *Coups d'état* is never cited.[11] Whether he thought he was making an original association between Clapmar's arcana and Naudé's magicians or not, the passage makes it clear that Machon refers Machiavellian illusion making to the mysteries of state of the ancients.

There is very little difference between tromperie and dissimulation, but they are separated by Machon's plan of treating maxims from *Il Principe* separately from those derived from the *Discorsi,* so that dissimulation, perhaps as distinct from simulation, has to wait until the second section of the book. Many of the issues are similar, but dissimulation seems to mean not so much deception as reserve, tact, a patient pretending not to notice the faults or insincerities of others. Like outright deception, dissimulation is ineradicable – "our prudence is composed of nothing else, and without it our life would be shameful and ridiculous" (p. 640). The motif of covering over the distasteful and shameful aspects of life seems to have a special psychological pressure for Machon, and he tells us that he sleeps with a sign posted above his bed: "Dissimulation is the mainstay of affiars" (p. 651). This prudential axiom is almost a decalogue to Machon, who reminds himself of its truth "when I go to bed and when I arise" (loc. cit.; cf. Deuter-

---

[11] In the 1668 text, Machon compares his project of defending Machiavelli to Naudé's defense of the magicians: "If M. Naudé, the librarian of Cardinal Mazarin, has made an apology for the great men accused of magic, and for popes, saints, kings, philosophers and so many wise men who have been charged with injury to the divine majesty; if the Jews imagined that Jesus Christ performed his miracles by perverse and diabolical magic because he accomplished them so quickly and easily, and were so rash and impudent, as Saints Jerome and Augustine noted, as to circulate and publish certain books entitled *Magia Jesu Christi ad Petram et Paulum Apostolos* which the same doctors demonstrated to be spurious . . . if, then, the Son of God has been so rashly accused of magic and sorcery, one may well charge Machiavelli with impiety atheism and libertinage, though he has asserted nothing against the divinity or the perfection of the God who cannot err" (1668, preface, pp. 35–6).

onomy 6:7). For Machon, dissimulation stands between him and shameful thoughts he cannot otherwise control:

When I hide to attend to my natural functions, is this not to dissimulate the human weakness that is in me? When I do not speak all reveries that are in my mind and the extravagances that present themselves there without my consent, is that not to dissimulate, since my words are other than my thoughts and I reveal only the hundredth part of them? When I deny the vices I am accused of, hide my bad humor, am generous against my will, do not speak to women of the favors which in my heart I desire of them, forget myself before those to whom I owe respect, and since all my life, like those of other men, is merely constraint, and ceremony, is it not to dissimulate, is it not in fact to practice what people want me to condemn in words? What would the world be without dissimulation? What would become of prudence, shame, modesty, discretion, reserve, honesty, civility, pleasure, estimation, reputation, honor, glory, reward, love, clemency, compassion, good deeds and all the best virtues that temper our malice and cover up our infirmities and our faults? (pp. 640–1)

Thus dissimulation is associated with those aspects of human self-consciousness that allow responsibility and judgment, and enable the individual to bring order out of the chaos of thoughts and feeling to which everyone is subject. As nature has given us facial features with which to express our inmost feelings, it has also given us a "secret cabinet" in the soul where those feelings may be concealed if need be – and dissimulation is the "curtain" that covers this inner chamber. This image may remind contemporary readers of Freud's notion of the censor, the part of the psyche that screens unconscious impulses, allowing or denying them conscious recognition and preventing an unmediated and destructive conflict between instinct and the moral standards of society, internalized as superego. The image of the secret chamber had more directly political connotations in the seventeenth century, however, and forms a link to the imagery of arcana. The word arcanum was thought to derive from *arx* – a citadel in which secrets of state were were sequestered (see Chapter 4, this volume). The English word "privy," which retains still its double reference to secrets of the body and of the state, perhaps approximates Machon's use of the word *secret:* The privy chamber, like the *cabinet secret,* was a place in which the intimate needs of nature as well as of the state could be shielded from public view. Because a king had two bodies, one word could refer both to the physical privacies he shared with all human beings and to those secret affairs of state that pertained not to the man but to his office. Both, in Machon's view, might be shameful, and needed a curtain drawn about them:

Dissimulation serves [the spirit] as a curtain . . . Those who bear their heart upon their forehead and who, in natural openness reveal in words, as through crystal, all that is within their souls are more fit for a table of good fellowship than for that of a political council and assembly, because in the theater of public affairs, the actors of necessity must wear divers masks, and change them in each scene, since the good and the safety of the state are the center and end of all their counsels. (pp. 662–3)

Secrets of state are analogous to secrets of the soul. The theatrical metaphor reminds the reader that privacy is required not only to mask the unseemly but also to prepare a spectacle. The possibility of order and decency in public life as well as in private depends upon masking the distressingly human realities of life, upon skills that, like the theatrical, entail pretense and deception.

Machon has no difficulty finding dissimulation in the Bible. Many of his instances overlap with those used to illustrate biblical *tromperie,* and Augustine and Gregory the Great provide patristic support (p. 645). Among the moderns, many of the systematic opponents of Machiavelli devoted lengthy sections of their treatises to licit dissimulation, and so Machon is able to quote from Ribadeneyra, Scribanus, Menochius, and others on the point (pp. 645–6). Dissimulation in the Bible is not merely a matter of human conduct, but, as also in the case of tromperie, of divine example as well:

God himself, who is all-powerful, and who in a moment could destroy the world . . . dissimulates nonetheless the sins of men to bring them to repentance: "He can do all things, and dissimulates the sins of men for repentance" – Wisdom 11:24. (p. 642)

The human world, left to itself, is one in which sin and vanity (in its extended scriptural sense of meaninglessness and unreliability) prevail. In such a world, a morality of absolute truth telling may be no more than misplaced fidelity to what is uncertain and unredeemed. The possibilities for individual redemption, as for political order, depend upon not accepting the fallen world of human evil and epistemological instability as final, upon the possibility of making it other than it is. The arts of illusion – whether that means the individual's pursuit of a better self through masking and transforming inchoate and sinful impulses or the politician's skillful use of Machiavellian simulation and dissimulation – may, in a world that is itself illusory, be redemptive.

Religio instrumentum regni

The idea that illusion may be redemptive informs Machon's treatment of the problem of Machiavelli's attitude toward religion as well. A serious charge of the critics had been that Machiavelli encouraged the manipulation of religion as an *instrumentum regni* without regard to its truth or falsehood, and that he taught that religion had to be accommodated to the needs of the state. Machon's discussion of the problem repeatedly distinguishes between religion as a human institution, and like all others subject to the rule of mutability and the distortions of sin, and religion as worship of the Creator. The Machiavellian passages most relevant to the question of the utility of religion are from *Discorsi* I:12, where the legislators' recourse to God is discussed. It was this chapter, as we have seen, that was most important for Gabriel Naudé's analysis of the fictional deifications of the ancient founders: Recourse to God continued to be a powerful and necessary political tool for contemporary practitioners of the *Coups d'état*. Machon's discussion of the lawgivers, unlike those of Machiavelli and Naudé, makes a very sharp distinction between Moses and the pagan lawgivers, who lacked the grace of God and so had to feign it. Solon, Lycurgus, Numa, and Mohammed pretended to have had conference with gods, and even Caligula, the greatest skeptic among the emperors, claimed to have spoken with Jupiter, and let it be known that he was the brother of Castor and Pollux and the lover of the lunar deity (pp. 79–80).

Machon also takes up more directly than Machiavelli or Naudé the question of the precise relation of the efficacy of pagan and Christian sanctity, and therefore leaves no room to suppose that Christianity is merely an instance of the power of superstitious beliefs, as his predecessors tended to suggest. Just as the false gods of the pagans were of immense political utility, so scorn for those gods often brought miraculous retribution. Machon draws on Pausanias, Aulus Gellius, and others for numerous stories of the harm that befell the violators of pagan temples (pp. 87–9). These are not superstitious stories for Machon, but evidence that God himself, the true Christian God, punished "the scorn they had for what they ought to have revered" (p. 90). As a quotation from Seneca that Machon cites here states, the violation of whatever is thought to be sacred will be revenged as if it were in fact sacred, for it is the violator's own belief that makes him guilty (p. 90). The fact that the gods worshipped at pagan shrines were false makes no difference, for "those who worshipped them held them to be true and wholly divine, and made a sacrilege in not revering them as such." The sanctity of pagan worship is sufficiently real for Machon for him to make an interesting slip of the pen in the manuscript here: First he writes "made a sacrilege in not recognizing [*reconestre*] them as such"; then he crosses it out and writes "reverer

comme tels" above the line. If he, like Machiavelli and Naudé, tends
to treat Christianity and other religions in similar ways, this is more
a consequence of the belief that all religions have some truth in them
than evidence of skepticism toward Christian revelation.

In fact, Machon's religious universalism is quite striking. The fact
that even pagan religion can have the effect of unifying and pacifying
political communities should lead us, in his view, to embrace an attitude
of religious tolerance. Writing with France's history of religous strife
in mind, he points out the paradox of humanity's universal respect
for religion and nearly as universal penchant for religious strife:

> Men are never so good, never in such universal accord as when they are
> establishing a religion: and never have they found among them a subject that
> has caused them so many benefits and so many evils. . . . There is no people
> so barbarous or disordered that they do not recognize some kind of religion,
> and who have no special ceremonies by which to recognize and practice it:
> and here is the universal agreement. But to establish whose is the purest and
> the most holy, it is here that hate, war, persecutions, martyrdoms and cruelties
> find their subject; this is the common cause of all disorders of the earth. (pp.
> 73–4)

The difference between the unity of humanity in worship and the
disunity in particular "ceremonies" is developed with reference to the
distinction between the inner and the outer man: If we recognized
the external aspects of religion as less important than the inner devotion, we would see that outward forms were not worth fighting
about, that particular practices might vary widely and might best be
left to statesmen, to use as political circumstances required. The individual should regard the religious conformity demanded by the state
as a merely external matter,

> and if the interior belies the exterior, what does it matter to the prince: he
> is not responsible for our thoughts, that is our affair; we are the masters and
> ministers of our salvation. It is enough that he be obeyed; it suffices that the
> republic be in good union, and that bad examples be banished from it. (pp.
> 91–2)

By the same token, it is not part of the office of the prince to reform
the existing religion, or even to attempt to interfere with belief in
miracles he knows to be false or with the worship of false relics. The
church itself permits such practices, they are in accord with "la bonne
police," and to reform them would do more spiritual and political
harm than good.

The doctrine of toleration – for the false miracles of one's own
religion, as well as for the religions of others – is extended in bold

ways in the 1668 text. Arguing that Machiavelli's analysis of religion referred to "ceremonies exterieures" rather than to "religion au fond," Machon holds that although it is true that the diversity of religions is quite great, it is even more certain that there is universal agreement that there is a god, so that religious variation is mostly a matter of outward ceremonies (1668, p. 99). The position implied is striking in its relativism, especially when illustrated, as it is in the 1668 text, by religious practices drawn from outside the Christian fold, like the practice of nudism for religious reasons or the various practices of the Chinese described in Trigault's *History of China* (p. 101). At points Machon seems to limit his toleration to varieties of religious practice within Christianity, as when he says that "everyone knows that all religions, good and bad, are founded on the Holy Scriptures, and that each finds its support there" (1668, p. 100). But certainly not all religions accept the Bible, as Machon knew, and his references to China make statements such as this appear to be deliberate blurrings of the boundary between Christian and non-Christian belief. This may be one of the places in which Machon is "not entirely at liberty" to say all he means,[12] for his ideas of the sanctity of all human religion press the limits of orthodoxy.

Expanding Machiavelli's remark that the Romans were more religious than Christian princes usually are, Machon endorses not only the religious impulse of ancient Rome but also certain aspects of its particular theology, holding that the Romans were moving in the direction of recognizing a single, all-powerful deity – "and if they had known him better, they would not have been more religious for that, but simply better instructed" (p. 120). Machon also claims that at least part of Roman polytheism can be explained as a matter of nomenclature, their plurality of gods being understood as manifestations of a single deity, just as the biblical God is called Rock of Jacob, Lord of Hosts, and many other names, though he is understood to be one deity (p. 120).

[12] See fol. M: "J'aurois pu traitter ce sujet plus amplement, plus clairement, plus naifvement, et plus fortement, si j'avois voulu, mais n'y le temps present, ny ma qualité, ny ma condition ne le permettent point, et m'en ostent entierement la liberté. Et comme les loix de la bien-seance et de la modestie deffendent de se monstrer nud et descouvert a touttes sortes de personnes, aussi la raison et la discretion ne m'empescheront d'exposer au publique ce qui doibt estre reservé pour les plus sages, et ce qui n'appartient qu'aux mieux denses et aux plus clair-voians, dont le nombre est, et a tousiours esté asses petit et asses rare."

This passage, with its hint of further revelations and its metaphor of nudity, shows the influence of Montaigne's *Essais* ("si j'eusse eté entre ces nations qu'on dit vivre encore sous la douce liberté des premieres lois de nature, je t'assure que je m'y fusse très-volontiers peint tout entier, et tout nud"; preface) but also makes its author one of those "rare spirits" capable of understanding the arcana.

Machiavelli repeatedly associates pagan and Christian religions, as his critics had noticed. But the association may serve to elevate paganism rather than to degrade Christianity. According to Machon, Machiavelli preferred the Catholic faith, but, believing that there was good in all religions, thought that other, even false, religions could be tolerated when politically necessary "by maxim of state" (pp. 95–8; 1668, p. 114).

The doctrine of accommodation: religion as "milieu"

In a key passage, Machon develops his argument concerning the accommodation of religion to the needs of state by characterizing religion as a link, or bond, between man and God. Etymologically, *religio* is a binding or connecting, and what is important is the connection made, not the nature of the medium, or *milieu*, through which it is made:

Since religion is only a *milieu* between God and men, what does it matter if one makes use of it, as it were, to create unity among subjects, not thereby distancing them from their Creator? When one joins them by this link, one gathers their hearts and vows in common prayer and sacrifice to God the Creator. God became man to communicate with us, to make himself known to our eyes and our spirits; yet we do not want the prince to lower himself at times to sustain his subjects in this love and eternal union. (pp. 133–4)

The accommodation of religion to the state is thus sanctioned by the accommodation of God to man. A long exegetical tradition held that God accommodated himself to our understanding in the Bible, which uses words, images, and anthropomorphic expressions in referring to a deity who is ineffable. The Incarnation itself is a kind of accommodation for Machon, in which God takes a human form to communicate his love. If God can accommodate himself to our limitations to the extent of taking upon himself our form, then the prince can lower himself to the level of his subjects' understanding in order to achieve unity in worship among them – even if this entails an accommodation with popular religious beliefs. In accommodating religion to the state, the prince actually acts in imitation of the Christian God.

Machon's typical doubleness of argument is in evidence here: The political manipulation of religion is defended partly because religion is a neutral symbolic medium (this is a secular or desacralizing claim) and partly because, in using religion as an instrument of rule, the prince acts in imitation of the Incarnation of Christ and thus participates, once again, by virtue of his sacred office, in the mysteries of faith as well as politics.

Where Machon deals with biblical texts concerning the accommodation of religion, the same duality occurs: It is not merely that the Bible seems to tolerate a wide variety of religious practices, and to forgive its protagonists their lapses into the forms of worship practiced by their neighbors, but also that one can discover a pattern in biblical accounts of idol worship whereby participation in wrong forms of religion seems almost to be required by the biblical God in order to show his superiority to all external forms. The principle of toleration, then, a principle that makes Machon's attitude toward religion seem so contemporary at times, alternates with a more mysterious and paradoxical doctrine of licensed transgression, of ritual violation of the very religious practices that the Bible itself mandates.

Machon's biblical examples of religious accommodation include Moses' marriage to the daughter of a Gentile priest, his neglect of circumcision, Jacob's toleration of household idols, and the interesting case of Samaritan religious practices at the time of the Exile. Foreigners transported into Samaria combined elements of their native cults with elements of Israelite religion: "They feared the Lord, but also served their own gods, after the manner of the nations from whom they had been carried away" (II Kings 17:41). Machon takes this verse as divine approval of mixed religious practice:

The king [of Assyria] was forced to allow this so as not to trouble his state, and moreover it seems that God did not reprove this, or find it wicked, for he said: "therefore these people indeed feared God, and nevertheless served their own idols," and this just goes to show that God wanted to declare clearly and definitively that the Assyrians were god-fearing people even though they served and sacrificed to their idols, allowing the humor of the people this idolatry by necessity of state, for the general order of the realm, and in accord with the custom of their fathers. (pp. 148–9)

The texts Machon selects do imply that the combination of Israelite and foreign worship was acceptable to God, but they are contradicted by adjacent texts that condemn eclecticism.[13] Modern scholarship explains such contradictions between an uncompromising and exclusive monotheism and a more eclectic and tolerant conception of religion on the theory that the text took shape over centuries and reflects stages in Israel's understanding of its faith. But the hypothesis of a historically evolving text was not available to Machon: For him the text was con-

[13] Compare 17:41, "these nations feared the Lord, and also served their graven images," with 17:34, "they do not fear the Lord, and they do not follow the statutes or the ordinances of the law."

sistent and sacred, and in a sacred text apparent contradictions reveal a hidden purpose or manifest a mystery.

The Bible appears to command purity of worship in a categorical manner, and yet undermines its own prohibitions and sanctions the very forms of idolatry the commandments exist to forbid. The golden calf is the archetypal idol in the Old Testament, but Aaron, its maker, is rewarded by an appointment as high priest. This is because, according to Machon, Aaron acted as a prudent political leader, accommodating himself to the superstitions of his people (pp. 142–5). Though Aaron made the idol, he was not punished for worshipping it, as the people who believed in it were, for "God only demands the inner self, and leaves appearances to men" (p. 146).

In the 1668 text, the significance of the golden calf is pressed even further in a discussion of Jeroboam's construction of calf idols at the schismatic shrines of Dan and Bethel. In 1643 Jeroboam is mentioned as an example of a politician who accommodated himself to his people, but in the later text, Machon connects the calves of Jeroboam to the calf of Aaron and to the cherubim of the Temple of Jerusalem. In expanding the discussion, Machon was influenced by Daniel Clasen's *De religione politica* (Magdeburg, 1655; 2nd ed. Zerbst, 1681), which praises Jeroboam as a prudent politician who turned religion to his own ends (Zerbst ed., pp. 226–7, 250–2), and by Franciscus Moncaeus's *Aaron purgatus, sive de vitulo aureo libri duo* (Arras, 1606; also printed in several editions of *Critici sacri*, J. Pearson et al., eds., including London, 1660, Vol. IX; Frankfurt-am-Main, 1695, Vol. VII, pp. 3273ff). Moncaeus argues, quite convincingly, that Jeroboam's calves had to be similar in form to the Temple cherubim they were meant to supplant. The narrative in I Kings 12:26–8 specifies Jeroboam's motive for making these idols as fear, lest the people return and worship at Jerusalem:

So the king took counsel and made two calves of gold. And he said to the people, "You have gone up to Jerusalem long enough. Behold your gods, O Israel, who brought you up out of the land of Egypt." (v. 28)

The same words were used by Aaron in Exodus 32:4. Moncaeus points out that in order for the shrines at Dan and Bethel to replace Jerusalem as holy places, they would have to resemble the Temple of Solomon, and therefore the cherubim – made according to the model shown to Moses on the mountain in Exodus 25, originally designed for the Tabernacle and ultimately incorporated into the Temple – were themselves in the form of calves. As Machon puts it:

It cannot be doubted that the cherubim of Moses were in the form of calves, since Jeroboam imitated them, and if they had been of another form, he would have made them the same, taking care not to make them different, since he wanted to maintain and conserve his people by the same cult that they practiced in Jerusalem. (1668, p. 172; cf. *De vitulo aureo* I:7)

The golden calf had already become something of a positive symbol for Machon by 1643, representing a kind of biblical sanction for the Machiavellian accommodation of religion to politics (p. 150). Machiavelli's advice concerning the manipulation of religion could thus be thought of not as a secular or agnostic rejection of religion but as a kind of mysteriously licensed idolatry, practiced by kings, in imitation of the high priest Aaron, as part of their sacred office. When Moncaeus' speculations concerning the identity of calves and cherubim are added to this already paradoxical line of thought, the effect is to locate the mystery of licensed idolatry at the very center of Israelite religion, for the cherubim in the Holy of Holies of the Temple were thought to be the seat upon which the invisible presence of God himself rested.[14]

The power and moral richness of the Old Testament lie partly in its tensions and contradictions, and Machon was not the first to find a complex synthesis of the worldly and the godly in it. In making even his more surprising comments, he often merely takes one step further an exegetical tradition as old as Christianity itself: His doctrine of licensed transgression is present, at least in germ, in Gospel interpretations of the Old Testament.

For example, the story of David's eating of the show bread, normally reserved for priests (I Samuel 21:3–6), is cited by Machon as an example of the prince's license, as sacred king, to transgress religious

---

[14] Moncaeus anticipated, in a number of ways, the conclusions of some modern biblical scholars. See, for example, Umberto Cassuto, *A Commentary on the Book of Exodus*, tr. Israel Abrahams (Jerusalem, 1967), p. 407: "The *kapporeth* over the ark, and particularly the wings of the cherubim spread over it, were a kind of throne for God who sits upon the cherubim, a vacant throne for the deity who is invisible to man. . . . In general the peoples of the ancient East were accustomed to portray the deities as standing or sitting upon wild beasts or cattle, such as lions, oxen or other animals. On this basis, several exegetes have in recent times put forward the view that the golden calves – that is, the golden bulls . . . both the one made in the wilderness and the two of Jeroboam, according to the account in I Kings XII, were not originally deemed to be actual gods, but were likewise regarded as the seat of the invisible godhead."

The biblical texts, on this view, exaggerate the differences between permitted and forbidden kinds of worship. In both form and function, the cherubim and the calves may have been closer than the Bible implies. Machon often discovers the same contradictions and the same cruxes in the biblical text as modern scholars do, but his assumption that the text is to be read as a unity, and synchronically, leads him to posit a mystery of state where historical criticism finds evidence of an imperfect fusion of traditions or source documents by later redactors.

prescriptions and accommodate religion to the state (1668, pp. 165–6). The interpretation of this act as a licensed violation of religious law is already standard in the New Testament (Matthew 12:4 and parallels) and is presented as Old Testament precedent for the violations of the Jewish Sabbath of Jesus' followers.[15]

In the New Testament, too, traces of a process by which early practices were harmonized with later orthodoxy are evident. As Israelite texts preserved traces of an idol-worshipping past, so Christian Scriptures retain evidence of early forms of worship rooted in Judaic practice. Inconsistencies that arose in this way were often explained by patristic exegetes as accommodations or simulated observances performed in order to ensure the survival of the new Christian faith within the matrix of Judaism. Jesus himself was circumcised, although he had come to abolish circumcision; he was baptized according to the practice of John the Baptist, whom he would supplant; he told the leper he healed to make sacrifice according to Mosaic law:

The New Testament has its examples as well as the Old, which are of no less authority, for the savior of the world himself, the king of kings, not merely taught them, but even practiced them, to introduce his law, establish his universal empire, and reduce his creatures to the obedience and submission he desired. The least learned in the Christian religion know that although Jesus Christ came to earth to abolish the law of the Jews and destroy all their ceremonies, nevertheless, not wishing to do so through absolute power, as he could have done, he accommodated himself to their manner of proceeding; and in order to act as a man, whose form and nature he had taken, he practiced with the Holy Virgin his mother almost all his life things which he did not approve, since he had come to destroy and abolish them. (pp. 155–6)

In the 1668 version (pp. 191–2), the accommodation of Christianity to Judaism is supported by a discussion of I Corinthians, where the question of the propriety of Christians eating meat previously sacrificed to idols is addressed. Paul's position is that everything depends upon how this practice is understood: As there is no reality to the supposed gods to whom the food was offered, the only problem arises in the case of new Christians, unsure of their faith, and the example experienced Christians set for them. The question is entirely symbolic, and the form the outward expression takes is to be accommodated to the level of understanding of the Christians involved. The passage supports Machon's view that particular religious practices derive their

[15] Actually, I Samuel 21:3–6 does not seem to support either Machon's interpretation or Matthew's: David's permission to take the show bread is granted by the priests in verse 5 on the basis of his supposed ritual purity.

significance from the inner reality they point to and from their value in representing or communicating that inner devotion to others. As in the case of the licensed idolatry of Aaron and Jeroboam, Paul maintains that there are circumstances in which apparent idol worship is not only permitted, but becomes a religious act in its own right.

Accommodating virtue and vice to the state

In *Il Principe* 15, Machiavelli put forth the view that a prudent politician cannot always conduct himself virtuously:

A man striving in every way to be good will meet his ruin among the great number who are not good. Hence it is necessary for a prince, if he wishes to remain in power, to learn how not to be good and to use his knowledge or refrain from using it as he may need.

Machon is even more skeptical, casting doubt upon the possibility of virtuous conduct itself. For him, virtue is "an object of idolatry," a "name that blinds" (p. 445). Excessive concern for it turns life into a stage play:

This is the theater in which each thinks he does better than his neighbor, but however well prepared one is, his expression is studied, his character is borrowed, and he represents what he does not understand. Here all is constrained, one does not act as one really is, and at the end, be it good or bad, the piece concludes in farce and mummery. We run after virtue, and know nothing about it; we seek what escapes us, and wish for what does not comport with our nature. (p. 446)

The theatrical metaphor functions in the argument in a way that is analogous to the discussion of outward ceremonies in the section on religion. If religion, or virtue, is merely an external show, then it has no inherent sanctity and can be manipulated for a good cause. Machon's tactic is to desanctify moral terminology. Aristotle has shown that virtue was merely a midpoint between opposed vices, and the Bible has revealed that virtue arises out of sin and lapses back into it, as Adam's repentance, the first human act that could be considered virtuous, was predicated upon his sin (p. 448).

Machon argues not for moral laxness, but for sensitivity to the way in which the word "virtue" can misrepresent or traduce the inner state it is meant to refer to, and for appreciation of the complexity, even the mystery, of ethical choices in a fallen world. If we are quick to affix moral labels, we may be unaware that "most things in this world have two handles by which they may be grasped" (p. 450). Even death, often thought of as an absolute evil, can be regarded as a liberation from the miseries of life (loc. cit.).

This attack on moral oversimplification has much in common with Charron, Naudé, and the other "libertine" writers. Like them, Machon's opponents are the "hypocrites and bigots," and his project is *déniaisement*, a freeing of the mind from popular prejudice. Yet he is also concerned with locating his own sense of moral complexity, and his relativism, in a firmly Christian context, and tries to demonstrate at length that the church fathers and the Bible support his views. Jerome, Basil, and Gregory the Great all stress, especially in their works of pastoral advice, the difficulty of distinguishing virtue from vice and the need for charity and caution in making moral judgments (pp. 454–5); Cyril's catechism taught that the vices imitate virtue and that the Devil himself could appear in the guise of an angel (p. 461); and John Chrysostom, like the libertines, had spoken of the distorting effect of popular consensus on moral judgment:

Many vices seem good, and many things seem bad that are not so, and thus we fly from what is truly good but does not seem so to the multitude, not having investigated the nature of things, but respecting the opinion of the multitude. (pp. 451–2, citing Chrysostom's commentary on I Corinthians; Homily 12, chap. 7. English tr. in *The Homilies of S. John Chrysostom* [A Select Library of the Nicene and post-Nicene Fathers (Grand Rapids, 1969; first published 1844), XII, p. 67])

Having established a Christian context, Machon cites Pliny on the ineradicably mysterious quality of human conduct – "true understanding of the actions of men is not only difficult, but entirely impossible: 'God has hidden the seeds of it, and the causes of many good and evil things are hidden under contrary appearances' " (p. 465; citing Pliny the Younger, *Panegyricus*) – as well as Brutus's remark at the battle of Phillipi to the effect that virtue, which he had followed as if it were real, was but an empty name (p. 457). Machon insists, however, on the Christian implication of this fact: It should remind us that we have not solved moral difficulties by naming them, that we must not be content with visible signs, but must, to use another metaphor drawn from the theater, "penetrate within, and know the secret and the motives that make the strings work" (p. 479).

The pursuit of virtue can be a kind of idolatry, because it erects a humanly conceived standard of judgment to replace the God-given one. Our preoccupation with virtue aligns us with the Pharisees and hypocrites of the Gospels, who, by adding to the commandments tranformed them into human rules. Virtue, in the Pharisaic sense, was the cause of the martyrdom of the early Christians, and even of the death of Christ (p. 491). As the Decalogue was turned into a "human commandment" by the Jews (p. 475), so Christians have betrayed the Gospel law, a doctrine of freedom they have turned into an idol:

The original naiveté is entirely effaced and corrupted. The fervor and simplicity of the first Christians is despised. We have made human commandments of the counsels of the divine. Our unjust and violent tyranny has exchanged the liberty we hold from heaven for a servitude and enslavement both shameful and insupportable. (p. 475)

Procacci has demonstrated the close relation that exists between this chapter and Pierre Charron's *La Sagesse* (Paris, 1604), which is often quoted in it.[16] Charron's remarks on those who attempt to transcend the human and achieve the bestial, who imitate the gods and become fools, undoing the fraternal union between human soul and body, provide Machon with welcome support in his attempt to defend Machiavelli's view that the virtues cannot always be practiced (*La sagesse*, p. 401; *Apologie*, pp. 482–3). Similarly, Charron's approval of the use of "bad means, to avoid and get out of a greater evil, or to achieve a good end" is cited in support of Machiavelli's view that the prince needs to know how not to be good, and to use his knowledge when required (*La Sagesse*, p. 185; *Apologie*, p. 470). The importance of Machon's use of Charron, as of other suspect or libertine writers, can be overstated, however. Like Machiavelli, Charron was a writer whose orthodoxy was questioned. Machon's purpose is to show that the apparent amoralism of writers in this tradition had sanction in Christian tradition; the heart of the case is not the similarity between Machiavelli and Charron, but the concord between Machiavelli and the church fathers.

This is an important point, because Machon's purpose is not simply to defend or embrace the liberal or secular direction of Renaissance political and ethical speculation, but to reclaim its sacred dimension. Machiavelli, Lipsius, Charron, and the many writers of the reason of state school all believed that a small evil was justified by a greater good, especially a greater political good, and in this they had ample Classical precedent. But Machon searches this paradox more fully, and, pressing his case for biblical sanction of Machiavellian principles, he elaborates a theory of the necessary commerce of virtue and vice.

One place in the Bible where Machon finds this mysterious "crossing over" of virtue is in the book of Joshua, where Rahab, the Canaanite prostitute, gives aid and comfort to the Israelite scouts. "Ceste histoire

---

[16] Procacci, *Studi sulla fortuna*, pp. 201ff; cf. Butler, p. 213.

n'est pas sans mistere" (p. 501): Not only does it show that the scouts rightly preferred the interest of the state to the preservation of their personal reputations for purity, and that virtue may be found among "sinners," but it also hints at a more mysterious transformation or elevation, for Jewish legend held that Rahab later married Joshua, and the Gospel of Matthew lists this Gentile prostitute as one of the ancestors of Jesus Christ. In fact, as Jerome had pointed out, the only women except Mary who are mentioned in the genealogy of Christ are Rahab; Tamar, who played the part of a prostitute in order to bear a child to Judah; and Bathsheba, who committed adultery with David and caused the death of her husband.

The savior of men did this in order to show the world that frailty may be honorable, to teach that he who came to win back sinners also came to honor them by deriving his birth from them. (1668, p. 588)[17]

As elsewhere in the *Apologie,* the Incarnation, with its mysterious fusion of divine and human, provides a model for the prince's derogation from moral perfection and a way of finding Christian imagery for Machiavelli's principle of necessary entry into evil (entrare nel malo, necessitato"; *Prin.* 18).

Interwoven with Machon's tracing of the biblical motif of crossing over into evil is the principle that this mystery is one reserved for princes, that the conscious use of evil means is a right that devolves upon them, and upon them alone, as a consequence of their special relation to God and their duty to imitate him. Thus, surprisingly, it is in this chapter, which concerns the prince's need to know "how not to be good," that the difference between the princely nature and that of ordinary mortals is most stressed and the doctrine of the "king's two bodies" is invoked. There was, of course, a long and not exclusively Christian tradition according to which the morality binding princes differed from that binding subjects, a difference between private and civic ethics, as in Aristotle. In Charron's words:

The justice, virtue, and the probity of the sovereign proceed quite otherwise than those of individuals. They have larger and freer scope on account of the great, weighty, and dangerous charge they bear. (*La Sagesse,* p. 489, quoted in *Apologie,* p. 508).

Machon, however, embeds this principle of Charron's in a context that makes this double standard a corollary of the godlike prerogative of sacred kings:

[17] Cf. Jerome's commentary on Matthew in Migne, *Patrologia latina* XXVI, col. 21, sect. 9, and Joan Marquez, *El governador christian* (Salamanca, 1612), p. 237.

His nature is human, but his condition elevates him and separates him from what he has in common with others. His quality gives him dispensation from thousands of subjections inseparable from private men and from all those who depend upon his scepter and his crown, there being nothing more certain than that the justice, virtue and probity of the sovereign proceed quite otherwise than those of individuals. (p. 508)

Machon uses King James's *Basilicon Doron* as well as Charron's *La Sagesse* in this section, citing him on page 510 and using the distinction between the king's "two bodies" throughout the section. Kings have two roles ("kings and sovereigns play two characters, that of a man and that of a king"; p. 532), one natural and one political, and the latter is sacred. When the king acts as head of the body politic, he "acts as the gods do" (p. 510). Thus Machon takes care to tie the doctrine of the two standards of conduct very firmly to the sacred office of the king.

Royal "kenosis": Machiavellian ethics as mystery of state

This tying together of the imagery of sacred kingship and the Machiavellian notion of the necessity of vice in politics culminates in a grand comparison between the king, the sun, and God in which all three are seen as perfect in themselves yet willing to act in an imperfect world.

Since the prince is, in his state, what God is in heaven, the sun is in nature, and the soul in the body; and since it is true that the sovereign creator accommodates his goodness and his mercy to the salvation of the Jews, as well as to that of the Christians and to that of the most criminal, as well as to that of those who are most innocent; if it is beyond doubt that the sun does not refuse its rays to sewers and to infected places any more than to flowers and altars; and since everyone knows that the soul lends itself and gives its faculties to the blackest actions, ones it approves of least as well as to the purest and most religious, why should the prince, who is constrained and obliged to live among and converse with so many different kinds of spirits, to govern so many different humors, and to accommodate himself to so many men who have nothing reasonable about them but the name ... why should he not be able to grant them certain things that are no less useful to them than to the wisest and most intelligent?. ... The prince in his own being, and in repose, is like God in heaven, without other meditation and with no other action than contemplation of himself. He is like the sun in its own essence, apart from the dispersal of its rays and the commerce it has with us through its light; and like the soul, detached from its agitated and disorderly body. But as father of his people and sovereign governor of his state he is like God, who, in order to communicate with men, seems to divest himself of his divinity; he is like the sun, which, to animate the world and vivify all things, seems to quit the sky and live on earth and join with it; and like the soul which, to accommodate itself to the body and give it the sustenance it receives, is so united to the body that most men, and almost all the wisest, have believed and still believe that they are one thing, so great and perfect is the joining. And as all these powers have received some blame in their operations, so one should not be surprised if so many small minds, who have no knowledge of themselves, confuse the actions of princes with those of common men. (pp. 521–3)

The idea of a God who put off his divinity in order to communicate with men is pauline. The crucial passage occurs in Philippians, where it is said that Christ, though divine, emptied himself to the condition of a slave. It is this self-emptying (*kenosis* in the original, *se depouiller* in Machon) that Machon conceives of here as a lowering of the divine nature to the point of participating in evil and as a biblical sanction for Machiavelli's idea that the prince must practice vice. The prince, imitating a divinity who put off his divinity in Christ in order to achieve the salvation of the world, puts off an ideal and otherworldly goodness in order to achieve the safety of the people, exchanging contemplative perfection for morally flawed action. It is precisely in giving up perfect goodness that the prince most fulfills his sacred charge: "when the prince lapses sometimes from narrow virtue, and when he does not refuse the help of vice for a general and necessary good for his state, he acts as a king, and not as a man" (p. 533).

Thus, by emphasizing theological doctrines such as accommodation and *kenosis,* and by pointing to the antithetical ways in which God's intentions work themselves out in the lives of imperfect human beings in biblical narrative, Machon is able to retain, together with his allegiance to Machiavelli, a paradoxically altered form of the ideology of the sacredness of kings. He recasts the idea that the king is an imitator of God so that *imitatio dei* includes mimesis not only of the unproblematic aspects of the divine image – power, justice, kindness, and mercy – but also of those modes of divine action that entail a lowering of the divine nature or a departure of that nature from its own repose and perfection in the interest of the salvation of mankind. So, in attempting to include the Machiavellian idea that the prince must enter into evil when he has to ("entrare nel male, necessitato"), the doctrine of the mystery of kings is made, by analogy with God's saving action, to include a departure of the royal nature from itself for the public safety.

The necessity of entering into evil is explicitly stated in *Principe* 18, and it was perhaps this phrase, with its refusal to call evil methods by another name, that most angered Machiavelli's critics. As Machon recognized, "this is the place where our author seems to have spoken most freely" (p. 670). In defending this difficult maxim, Machon extends the idea of royal imitation of divine *kenosis* so that the moral self-lowering of the prince includes the risk of damnation. Biblical sanction for self-sacrifice was easy to demonstrate. John 10:11 and 15:13 taught that the greatest love is to give one's life for one's friends and that the good shepherd gives his life for his flock. What the prince does, in accepting the principles of *Il Principe* in order to rule well, is to risk eternal life itself for his "flock": "It is only a good prince who will hazard his own salvation to seek that of the subjects whom he governs" (1668, p. 778).[18] Machon's prince accepts estrangement from God for his people, abandoning the moral perfection that is his by nature and entering into the problematic areas of moral ambiguity and hard choice that characterize the political world as described by Machiavelli. By risking his soul and adopting the principles of *Principe* 15 and 18, the prince enacts the mystery of self-sacrifice for the good of others.

Science royale: *Il Principe* and *I Discorsi* as arcana

It must be emphasized that at no point does Machon imagine that either his own ethical principles or those of Machiavelli are generally applicable. Machiavelli's teaching is

meat for kings, and for those they wish to render worthy and capable of it. I would not wish it to be more common, for it is reserved for the gods and sovereigns of the earth. (p. 804)

There is no evidence in the *Apologie* that Machon was conscious that the evident republican tendency of the *Discorsi* constituted a stumbling block to this view of Machiavelli's intended audience. He was not alone in this, nor, as this study has demonstrated, in regarding Machiavelli's works, despite the fact of their publication, as private manuals of instruction for princes. From the time of the 1643 preface on, Machon makes the limitation of audience a central part of his defense. Those

---

[18] In places the Bible does seem to advance some such notion of the self-sacrifice of the leader (not only of Christ but also of the prophets and apostles), though it is not quite so Machiavellian. For example, both Moses and Paul appear to offer their own salvation as intercession for their sinning people: In Exodus 32:32, Moses asks to be blotted out of the book of life if God will not forgive Israel's apostasy, and Paul makes a similar offer in Romans 9:3 ("I could wish that I myself were accursed and cut off from Christ for the sake of my brethren, my kinsmen by race"). Both passages could be taken as a hazard of salvation, but not in the sense of being willing to sin for the people, as in Machon's text.

who are not "capable of penetrating the secret movements of state" may indeed make bad use of Machiavelli, for "what is sweet in the mouths of kings and monarchs is often bitter and disagreeable in the mouths of their subjects and of the common people" (fol. C).

The notion of a secret wisdom of kings is implicit throughout the *Apologie* but gets special attention in the section devoted to *Principe* 23, which deals with the subject of avoiding flatterers and taking advice. Because the prince must take responsibility not only for selecting his ministers but also for accepting or rejecting any advice they offer, Machiavelli says that

the prudence of the prince does not come from the advice given him but, to the contrary, good advice, whatever be its immediate source, has its true origin in the wisdom [*prudenzia*] of the prince.

This is hardly a doctrine of royal infallibility, for it makes no assumption that the prince will in fact be wise: It is rather the statement of an observed administrative reality that would apply to any situation in which decisions were taken by one person on the advice of others. But for Machon, it provides the occasion for attaching the doctrine of a specifically royal wisdom (or *science royale*, as it was called in several books of the period)[19] to Machiavelli's text. For Machon, wisdom emanates from the king and not from his ministers not merely, as in Machiavelli, because government happens to be arranged that way, but because the king is different from ordinary mortals:

To have the thoughts of a king, it is necessary to have been born one, and he who is not one and tries to counterfeit it will succeed as badly as a lover in a counterfeit passion set beside one who is actually so smitten that he loses appetite for food and drink, who loses spirit and rest. (p. 732).

Machon finds his views of the special and sacred character of kings mirrored in the Bible. In fact, in the context of the ancient Near East, the biblical doctrines of sacral kingship are much qualified in the Bible: Kingship is a concession to the demands of the people and, in some respects, always remained subordinate to prophecy. In certain texts in Judges (e.g., 8:22–3), Israel's desire to have a king is presented as a rejection of the rule of God, and at the very moment at which the kingship of Israel is established, its dangers and the potential for both social oppression and the theocratic traditions of Israel are delineated (I Samuel 8). But, though extreme statements of a sacral or divine

[19] Pierre de La Mare, *Discours de la justice et science royale* (Paris, 1618); Francois Marchant, *La science royale* (Saumur, 1625). See Church, *Richelieu*, p. 31n., for other references.

conception of kingship are not dominant in the Bible,[20] there is enough material so that, during periods of the revival of sacred kingship in the West, the Bible could be mined for proof texts supporting an almost magical conception of kingship, as Machon does here. According to such texts, the king is not merely the leader of his people but represents a kind of corporate identity, so that the soundness of the body politic depends upon the king in a quasimagical fashion; the king is worth 10,000 of his subjects and is the foundation of his people; his character determines theirs (pp. 737–9; Wisdom 6:24; II Samuel 18:3; Ecclesiasticus 10:3). Kings are the anointed lieutenants of God; they have special "geniuses" appointed to watch over them, are granted special grace, and have "sentiments that are proper to them and reserved for their rank" (p. 737). "Inspired decisions [Vulg.: *divinatio*] are on the lips of a king" (Proverbs 16:10); a king who sits upon the seat of judgment scatters evil by his glance (Proverbs 20:8; *Apologie*, p. 737). In keeping with such a mystical view of royal infallibility, the counsels of kings are not only to be kept secret, but are to be regarded as sacrosanct:

The secret of kings must be hidden and covered with a veil like a sacred object, not allowed to be known by everyone. *Sacramentum regis abscondere bonum est* (Tobit 12:7); the thoughts and the designs of princes, not being like those of other men, since they are as mysteries and sacraments whose causes, invisible and unknown, ought to stay within the souls of princes, it being enough that the subjects discover their marks and apparent signs by the well-being and utility they receive and feel from the wise conduct of their sovereigns. (1668, p. 870; cf. 1643, p. 742)

The king is a living law, a *lex animata*, and beyond the law in his conduct, as his motives ought to be beyond public scrutiny. The argument continues, deriving, again, much of its strength from the *imitatio dei* trope:

Further, if it is true, as Scripture everywhere asserts, that kings are gods on earth, that they derive from and depend immediately upon heaven, with the Apostle adding that no one ever knew the things of God but God himself (I Corinthians 2:11: *quae dei sunt, nemo cognovit nisi spiritus Dei*), then kings, having something of divinity, and possessing advantages not at all common to other men, it is very difficult for spirits of another temper, and of less substance than theirs, to be able to have sentiments worthy of the thought of kings, or corresponding to the greatness of their being. (pp. 742–3)

We see here a form of what Kantorowicz, in his well-known work on

---

[20] See A. R. Johnson, *Sacral Kingship in Ancient Israel*, 2nd ed. (Cardiff, 1967), for a full account of this subject.

mystery of state, called "monopolization by exclusion." The knowledge
of God referred to in I Corinthians, to which the *spiritus dei* gave access,
was available to all Christians. By limiting New Testament promises
of participation in divine mysteries to the papacy, or, here, to the
king, a mystery of state is created where none was intended by the
biblical text.[21]

In his development of the idea of royal wisdom, Machon has the
French monarchy very much in mind and, in one of his relatively rare
direct discussions of contemporary history, applies his concept of the
sacredness of royal prerogative to the Declaration of February 1641,
by which Louis XIII forbade Parliament to discuss matters pertaining
to his "state." This declaration of the king's

removed him from slavery and established him in liberty: it was a recognition of what he could do and of what he was, the work of a perfect king,
of a terrestrial god, and the first and highest degree of human wisdom. (pp.
770–1)

Machon's view of the royal prerogative, or "mystery of state," a phrase
that was used of the prerogative in contemporary discussion, bases
the freedom of the sovereign from parliamentary restraint upon New
Testament promises of Christian liberty and godlikeness, interpreted
as specially applicable to the king, who was, in ways not allowed to
other men, an imitator of the power and the freedom from law and
scrutiny enjoyed by God. Such claims were far from being unusual
in French political writing of the seventeenth century: What makes
Machon's speculations on mystery of state in this chapter different is
that he believes the sacred mystery of kingship to have been a doctrine
implicit in the Bible and taught by Machiavelli.

We have seen that Machon's defense of Machiavelli depends on
regarding *Il Principe* and the *Discorsi* as treatises on sacred kingship,
with their apparent amoralism interpreted as the special prerogative
of the divinely appointed sovereign, a reflection of mysterious biblical
patterns of licensed transgression. These patterns find their ultimate
expression in the Incarnation, which Machon reads as a lowering of
divine perfection and a model for the moral self-lowering of the Machiavellian prince. Such a reading of Machiavelli, as of the Bible, is a
strained one; yet the commerce of the holy with the profane is surely
a central biblical theme, both on the individual, ethical level and on
the plane of history, where God's chosen people interact with other
nations. The Old Testament not only offers numerous examples of

[21] Ernst H. Kantorowicz, "Mysteries of state: an absolutist concept and its late medieval
origins," *Harvard Theological Review* XLVIII (1955), 65–91; see esp. pp. 74ff.

the failure to observe the divine commandments and sustain the rituals by which Israel was distinguished from "the nations," but often seems to present such breaches of the boundary between sacred and profane as, paradoxically, the means by which God's purposes are advanced. Whatever the actual reasons for this tension between the commandments and their transgression in the Old Testament, the New Testament tends to regard it as a prefiguring of Christian liberty and Christian universalism. When Israel disobeys the commandments and becomes "like the nations," the sin of its disobedience is not the only moral to be drawn from the event, for apostasy also prefigures the abolition of the distinctions between Jews and Gentiles of the New Covenant.

The institution of kingship is a special instance of this paradox, for it was undoubtedly sacred and inevitably profane at the same time. God chooses the first kings of Israel (Saul and David) establishes a special covenant with the House of David in perpetuity, and this house becomes, in time, the bearer of the messianic hope. Yet kingship, though divinely sanctioned, has its origins in the wish of the people to be like their neighbors, to abandon the theocratic institution of judgeship in favor of the forms of sacred kingship more prevalent in the region – forms that potentially conflicted with monotheism and the injunctions against idol worship. The establishment of the monarchy is thus partly a concession to paganism and eclecticism, and the biographies of the kings show the potential conflict being realized – in Solomon's tolerance of foreign cults and in the frequent reversions to idol worship of those who succeeded him, both in Judah and in the schismatic north. In addition, this institutional ambivalence is mirrored in the personal lives of the kings, many of whom are very great sinners indeed. Even David, the greatest of them, is shown in this double light, violating the institutional tenets of Hebrew religion in the eating of the showbread and the taking of the census, and breaking the moral law by contriving the death of Uriah, the husband of Bathsheba. Yet the union between Bathsheba and David gives rise to the messianic line, and the sin of the census is connected to the founding of the Temple. Thus, in the Israelite kingship, the sacredness of the institution does seem to be connected, as Machon thought, to its potential for eclecticism, and the holiness of the kings themselves is inseparable from their human failings. For Machon, the mystery of the royal office lay precisely in this interplay between the sacred and the profane, between the king's imitation of God and his necessary involvement in the world of sin. The mystery of kingship, at its most paradoxical, required that the sacred king become a follower of Machiavelli, not only because the king had special license to transgress the law, but because that transgression itself reflected the mysterious process whereby God sanctified and reconciled to himself a sinning world.

We have seen that the attempt to combine Machiavellian politics with the principle of *imitatio dei* led Gabriel Naudé to a view of politics that was in some respects initiatory: He makes a distinction between the moral beliefs held by ordinary people and another set of values into which kings, counselors, and *esprits forts* would be initiated by reading books (like his own *Coups d'état*) that revealed the *arcana imperii.* Machon's *Apologie,* too, offers a kind of initiation: The conventional, "bigoted" understanding of politics, of moral principles, and of the Bible is contrasted with a more vigorous, complex, and paradoxical interpretation, appropriate to princes and taught by Machiavelli. As with Naudé, the *déniaisement* that leads to knowledge of mysteries of state entails a recognition of the role of fiction and illusion in political life.

Yet the differences between Naudé and Machon may perhaps be seen most clearly in the way each develops this Machiavellian theme. For Naudé, political fiction making explains magic and suggests that the origin of religion lies in imposture. Machon does not develop this principle in a skeptical direction. Rather, for him, Machiavelli's insight into the fictive or illusion-making aspect of politics is regarded as a religious insight, a recognition of the merely symbolic importance of all things in the human world, in contrast to the divine. Appearances are manipulable for Machon not because there are no solid realities, but because the sacred truths of religion may only be symbolized, not reproduced, in the imperfect human media in which we must communicate. Machon's Machiavellian prince is an imitator of a God who himself employed illusion and deception in the interests of salvation.

As a final contrast, one may note that Naudé, despite his allegiance to monarchy, is really more interested in the potential counselor than in the prince, that he is interested in revealing the arcana to a select circle of *esprits forts,* undeceived intellectuals whose perception of the fictional character of sacred kingship will make them, like Machiavelli's founders, able to acquire and maintain power by the manipulation of appearances of the supernatural. But for Machon the deceptions and illusions of politics that Machiavelli described are necessary means employed by kings who *in fact* enjoy divine favor and exercise divine exemption from ordinary laws. Machon's audience is not the *esprit fort* but the monarch, and the initiation Machon envisions is one in which the monarch will come to understand his own special license in Machiavellian terms.

Machon's *Apologie pour Machiavel* offers a radically transformed belief in the mystery of kings, in which the divine character of their office is seen most clearly in their willingness to, as Machiavelli had said they must, enter into evil when required.

Index